Portal Peak, Chiricahua Mountains

Oil painting on canvas by Crystal Foreman Brown

The Friends of Cave Creek Canyon

Our mission is to inspire appreciation and understanding of the beauty, biodiversity, and legacy of Cave Creek Canyon.

We work closely with the Coronado National Forest to support their work in Cave Creek Canyon. We seek to provide educational opportunities for area residents, visitors, school groups, scientific researchers, and others who cherish the special qualities of our region.

We are a 501(c)(3) organization. Donations may be tax-deductible.

We are an all-volunteer organization. All donations and membership fees are used to advance the mission of FOCCC.

Friends of Cave Creek Canyon
P.O. Box 16126
Portal AZ 85632

www.friendsofcavecreekcanyon.org

CAVE CREEK CANYON

Revealing the Heart of Arizona's Chiricahua Mountains

Edited by
Wynne Brown and Reed Peters

Foreword by Jeanne Williams

ECO Wear & Publishing

This book is typeset in Minion Pro and Myriad Pro.

CAVE CREEK CANYON (hardback) 978-1-938850-15-8
CAVE CREEK CANYON (paperback) 978-1-938850-16-5
Revealing the Heart of Arizona's Chiricahua Mountains
Hardcover with dust jacket $49.95
Paperback $19.95

Design and production by Wynne Brown LLC and printed in China.

Cover photo by Sarah Thomson, www.thegreybarnlansing.com

Frontispiece: *Portal Peak, Chiricahua Mountains* by Crystal Foreman Brown

ECO Wear & Publishing
P.O. Box 376
Rodeo, NM 88056
USA
575-557-5757
575-557-7575 fax
ecoorders@hotmail.com
www.ecouniverse.com

ACKNOWLEDGMENTS

A book of this scope would never have happened without the help and support of so many people—this is indeed an extraordinary community!

Forty-three remarkable authors have freely shared their passion for their subjects. Many have reviewed several chapters, made valuable suggestions, submitted graphics and photos for their own and others' chapters, and more. Thank you, all!

It could not have happened without Bob and Sheri Ashley, owners of ECO Wear & Publishing, Rodeo, N.M., as well as the Chiricahua Desert Museum, who provided the publication knowledge and advice to bring this book to life ...

Our thanks also to Narca Moore-Craig, art editor, Photoshop whiz, and donor of multiple illustrations ...

And to Fran Zweifel, scientific illustrator, who generously created special drawings of butterflies (one of which is the Chiricahua White), for the chapter headings ...

Our thanks to Pat Owens, who took on chasing down and editing the author bios, in addition to creating and editing the glossary ...

And to Kathleen Talbot who brought her librarian skills to wrangling the Further Reading section ...

And to Bootheel Maps for creating the stunning maps of the Cave Creek watershed ...

And to JoAnn Julian for forwarding to the community our incessant requests for artwork, photos, information, chapters, funding, etc. ...

And to Laura Zeuner who cheerfully typed everything we handed her, no matter how long or how weirdly formatted ...

And to the photographers and artists who were not authors and who donated their work, including Dori and Ray Brooks, Crystal

Foreman Brown, David E. Brown, Wynne Brown, John Chenger, Chris Conlan, Orchid Davis, Maya Decker, Pierre Deviche, Rene Donaldson, Fred Espenak, Harold Farmer, Deby Galloway, Warner Glenn, Jackie Lewis, Bill Love, Joy Comstock Mendez, Ray Mendez, Wyatt Mendez, Michael Morrow, Stephen Mullin, Sherry Nelson, Rose Ann Rowlett, Sarah Thomson, Eskild Petersen, Sandy Urban, Cecil Williams ...

People who generously contributed artwork or historic photographs from their personal collections include Marge Fagan, Eric Hayes, Reed Peters, Zola Stolz, Ted Troller, Jeanne Williams ...

Organizations that graciously shared photographs from their collections include Alden Hayes Collection, Arizona Historical Society, Arizona State Library Archives, Chiricahua-Peloncillo Historical Society, Cochise County Historical Society, Coronado National Forest, Southwestern Research Station ...

We owe a special debt of gratitude to all the Board Members and Advisors of Friends of Cave Creek Canyon who provided welcome comments, suggestions, and cheerleading.

Proofreaders included Bonnie Bowen, David Brooks, Alan Craig, Susan Dalby, Freddy Davis, Pat Espenak, Bud Fackelman, Kate Fackelman, Eric Hayes, Dave Jasper, Rolf Koford, Peter LaRue, Narca Moore-Craig, Dick Parran, Pat Parran, Wade Sherbrooke, Helen Snyder, Noel Snyder, Mike Sredl, Howard Topoff, Kim Vacariu, Mike Van Buskirk, Peter Waser, Cecil Williams, Jeanne Williams, Mike Williams, and Dick Zweifel.

For all the others whose names escaped this list, we are forever grateful!

The extraordinary faith and generosity of nearly 150 individual donors have made the dream of this book a reality. By fully funding it in advance, all proceeds from the sale of *Cave Creek Canyon: Revealing the Heart of Arizona's Chiricahua Mountains* can go toward projects benefitting the Canyon.

— *Wynne Brown and Reed Peters, co-editors*

IN MEMORY

Lee Abbott

H. Bernard W. Ashley

Herbert Barker

Mickie and Charles Bogert

Matt Caron

Jack Carson

Mont Cazier

Bob Chew

Jemma Dant

Bob Fagan

Wynne Byard Fooshee

Janet L. Gee

Wendy Glenn

Devorie Griffiths

Edna Hastings

Alden Hayes

Joanne Hilligus

Justin Sinclair Jarosak

Penny Johnston

Aldo Leopold

Audrey and Guy Miller

Ralph Morrow

Wayne Morrow

Bob Morse and Leon

Kay and Martin Muma

Jerry Parks

Lee Penwell

Robert H. Peters

James Finley Richards

Vince Roth

Findlay Russell

Katie and Bob Scholes

Sally and Walter Spofford

O'Leary and Bob Squier

Arch Steele

Dave Utterback

Peter Warshall

Bill Willy

Pat Willy

Contents

Foreword
Jeanne Williams

*I*n this unique book, 43 writers share their passion and knowledge of what is for many of them their life work. Learn when and where to find which butterflies. Locate the lizard that needs no male to reproduce. Consider, before you destroy an anthill, that these insects work the soil as efficiently as earthworms. Listen to a diversity of owls from night hunters to those of the day. Admire trogons and soaring raptors. Meet a troop of coatis feeding on madrone berries, or glimpse a bear or mountain lion.

Watch bats darken the twilight as they leave their caves. Bend to a tiny flower, fern, or mushroom sheltered by giant trees. Visit Sally Spofford's world-renowned feeders and be dazzled by hummingbirds. Find traces of the earliest dwellers and Apaches. Get a glimpse at how miners, homesteaders, ranchers, woodcutters, and sawmill workers made a living.

The scope of this guide is amazing, but no more so than the vision, tenacity, and just plain hard work put into it by co-editors Wynne Brown and Reed Peters. Reed was elected first president of Friends of Cave Creek Canyon, fledged only a few months before the Horseshoe 2 Fire destroyed much habitat for wildlife, burned old-growth forest, and stripped slopes of erosion-checking trees. In those crucial times, FOCCC volunteered countless hours to clear debris, restore trails, and help rebuild picnic areas and campgrounds.

Since then, a Nature Day for area schools gives students an opportunity to learn about different aspects of the Canyon and question experts. A professionally designed butterfly/bird garden near the Visitor Information Center has paths, benches, and a picnic table. Work days are held as needed to keep it weeded. One task force has even begun removal of invasive weeds.

After Hurricane Odile, there will be daunting challenges.

Cave Creek Canyon, born of volcanic convulsions that hurled magma and ash over the land for millennia, has been formed, altered and re-shaped by crashing meteors, earthquakes, fires, floods and forces beyond our imagining. During the brief human sojourn here of perhaps 12,000 years, cave and pit-house dwellers fled with whatever they could carry, as did the Apaches who moved with the seasons. They lived lightly on the earth with no paved roads, permanent homes, fences, or heavy belongings.

That had changed by 1912 when Stephen Reed refused to leave his cabin as Cave Creek roared at both doors. Sally Spofford in 1978 watched huge trees and a refrigerator tumbling past. The Rattlesnake Fire of 1994 left moonscapes and skeletal trees that fell for years like giant jackstraws.

Smoke shrouded Cathedral Rock and stung throats and eyes days after the 2011 Horseshoe 2 Fire finally died. The entire community was grieving over charred trees, incinerated nests and what wild creatures would do.

The newly formed Friends group found an immediate niche in assisting with post-fire projects. This book is going to press two weeks after the remnants of Hurricane Odile caused massive flooding and erosion in the Canyon. Proceeds from the sale of *Cave Creek Canyon: Revealing the Heart of Arizona's Chiricahua Mountains* will help fund projects to assist the Canyon.

The Canyon is ever-changing, still being altered before our eyes by the powerful forces of nature.

This book will help you appreciate and understand it.

Pinnacles on the shoulder of Silver Peak   *Noel Snyder*

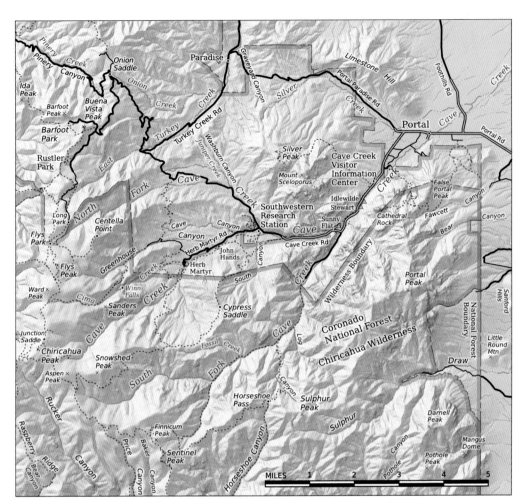

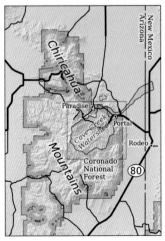

Cave Creek Watershed

The large map above shows most of the watershed of Cave Creek, including its North, Middle or Main, and South forks, as well as Silver Creek.

The small map to the left shows the entire watershed, surrounded by an orange line, in relation to the Chiricahua Mountains.

www.BootheelMaps.com

Introduction
Reed Peters

C ave Creek Canyon in the Chiricahua Mountains has been drawing people and animals for thousands of years. The most extensive watershed in Arizona's largest Sky Island, Cave Creek and its forks form abundant riparian areas. Situated at the convergence of four ecozones—the Sonoran and Chihuahuan deserts, and the Rocky Mountains and Sierra Madre Occidental—the canyon and surrounding areas constitute the most biodiverse land area in North America!

As the following chapters will reveal, Cave Creek Canyon and its surrounding mountains and valley are one of the extraordinary jewels of this continent. The sheer diversity of flora and fauna species, including half of North American birds, half of the bats, and a large proportion of the ants, offers a richness of nature that continually astounds. The magnificent canyon walls and pinnacles are a breathtaking backdrop to the wonders below. The varying shades of rhyolite are altered by numerous species of colored lichens, changing tone and mood with the passage of clouds and sun, providing an ever-changing setting. Above this, the clarity and purity of the air and the dark skies at night encompass the canyon in what are increasingly rare and precious conditions on this continent.

Archaeologists have estimated that there were more people near the canyon a thousand years ago than there are today! Remains of dwellings scattered downhill from the mouth of Cave Creek suggest that around 300 people made their homes here. Nearby canyons show similar remains. Paintings in caves in the canyon, while mostly inaccessible by trail, attest to the early creative presence of humanity.

This book is merely an introduction to the canyon. Volumes have been written about each of the topics introduced here in short chapters. The book is intended to give answers to some of the first questions that occur to residents and visitors. Sources for more information may be found at the end of the book in the **Further Reading** section.

Cave Creek Canyon: Revealing the Heart of Arizona's Chiricahua Mountains is an extraordinary community effort by residents of Paradise, Portal, Rodeo, Whitetail Canyon, and their friends, who have given their time, expertise, and talent in writing chapters, contributing photographs and artwork, editing, reviewing, or assisting with the creation of the book. It is sponsored and produced by the Friends of Cave Creek Canyon, whose mission is to "inspire appreciation and understanding of the beauty, biodiversity, and legacy of Cave Creek Canyon."

As you explore this wondrous area, remember that every paradise has its serpent, both literally and figuratively. In snake season, watch where you walk, and don't put your hand in dark holes! Take water, let a friend know where you'll be if hiking alone, and avoid washes running with water.

Above all, let the peace and magic and beauty of the area refresh your spirit.

View from Cave Creek Ranch

Pastel by Marge Fagan, courtesy of Reed Peters

The Physical Canyon

Wind, water, fire, and, most of all, time forged the Cave Creek Canyon we know today.   *©Raymond A. Mendez 2014*

The cliffs above the Ranger Station   *Noel Snyder*

1 Geology
Sharon Minchak

The geology of the Chiricahua Mountains plays a feature role in the dramatic natural beauty of southeast Arizona and provides the foundation upon which the region's rich biologic diversity has anchored itself. These mountains tell a story of billions of years of Earth's history that is otherwise hidden in the surrounding valleys by the sands of time. The sections below briefly describe the geologic history and resulting present-day rock formations of the area around Portal and Paradise, including Cave Creek Canyon.

Proterozoic Era Rock Formations (2.5 billion years to 570 million years old)

The Proterozoic Era, in geologic nomenclature, is the period from roughly 2.5 billion years to 570 million years before present. The most ancient rocks exposed in the Portal area, the Pinal Schist and an unnamed granodiorite, are from this time period and are each more than 1 billion years old. These rocks were formed as an ancient magma chamber cooled deep below the Earth's surface. Erosion and tectonic activity over the last 1 billion years have brought these rocks to the surface, and they now are the foundation on which the much younger, and more visible, geologic units of the Chiricahua Mountains stand. The blocky fracturing and easily broken nature of the granite-like rocks

Fracturing is the result of billions of years of tectonic activity.
All photos by Sharon Minchak

are the result of billions of years of regional deformation and volcanism. These rocks are best exposed on the east-facing flanks of the hills along Foothills Road as you approach the Portal area from the north. While the ancient Pinal Schist and granodiorite are somewhat nondescript in appearance, a hike to the base of the hills along East Turkey Creek or Round Valley, armed with an understanding of their staggering age, offers an opportunity to reflect on the vastly different scales of geologic and human time.

Paleozoic Era Rock Formations (570 to 250 million years old)

The upper surface of the Pinal Schist and granodiorite mark what geologists call an *unconformity*, a distinct missing period in the geologic rock record. This means that sequences of rocks have been eroded away, and there is a notable gap between the age of the underlying and

(Top) Limestone in the Portal area often includes tiny fossil brachiopods.
(Bottom) Basalt has been forced through fractures in the Earth's crust.

overlying units. In the Portal area, this geologic unconformity represents a time gap of as much as possibly 1 billion years of geologic history that were erased by erosion. What environments or geologic activity may have occurred in this area during that time remain a mystery.

The younger rocks that overlie the unconformity are Paleozoic Era sandstones, limestones, and shales deposited along or near the shoreline of an ancient sea that ebbed back and forth in this area for roughly 300 million years. Fossils can be found in some of the limestones including specimens like the small brachiopods shown above.

Mesozoic Era Rock Formations (250 to 65 million years old)

During the Mesozoic Era, shallow sea and shoreline conditions persisted in the Portal area, depositing thick sequences of shale, siltstone, and coarser grained formations called conglomerates. Conglomerates are collections of smaller pebbles and rock fragments that have been cemented together over time into something similar to natural concrete. But, unlike during the Paleozoic Era, this area was no longer quietly sitting on the edge of a passive continental seashore. Highlands began to rise to the west as a series of small land masses crashed into the western margin of what would become modern-day North America. Those land masses arrived—as if on a conveyor belt—as an oceanic plate dove beneath the North American continental plate, creating what is called a subduction zone. As an oceanic plate hits a continental plate edge and begins to be forced underneath, it creates earthquakes, uplift, folding, and faulting similar to a rug being crumpled up if another rug is forced underneath its edge.

As the oceanic plate plunges back into Earth's mantle (as it is subducted), it begins to melt and the less dense liquid rises up towards the planet's surface. Such melting rock daylighted in the Portal area as basalt that squeezed out on the sea floor like toothpaste and hardened into rocky pillows, or that was forced through fractures in the buckling Earth's crust. These Mesozoic Era basalts were the first stirrings of deep-seated volcanism that would culminate, some 50 million years later, in a cataclysmic event responsible for many of the dominant geologic features we see in the landscape today.

Cenozoic Era Formations and Volcanism (65 million years old to present)

As subduction continued along the western edge of the North American continent, the subducting tectonic plate continued melting and formed large underground magma chambers in the region. Magma rose through the deforming Earth's crust, melting more and more of the overlying rock as it did so, and eventually reached the

Rhyolite, silica, and quartz are just some of the minerals that color the canyon cliffs.

surface 28 to 29 million years ago as broad flows of lava. Standing at the mouth of Cave Creek Canyon today, the majestic purple and reddish-brown peaks that dominate the view are flows of Silver Peak dacite, Cave Creek rhyolite, and Horseshoe Canyon tuff, to name a few. Containing more silica than the basalts that erupted in the Mesozoic Era, these rocks are rich in minerals such as quartz and plagioclase that contribute to the distinct hues seen today in the canyon cliffs.

Hikers often find rocks that contain the bright green and blue malachite and azurite.

However, the eruption of these large flows of lava was only the beginning of a chapter in volcanism in the canyon that would culminate in a truly earthshaking event. As a magma chamber grows, pressure builds within as gasses and water vapor are liberated from the melting rocks. The pressure is held in check by the crushing weight of the overlying crust. However, as magma creeps closer to the Earth's surface, with less and less crust to provide a sufficient lid over top of it, the pressure may reach a point when it can no longer

be contained. The result is like releasing the lid on a pressure cooker. Roughly 27 million years ago, the lid on the magma chamber underlying the Portal region blew open, resulting in the explosive ejection of a huge volume of melted rock as the Turkey Creek Caldera erupted. The explosion was similar to that of Mount St. Helens in 1980—although

Old mine shafts and other evidence of early mining exploration are common in the Portal area.

probably more than 1,000 times larger. The material that erupted blanketed more than 1,000 square miles with acres of hot ash and volcanic rock. In the Portal area, the rock layers formed from this fiery blanket have been eroded by wind and water; however, the remnants can be easily seen further west where they form the soaring spires of the Chiricahua National Monument.

What We See In the Cave Creek Area Today

Many of the unusual and beautiful features we see in the canyon today are a result of local geologic history. As described earlier, the magnificent purple and red cliffs that dominate the Cave Creek Canyon vistas are the direct result of massive volcanic lava flows that covered this region 25 to 30 million years ago. But many other pleasant surprises in the area can be tied back to geology as well.

It is not unusual while hiking in the area to find rocks that contain the striking bright green and blue minerals of malachite and azurite, both copper carbonate minerals. These minerals formed as superheated fluids, laden with copper and other heavy metals, pushed ahead of the magma that was welling into the area's crust during the region's volcanic episodes. As those liquids, called hydrothermal fluids, moved through the existing limestone, malachite and azurite and other brightly colored carbonate minerals were deposited within those existing rocks throughout the region. And of course more than just the brightly colored minerals were deposited; actual copper and iron ores were also deposited, such as in the nearby Bisbee mining area. While extensive deposits of precious metal ore do not

Quartz crystals often lurk in cracks and open spaces of rocks.

occur in the Portal area, evidence of hopeful mining exploration in years gone by can be seen in abandoned mining shafts and workings throughout the region.

Also readily found along some hiking trails in the area are well-formed and abundant quartz crystals nestled in cracks and open spaces of rocks or intergrown in sparkling stripes cross-cutting some rocks. These crystals also represent a secondary geologic deposit that was created as heated fluids migrated, or were forced under pressure, into cracks and fractures in older rocks. As the fluids flowed further from their fiery source, they cooled and were no longer able to carry their load of dissolved minerals in solution. As a result, sparkling crystals precipitated out in open gaps in the rock.

Conclusion

The modern-day beauty and grandeur of the geologic features in the Cave Creek Canyon area cannot be missed. The rocks tell a timeless story of the varied and sometimes turbulent events Earth has undergone in this region—a story that can be appreciated regardless of whether you are a geologist, a weekend rock hound, or a casual observer.

View into the cliffs of the Canyon   *Deby Galloway*

2 Hydrology
Harry Ridgway

a water molecule (H_2O) measures about 0.14 nanometers (1 nm = 1 billionth of a meter), which is so astonishingly small that it defies imagination. What water lacks in stature, however, it makes up for in numbers. More than a trillion (1×10^{12}) water molecules can fit onto the period at the end of this sentence. In a cup of liquid water, roughly 10^{24} molecules are feverishly jostling about to find a thermodynamically comfortable space among their myriad brethren. Water is the most abundant substance on Earth, with nearly a billion cubic kilometers held in the world's oceans, and it is the third most common molecule in the universe, following hydrogen (H_2) and carbon monoxide (CO).

A brief history of water

Having been detected at the farthest reaches of the cosmos, water probably first formed ~12 billion years ago. Water arrived on Earth from comet and asteroid impacts, but also was associated with the earliest stages of planetary accretion ~4.5 billion years ago. Recently geophysicists discovered vast quantities of water, perhaps three times more than is in the world's oceans, trapped in a bluish crystalline mineral (ringwoodite) located in Earth's mantle 400 miles beneath North America. As part of a whole-earth water cycle, the mantle water slowly exchanges with our oceans by tectonic and volcanic processes. Water is woven into the fabric of life at every level, and our existence depends on an uninterrupted supply. In cells, water is transported by "aquaporins" that span the membranes of all life forms. So efficient are these miniscule water pumps that a single Aquaporin-1 channel can transport about 3 billion water molecules per second.

Water in the Chiricahua Mountains

In spite of its miniscule size and seemingly placid nature, water in its liquid, solid (ice), and gaseous forms is arguably the most powerful, dynamic and virtually unstoppable force that shapes not only the present-day

physiography and **geomorphology** of the Chiricahua Mountains and Cave Creek Canyon in particular, but also the diversity and distribution of wildlife throughout the "Sky Island" mountain ranges that cover much of southeast Arizona and southwest New Mexico. Over geologic time frames ranging from many thousands to tens of millions of years, water has created and/or severely modified all of the primary drainages and natural springs of the Chiricahua Mountains, including the North and South Forks of Cave Creek, East Turkey Creek and Greenhouse, Cima, and Snowshed creeks. Through various **hydrogeologic** processes such as abrasive erosion, sediment transport, and mineral dissolution (leaching), water inexorably, and sometimes catastrophically (*e.g.,* following major forest fires), alters and sculpts the land (see Chapter 1).

The monsoon rains that move into southeast Arizona and southwest New Mexico in early July represent the northernmost fringes of a much more powerful monsoon season that sweeps across northern Mexico beginning in early May (see Chapter 3). The long-term average rainfall measured from 1930-2002 for the Coronado National Forest Planning (CNFP) area, which includes the Chiricahua Mountains and extends from the U.S. border north to the San Carlos area and west almost to Tucson, is about 14.7 inches, with an average 30 percent occurring as snow. But *average* snow and rainfall values by themselves can be highly misleading and do not reflect the extreme geographic and historical variability of seasonal rainfall amounts. Indeed, the occurrence of monsoon storm cells in the Coronado National Forest and the Sky Island region is nearly random over space and time, making accurate short-term weather prediction practically impossible during the summer months. Even on relatively small **geophysical** scales of 1-2 kilometers, there is marked discontinuity in storm cell frequency and magnitude.

Similar precipitation variability is observed even in the winter months. For example, during the 2005-2006 winter months the CNFP area received more than 6.3 inches less rain than during the 2004-2005 winter. This kind of variation is also observed across much longer time frames as well. The 1950s were, for example, a comparatively dry decade, with an average annual precipitation shortfall (departure from the mean) of about 1.46 inches. On the other hand, the 1980s was a notably wetter period with an average annual rain surplus of 1.86 inches. It should also be emphasized that high summer temperatures (averaging about 80°F across the entire CNFP area) tend to result in increased evaporation rates directly from surface streams, springs, creeks, and catchments, as well as greatly enhanced **evapotranspiration** from plants. Reduced rates of water drainage from high-elevation spring snowmelt coupled with low evaporation rates tend to make winter precipitation more hydrologically efficient in terms of percolation into unsaturated root zones and deep drainage into subsurface aquifers.

A recent study by Earman *et al.* provided new insight into tectonic influences on groundwater systems in the magmatically active Sky Island region of southeast Arizona and southwest New Mexico. Aside from limited "hotspots" where intensive (*i.e.,* focused) natural recharge from valley floor precipitation occurs, the main San Bernardino and San Simon Valley aquifers receive their recharge from the bounding mountain ranges. For example, approximately two-thirds of the recharge to the San Bernardino Valley aquifer (located south and east of the Chiricahua Wilderness and extending into Mexico) is derived from the Chiricahua Mountains, which are the highest bounding range at nearly 10,000 feet above mean sea level. Precipitation occurring above about 7,000 feet accounts for the bulk of recharge from the Chiricahua Mountains, with spring snowmelt contributing the largest portion of that recharge. For the San Bernardino aquifer, derived from pumping tests and a method using ^{14}C dating, water percolates through the substrate very slowly, from about 8.18×10^{-6} to 2×10^{-5} m/s. That's 8 millionths of a meter per second—all the way up to 200,000ths of a meter per second—very slow indeed. The flux (that is, the volume) of water across the U.S./Mexico border, calculated to be about 2×10^5 m^3/year (200,000 cubic meters per year), provides a conservative estimate for annual recharge in the U.S. portion of the San

South Fork running
Eskild Petersen

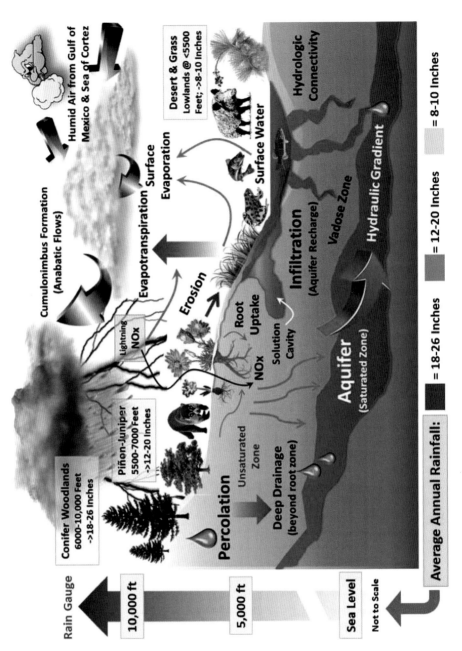

The water cycle in the Chiricahua Mountains is inextricably linked to the powerful summer monsoon season, as well as the higher-elevation snowmelt, that occurs throughout the desert southwest. The monsoons originate from warm moist air masses that migrate into northern Mexico and the American Southwest from the Gulf of Mexico and the Sea of Cortez. These moisture-laden air masses upwell (via **anabatic** flows) in the Chiricahuas and other surrounding mountainous areas. Anabatic flows can be extremely violent and rapid, with powerful air currents

18

Bernardino aquifer. The isotopic signature of the groundwater has been used to estimate the age of water underlying the Chiricahua Mountains and the surrounding alluvial deposits. Based on such measurements, groundwater in the central region of the San Bernardino Basin is about 6,500 years old.

Despite its seemingly simple and unpretentious structure, water behavior appears to be exceedingly complex and unique (indeed anomalous) in many respects compared to other liquid substances. Moreover, all life depends on the peculiar properties of water! For one thing, water is the only inorganic (i.e., non-carbon-containing) liquid at normal temperatures and pressures. In addition, its molecules at room temperature (~23°C) are not randomly organized and haphazardly bouncing about but rather spontaneously arrange themselves in loose (quasi-stable) tetrahedral clusters that give liquid water an identifiable, semi-crystalline structure that can be resolved and measured by suitable instrumentation. These clusters, which tend to be more pronounced on surfaces, represent a thermodynamically low-energy conformation for liquid water that derives from how the individual water molecules tend to associate with one another or with dissolved substances in the water. When monsoon rains tumble earthward in the summer months, raindrops capture (by **solvation** and dissolution) oxygen, nitrogen and other normal and anthropomorphic atmospheric trace substances (*e.g.*, CO_2, methane, sulfuric acid, etc.), as well as lightning-generated nitrogen-oxide species (*e.g.*, NO, NO_2, NO_3).

As might be expected, the major groundwater basins in the Sky Island region lie in the lowland areas between the major mountain ranges, such

---

traveling upwards at thousands of vertical feet per minute. Such rapidly moving air masses can extend to the upper reaches of the troposphere, some 7-8 miles high. Air temperatures at such altitudes can drop well below -50°C resulting in rapid condensation and/or freezing of water vapor to form rain and hailstones. Electrical activity in the form of lightning strikes results in the formation of nitrogen oxides (e.g., NO, NO_2, NO_3) from ionization of the nitrogen and oxygen in the atmosphere. The NOx compounds dissolve into rain droplets that are carried to Earth where they percolate into the soil providing a form of nitrogen fertilizer that stimulates soil microbial activity (in the Nitrogen Cycle) and plant growth. If the amount of rainfall exceeds the capacity of the soil to absorb it, the water quickly forms streams and creeks that flow under the influence of gravity into natural or man-made catchments. Water that percolates into the subsurface environment generally passes through an unsaturated zone and eventually accumulates in underground aquifers consisting of highly porous unconsolidated sedimentary and fractured volcanic rocks.

as the San Simon and San Bernardino Valleys, where artesian springs can still be found. The main inflow contributions for these aquifers come from mountain-front natural recharge and streambed infiltration, with some underflow from adjacent up-gradient basins. The main outflow components consist of solar evaporation, evapotranspiration, extraction by humans for domestic and agricultural purposes, and some underflow to down-gradient basins, including into Mexico.

During its multifarious journey, water constantly undergoes intimate interactions with minerals and living substances, some of which become dissolved and/or suspended in solution. Thus, it is a general principle that surface and groundwater (including oceans and inland seas) take on **physicochemical** and microbial identities or profiles that are characteristic of (and often unique to) their geological surroundings. For example, following major forest fires in 1994 and 2011, Cave Creek and its tributaries became heavily overburdened with sediments and ash during the subsequent monsoon seasons. The periodic destruction of forest canopy and ground-level vegetation following historic fire events in the region result in catastrophic erosion and sediment flows throughout the drainage area. During these events, water quality parameters are radically and suddenly altered, leading to precipitous fish and amphibian die-offs.

Conclusion

With its life-giving seasonal and perennial streams and springs, the Sky Island region of southeast Arizona and southwest New Mexico is able to sustain an enormous diversity of native flora and fauna, much of which is characteristic of, or entirely endemic to, the region. However, the geographic distribution and magnitude of the monsoon season can be capricious, often varying dramatically from one year to the next, which keeps life living on the edge, uncertain as to where the next sip of water will come from.

From a hydrological perspective, the winter snows combined with the spring snowmelt provide the greatest proportion of the annual groundwater recharge to the canyons and valley floor. Because of this, there is concern that accelerated climate change in the years ahead could reduce the annual snowpack and thereby alter the historical hydrological balance. Monitoring of annual rainfall and temperatures throughout the region, combined with judicious inventories of animal and plant species that are characteristic of the region could provide critical indications of climate impacts and the health of the diverse biomes that comprise the region.

In September 2014, remnants of Hurricane Odile passed over the Chiricahuas, dropping 6 inches of rain in 12 hours. Cochise County declared the canyon and vicinity a disaster area.

FS 42 was impassable.
Rene Donaldson

(Middle photo) The South Fork road became the new creek bed.
Harold Farmer

Catastrophic erosion: A raging Cave Creek buried the Foothills Road crossing under a massive boulder field.
Dori and Ray Brooks

So much rain fell in the upper drainages of Cave Creek that the resulting flooding tore out nine power poles. ©Ray Mendez 2014

3   **Weather**
Bob Maddox

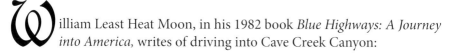illiam Least Heat Moon, in his 1982 book *Blue Highways: A Journey into America,* writes of driving into Cave Creek Canyon:

> *Then the road turned and went directly for an immense wall of mountain that looked impossible to drive through and improbable to drive around ... It had to be a dead end – there could be no opening in that sheer stone obtrusion, that invasion of mountain ... Where the canopy opened, I could see canyon walls of yellow and orange pinnacles and turrets, fluted and twisted, everything rising hundreds of feet. I couldn't have been more surprised ... I'd never heard of the Chiricahuas. I expected nothing.*

The Chiricahua Mountains are the most distinct Sky Island of southeastern Arizona. Sky Islands are mountain formations that are isolated from similar formations—for example, the Huachuca Mountains are a Sky Island to the west-southwest of the Chiricahuas, while the Pinaleño Mountains are a Sky Island to the north-northwest. The mountains that comprise a Sky Island are typically surrounded by lower elevation terrain that is desert or grasslands, so that each "island" is physically and somewhat ecologically isolated from others. There are distinct ecological zones within the Sky Islands that are the result of significant gradients of temperature and precipitation from the surrounding lowlands to the highest elevations.

The Chiricahua Sky Island is uniquely situated since it lies along the northwest margins of the Chihuahuan Desert and near the southeastern-most extensions of the Sonoran Desert. Thus, the two major deserts of the U.S./Mexico Borderlands have influenced the ecology of the Chiricahua Sky Island. The Continental Divide lies only about 25 miles east of the Chiricahuas and has a relatively low elevation of about 4,500 feet.

"Road Closed: Unsafe for Travel"— December 1978 USFS sign after a warm rain melted the substantial snowpack, resulting in massive flooding and damage in the Canyon. *Sally Spofford*

From December to March the Portal and Cave Creek Canyon area can be affected by weather systems and cold fronts moving from both west and east. Strong cold fronts from the Plains can push westward and breach the Continental Divide, especially at the lower elevations along the Divide, such as those near the Chiricahuas. These fronts tend to bring dust but can sometimes be accompanied by showers and light rains or snow. Weather systems from the west are more prolific producers of precipitation, rain and/or snow, especially if they have moved southward to positions west of Baja, picking up substantial moisture from the Pacific, before they move ashore.

The warm season is dominated by **convective** storms, with frequent lightning and thunder, as well as heavy rains and occasional flash flooding. The months of July and August are easily the wettest period of the year. The low-level moist air that feeds thunderstorms can move into the Chiricahua Sky Island from the east because of the low elevations of the Continental Divide from south of Silver City to east of Lordsburg south through the New Mexico Bootheel to the Mexican border. But the most important moisture, as well as many thunderstorms and nighttime complexes of storms, tends to move northward from the Mexican Sierra Madre Occidental mountains and their western foothills.

Finally, low-level moisture frequently moves north and eastward from the Gulf of California and the Sonoran Desert to feed storms and rains over the Chiricahuas. All of the summer weather features have come to be referred to as "the monsoon season." While the summer circulations over Arizona and New Mexico have similarities to more classical monsoons, such as those that occur over southwest Asia, the rain amounts are much less. The summer rains to the south, along and west of the Mexican mountains, are much heavier than those over southeastern Arizona.

The seasons tend to be more distinct in the Sky Islands than they are at lower elevations, with the march of seasons being most distinct at higher elevations. The Chiricahuas experience a winter season (December into March) that brings increased rainfall and snow at higher elevations, mostly due to weather systems from the Pacific. Spring (late March into the first half of June) is a dry, pre-monsoon season with warm-to-hot days and cool nights. Winds at this time can bring occasional dust storms, and late spring thunderstorms can produce locally intense dust storms due to strong outflow winds.

The summer monsoon season extends from mid-to-late June into September with rainfall amounts being about double those of the winter season. The fall season from mid-September through November often has an either/or character to it. If southeast Arizona is affected by several decaying hurricanes or tropical storms from the Pacific, the season will be wet. But in years without influences from tropical storms, fall can be mild and very dry, somewhat similar to the pre-monsoon spring season.

Local weather observations

According to Sellers *et al.*, the earliest weather observations near the Chiricahua Mountains were taken by the U.S. Army at Ft. Bowie beginning in the summer of 1867. More modern observations are fairly scarce. The longest continuous record of weather data—1893 to the present—is from Rucker Canyon but contains only precipitation observations until recently. The second longest continuous record of observations is from the Chiricahua National Monument and extends from 1909 to the present. The long-term record at the Monument is of temperatures and precipitation.

Summer thunderstorms building over the Chiricahuas. July and August are the wettest months with moisture moving in from the east.
Carol A. Simon

25

Staff at the Southwestern Research Station have also been recording temperature and precipitation since 1965 (designated as "Portal 4SW").

However, the recent installation of Remote Automated Weather Stations (RAWS) by Federal Agencies at Chiricahua National Monument (beginning January 1995) and at Rucker Canyon (beginning May 2000) have dramatically increased the weather data available from these two locations. Background on these stations can be found at http://raws.fam.nwcg.gov/ and the observations can be examined in real-time at http://www.wrh.noaa.gov/twc/raws.php.

All the weather observations currently taken in the Chiricahua Mountains are from elevations between 5,300 to 5,700 feet. Unfortunately, there are no weather or climate data available for the higher elevations west of Cave Creek Canyon.

Climate Data

The graph below presents long-term, average precipitation data for Chiricahua National Monument (annual precipitation 19.3"), Portal 4SW (annual precipitation 20.84"), Rucker Canyon (annual precipitation 19.26"),

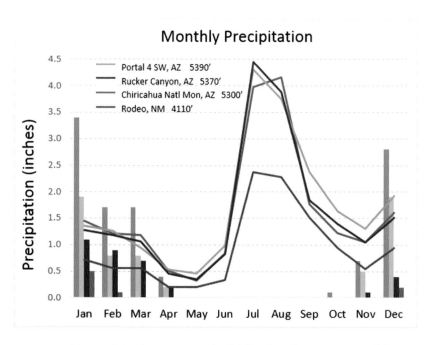

Average monthly precipitation amounts (solid lines) and average snowfall amounts (bars). Note that 1 inch of snow contains, typically, about a tenth of an inch of water equivalent.

and Rodeo, N.M. (annual precipitation 11.22"), for comparison. Note that Rodeo is only about 10 miles east-southeast of the Portal 4SW observation site but is more than 1,000 ft lower in elevation.

The long-term average precipitation data are similar for the three sites in the Chiricahuas. July and August are the wettest months with rainfall of approximately 4 inches each month. There is a second peak of precipitation in the winter (December), but it is not nearly as pronounced as the summer maximum. Annual snowfall amounts are: National Monument 10.8"; Portal 4SW 6.1"; Rucker Canyon 3.4"; and Rodeo N.M. 0.8".

Note that Rodeo's precipitation is more than 8 inches/year less than that at the other three sites. The mountain uplift of the winds produced by the Chiricahua Sky Island results in a much wetter climate than that over the nearby desert shrublands and grasslands.

In the Chiricahuas the heaviest single-day rainfalls are very significant: at the Monument 4.5" fell in one day during June 1911, and the next heaviest was 4.3" in July of 1919; at Portal 4SW 2.79" fell in December 1967, and 2.16" occurred on a day during July 1975; and at Rucker Canyon 3.90" fell on a day in June 1971. Rucker Canyon has had days with more than 3" of rain every month from July through October.

These record amounts were reported only up through 1985, and heavier amounts may have occurred since. Locally intense rains are mostly

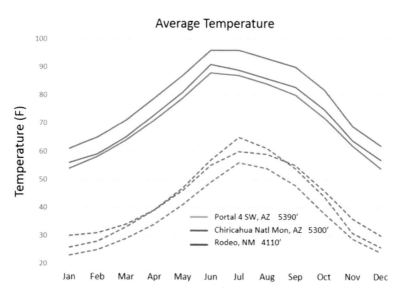

Average monthly temperatures—highs are in solid lines and lows are dashed.

Snow and sun over Cave Creek Canyon   ©Ray A. Mendez 2014

produced by summer and fall thunderstorms; hikers should stay weather-alert because of the potential for flash floods.

Average maximum and minimum temperatures are shown in the graph above. High temperatures at the Monument and Portal 4SW are mild during most seasons and remain near or below 90°F during the summer months, when high temperatures in the Sonoran Desert to the west can be much higher. Average low temperatures are in the 20s and 30s (mostly below freezing) from November through March. Because of cool air drainage into Cave Creek Canyon, the average temperatures are lower at Portal 4SW than at the National Monument.

Temperatures are more extreme just a few miles to the east at Rodeo where summer highs are nearly 10°F warmer than in Cave Creek Canyon, although winter lows are also a bit warmer. Record highs and lows at the Monument were 109°F in July of 1909 and -10°F in January of 1913. At Portal 4SW (where the data cover a much shorter time period) the record high was 100°F during June of 1980, while the coldest was -5°F in December of 1978.

It is important to remember that elevations in the Chiricahuas near the Canyon reach well above 9,000 feet and that all the weather observations available are taken at much lower elevations. Typically precipitation amounts increase substantially with elevation, as do local wind speeds. Depending on the season and the weather pattern, temperatures at higher elevations can be either colder or warmer than those at lower elevations.

28

Radar and Lightning Observations

Radar data can be used to monitor thunderstorm activity over the Chiricahuas when storms are expected. These data are available in real time from the National Weather Service (NWS) Office located in Tucson (the radar is located east-southeast of Tucson at an elevation of over 5,000 feet in the Empire Mountains). Because of the distance from the radar to the Chiricahuas, as well as blockage by the Whetstone Mountains, the radar beam is quite high above the surface by the time it is over the Chiricahuas. The radar beam is so high (~10,000 to 20,000 ft) above the land surface that it cannot detect precipitation falling from low clouds, for example, snow during winter. However, the radar can detect upper portions of deep cloud systems and thunderstorms over the Chiricahuas, and intense storms are accurately monitored. Because the radar beam is high above the mountains,

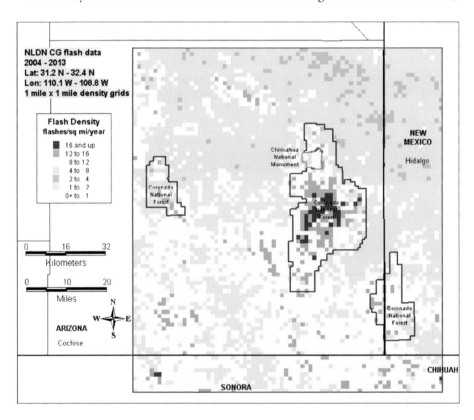

Annual average cloud-to-ground lightning flashes for each 1 mile square of area, based on 10 years of lightning data. Maximum average count is greater than 22 flashes per year over the square mile that includes Sentinel Peak. This map has been provided by Vaisala, Inc., which owns and operates the National Lightning Detection Network (NLDN).

one can not expect rainfall estimates made from the radar data to be accurate. The NWS radar data from Tucson can be accessed at http://radar. weather.gov/radar.php?rid=emx&product=NCR&overlay=11101111&loop =no, which is at the NWS Tucson website.

Finally, there is a monitoring system across the U.S. that detects cloud-to-ground lightning flashes. These data, although only available in real-time at the NWS, can be very useful in determining storm intensity and alerting forecasters to the potential for locally heavy rains and flash flooding. The highest frequency of occurrence of cloud-to-ground flashes occurs over the highest peaks of the Chiricahuas. The maxima during these 10 years appear to be centered on Sentinel Peak (more than 22 lightning flashes per year), and there is also a distinct lightning maximum over Portal Peak.

Because thunderstorms over the Chiricahuas can be intense, weather awareness on the part of hikers and other recreationalists is extremely important. In the Arizona Sky Islands, weather conditions can change very rapidly and people who will be out-of-doors should monitor the regional forecasts and keep a careful eye to the sky.

Rainbow over Cave Creek Canyon   *Barbara Miller*

4 Skies

Rick Beno

In the 19th century, Manifest Destiny was the concept that America should expand its reach from coast to coast. Without question, that concept has been fulfilled. Now, in the 21st century, our growth is tending skyward. While our population may not be growing skyward, we are continually and rapidly expanding our air and light pollution toward the stars—while slowly shrinking our clear dark sky territories. Sure, there are still places where the stars shine bright and the Milky Way glistens just as it did back in the 1800s. But these areas are rapidly becoming smaller, pushing those people who love the sky out of the cities, out of the suburbs, and farther and farther into the country—many all the way to the Chiricahuas and our wonderful Cave Creek Canyon and its surrounding deserts.

So, what prompted 80 plus regular people (who call themselves astronomers) to build more than 60 homes and observatories within 20 miles of Cave Creek Canyon? Much of the attraction is the residents already in the area: the naturalists, birders, and biologists who wish to maintain an environment that will remain natural for the animals and birds who make their homes here too.

The effort to build and live here is also a draw, for it is this

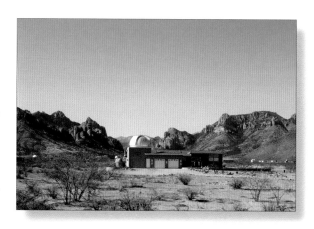

Eighty or more astronomers have moved to within 20 miles of Cave Creek Canyon.
Rick Beno

31

very inconvenience that we hope will keep the region natural for years to come. Of course, having the beauty of Cave Creek Canyon as our backdrop to the sky helps a lot too!

The darkness and clarity of the sky here in the Canyon's vicinity are necessary for us astronomers to fully utilize our equipment and practice our obsession with stars, nebulae, galaxies, and other night-time objects that we seek to explore and understand more fully.

But you don't have to be an astronomer to appreciate the skies here. With the lights turned off, look up—and you can enjoy all sorts of wonderful sights.

Yes, the moon and bright planets and stars are visible here, just like almost everywhere else. But, from a dark sky site like Cave Creek Canyon, expect to see the unexpected. Start by noticing the band of cloud-like light that stretches from horizon to horizon. That's not a real cloud, or any form of light pollution.

That is our very own Milky Way galaxy.

It doesn't matter what time of the year you

The Milky Way extends across the entire breadth of the night sky.
Fred Espenak

look, you'll see the Milky Way. During the summer you're looking towards the center of our galaxy and the constellation Sagittarius, while winter puts the outer regions on display. That "cloud" of our Milky Way is the combined light of hundreds of billions of stars shining from so far away that they come together as a faint brush stroke of light. Those darker regions in the Milky Way are dust particles scattered from long ago dying stars, still to form new stars, and planets waiting to be "born."

Another sight visible from a truly dark observing location is the zodiacal light. If you look in the direction where the sun set about one to two hours after sunset, you will notice a triangular patch of light rising above the horizon. Although this resembles the light domes that arise from cities just beyond the horizon, in reality this zodiacal light is scattered sunlight reflecting off dust particles orbiting our sun.

To carry this thought even further, keen observers should be able to see the gegenschein by looking exactly opposite the sun on particularly clear nights. The gegenschein is the back-scattered light of the sun reflecting back toward Earth from those same kinds of particles that also cause the zodiacal light.

Now let's go even deeper into our clear night sky.

Have you ever wondered just how far you can see on a clear night? City dwellers may talk in terms of miles. Like 240,000 miles to the moon. Or a few light years to the few bright stars visible when they look up into the "darkness" of their skies.

How about 2.5 million light-years to the Andromeda galaxy, which

Zodiacal light is a triangular ray of light that stretches up from the horizon.
Fred Espenak

33

The Andromeda Galaxy lies 2.5 million light-years away.

Rick Beno

is regularly visible from the Cave Creek Canyon area? Or 3 million light-years to the Triangulum galaxy?

And these impressive distances are without binoculars or telescopes. Add binoculars, and these distances quickly jump to the tens of millions of light-years.

Add telescopes—and literally, the sky's the limit!

If you're among those lucky enough to see the night skies from near Cave Creek Canyon, you already realize just how dark and amazing this area can be. There's a good chance that's why you came here in the first place.

But a question I hope each and every one of us asks ourselves is: "What can I do to help preserve this wonderful and natural environment?"

You can start by using shielded outdoor lighting—and only when you need it. You can use timers and sensors to turn off the lights when they're not needed. Also, only use enough light to get the job done. Shaded yellow or red lights are less disruptive than white lights. In addition, be sure to work with your neighbors and local government to spread the word regarding the preservation of dark skies and a natural environment.

For more information on keeping our skies dark, go to www.darksky.org. Remember, every little bit helps. Your local astronomers and all the local animals appreciate your efforts.

5   Fire History
Ronald Quinn

ave Creek Canyon and the surrounding Chiricahua Mountains have burned periodically for many thousands of years. Fire is as much a part of the mountain environment as wind and rain. The interplay between plants, animals, and fire has shaped a living landscape that would neither function nor look as it does without it. Living with fire, rather than attempting to totally suppress it, is essential to the maintenance and survival of our beautiful canyon and mountain range.

Scientists read Southwestern fire history from the scars that remain on old trees that burned, healed, and continued to grow. Each fire injury leaves its

A night view of the Horseshoe 2 Fire above Cave Creek Canyon. The fire is burning the forested ridges of the Chiricahua Wilderness. High flames at night indicate severe burning conditions.   *©2011 Fred Espenak*

mark, which can be dated by counting the number of annual growth rings formed beyond it. Researchers can construct chronologies from these scars that show when and where fires have occurred.

The fire history of the Chiricahuas follows the general pattern of the Southwest: Fires occurred at intervals of a decade or two for as far back as we have records from old trees, usually 300–500 years.

In 1902, Royal S. Kellogg made the first thorough study of the trees of the Chiricahua Mountains. He wrote, "I do not know of a single region in these mountains that has not been burned over in the last 20 or 30 years, and repeated fires have occurred in many places." Most of these fires were relatively small and patchy, and burned beneath the trees at low to moderate intensities. At about that time, this pattern ended almost everywhere in the Mountain West. Fires became relatively rare on public forestlands because of the new national policy of immediately putting out all wildfires.

Frequent fires in the Chiricahuas ceased in the 1890s. For almost the entire 20th century, small fires occurred almost every year, mostly started by lightning, but none grew to become large fires. This pattern dramatically ended in 1994, when the lightning-caused Rattlesnake Fire burned 24,000 acres through most of the higher elevation forests of the Chiricahuas. The fire burned out of control for more than three weeks until monsoon rains put it out—a natural fire with a natural ending.

In 2011, the Horseshoe 2 Fire, caused by humans, was nearly ten times larger, covering 222,000 acres. It burned across almost the entire range, including areas covered by the Rattlesnake Fire 17 years earlier. Huge fires

Natural air movement often causes smoke, here from backfires during the Horseshoe 2 Fire, to accumulate in canyons. Smoke patterns help fire fighters understand burning conditions.
Joy Comstock Mendez

like these two, now called "megafires," have become increasingly common throughout the Mountain West over the past 30 years. This change has been caused by a century of fuel buildup due to deliberate fire suppression, and, quite possibly, by climate change. The historical fire regime of frequent low-intensity fires had left most healthy tall trees and some shrubs alive and standing, removed dead plant material from the forest floor, and prevented the growth of dense thickets of more flammable trees and shrubs.

After such fires became rare, most forested areas gradually became crowded with spindly trees growing too close to one another, and the forest floor steadily accumulated dead plant materials. When wildfire ignites this long accumulation of fuels, the high-intensity flames kill all trees by leaping through the treetops. The intense heat penetrates the soil, killing seeds and soil organisms, leaving behind sterile powder and sand devoid of life. Wind and water then carry away this loose, exposed mineral material. It is a slow and difficult process for the forest to return to these impoverished sites.

Wildfire in Cave Creek and other large local canyons is a more complex event than the towering conflagrations of the higher mountains. Natural fires, caused by lightning, are more likely to start at higher elevations and spread downhill toward canyon bottoms. Generally, fire spreads more slowly downhill than uphill, and the rocky cliffs and outcrops of canyon walls form irregular firebreaks. Consequently, wildfires often come toward large canyons, like Cave Creek, from different directions and burn at varying intensities, pushed by erratic winds. The vegetation in larger canyons is uneven in stature, and wildfires can be patchy. Some trees and shrubs—such as maples, cottonwoods, sycamores, and chokecherries—are more resistant to burning because they contain quite a bit of water. These

A fire crew igniting a backfire with cans that drip flames on vegetation. The extensive use of backfires in Cave Creek and its tributaries protected structures and important canyon ecosystems.
Joy Comstock Mendez

may not burn at all, while partly burned ones can recover quickly. The resulting vegetation is more open and patchy, supporting more animal numbers and species.

In the Chiricahuas, so far, the relatively slow approach of megafires toward canyon bottoms has given fire fighters time to make and execute plans to stop wildfires before they reach critical areas. Since our canyons have most of the buildings, campgrounds, roads, and other centers of human activity, they are given priority for fire defense. During the Horseshoe 2 Fire, parts of Cave Creek Canyon, for example above the Southwestern Research Station and in South Fork, were deliberately burned by backfires set by firefighters. These were set where they would burn toward the wildfire at moderate intensities, creating firebreaks to stop the approach of the big fire.

These backfires were successful, helping save homes and structures in the canyon, while preserving the unique plant and wildlife diversity that makes Cave Creek Canyon so special. Three years later, those areas look much as they did before the fire.

As more and more people visit and live in and around the Chiricahua Mountains, the danger of wildfires caused by humans is steadily increasing. Lightning in the monsoon months starts natural fires, many of which, including the megafire of 1994, are naturally extinguished by rainfall. Wildfires caused by humans can and do occur any time when rainfall has been scarce and vegetation is flammable.

Since the Chiricahua Mountains are naturally arid with long dry periods, fire season can now be any season. An obvious prediction of climate change is more hot weather, causing more dry vegetation, more often. Another prediction is more and longer droughts. If large wildfires become more frequent and more intense, they could generate widespread changes in patterns of vegetation and wildlife. Generally, most woody shrubs and trees would become less common, and species that are favored by frequent burning would take their place. Fires in the spring, when many plants and animals are breeding and reproducing, would be particularly disruptive.

Given these uncertainties, it is extremely important that we take every precaution to prevent accidental human-caused wildfires. Fire safety here means obeying rules and regulations about all outdoor fires, and creating defensible spaces around structures where natural plants, landscaping, and all other flammable materials are carefully cleared away.

In this respect Smokey Bear is still right.

Plants and Animals

The diversity of plant and animal adaptations, such as this horned lizard's ability to squirt blood from its eyes, is part of the attraction of Cave Creek Canyon.
©Raymond A. Mendez 2014

Montezuma Quail   *Noel Snyder*

6 Habitat Zones
Peg Abbott

The dramatic drive into Cave Creek Canyon appears as a marvelous and stunning accident of geography. The canyon view is so grand and unexpected with vibrant rock colors and alluring vegetation that one marvels at its conception. Grand but not chaotic, the distribution of plants and animals in the canyon is organized, and is governed by living (biotic) and non-living (abiotic) factors. Each species encountered has established itself in a community or habitat zone here over time: Some cling tightly to one habitat zone, while others, more flexible, occur in more than one. Each species finds success by tolerating the climate (particularly temperature and rainfall variation), by co-existing with other species established here, and by being resilient to disease, fire, predation, and the other formative factors that shape ecological communities.

Cave Creek Canyon is considered by many to be one of the best and most accessible ecological classrooms on Earth. Its extraordinary biodiversity draws professional and amateur naturalists from around the world to study and enjoy. The prestigious American Museum of Natural History established a biological field station here in 1955. The living laboratory of Cave Creek Canyon is recognized as part of the Madrean Sky Islands, one of Conservation International's 34 Global Biodiversity Hotspots. This prominent designation validates the canyon's biological integrity. Cave Creek Canyon is embedded in that short list of Earth's richest and most endangered terrestrial ecosystems.

By all measures it is a unique and globally special place.

Of the world's estimated twenty Sky Island complexes, only the Madrean Archipelago spans habitats from cold to tropical/subtropical zones. From space, the Madrean Sky Islands appear as steppingstones between great contiguous mountain masses. Cave Creek Canyon's position as a stepping-stone is just south of the Madrean Line, an imaginary line running the same course as Interstate 10 and the route of the Union Pacific Railroad, at about 32° North Latitude. The Madrean Line is central to the 40 or so islands (Brusca and Moore now describe 65) of the U.S. side of the Madrean Archipelago. Like Wallace's Line, which marks the faunal boundary between Australia and Asia, this route roughly divides mountain islands to the south that are dominated by species from Mexico's Sierra Madre ranges (Madrean elements), and those to the north more influenced by species of cold-temperate Rocky Mountain origin (Petran elements). The Chiricahuas have a decidedly strong Madrean influence. No address to the north could host such diversity; few places in this latitude zone can compare.

Several key factors contribute to species richness in the archipelago and the way that communities are organized as visibly stacked habitat zones in each of the Sky Islands. Factors for Cave Creek Canyon can be summarized as:

• Our geographic position at the convergence of four biological realms;

• Our prominent position at a connecting route for species called the Deming, or Cordilleran Gap,

• Our placement in the Chiricahua Mountains, largest of the Sky Islands, and the canyon's range of elevation and topographic complexity that

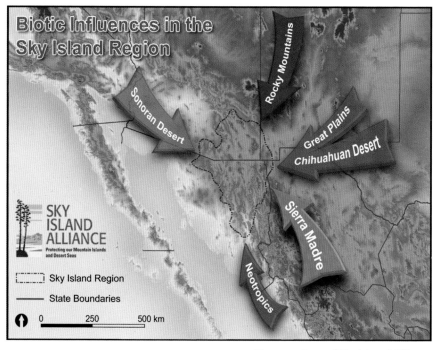

Map courtesy of Sky Island Alliance

42

create microclimates and expand niche opportunities,

- Our geologic heritage, and

- Our sparse human development due to low population.

Habitat Zones as Ecological Biomes
• Desert Scrub (mainly on limestone soils at base of Chiricahuas)
• Chihuahuan Desert Grassland
• Oak Savanna (Grassland)
• Chaparral Pine–Oak Woodland
• Pine Forest
• Mixed Conifer Forest

If biodiversity can be likened to a menu, then Cave Creek Canyon's rich choice of entrees is based on having an extraordinary array of ingredients in the cupboard. Cave Creek Canyon's habitat zones hold plant and animal communities based on a blend of ingredients from two mountain and two desert regions located at the convergence of four major biotic realms.

In Cave Creek Canyon, species that might normally occur hundreds of miles apart find themselves close together, taking root around a spring or vying for the same nest hole. Of the dozen or so U.S. Sky Islands that rise from a sea of grass at this convergence, the Chiricahuas sit closest to the lowest elevation gap of the entire Cordillera, an area of parallel ranges that spreads from the Continental Divide east of Animas and west of Deming, New Mexico. This gap sits in a slightly higher grassland habitat zone that bridges two deserts, the Chihuahuan to the east, and Sonoran to the west. This is the lowest elevation of the 4,500-mile long continental spine of the Rockies/Sierra Madre Cordillera. The gap allows even farther-reaching elements of the Great Plains to come through from the East (such as wintering sparrows, buntings and longspurs), and some species of the more diverse chaparral of Nevada and California (such as manzanita and other evergreen shrubs) to intermingle from the West.

The climate of Cave Creek Canyon results from its latitude, longitude, and position in the interior of a continent. It is semi-arid with bi-seasonal periods of rain, winter and summer. As patterns of rainfall are critical to forming plant communities, this bi-seasonal pattern invites high biodiversity by attracting summer and winter moisture adapted species. The Cave Creek watershed's upper elevation pine and mixed conifer habitats are typical of northern (Petran) cool temperate zones, with moisture augmented by winter snow. Its southern-influenced (Encinal or oak) habitat zones of pine-oak and oak woodlands as well as oak grasslands respond to summer monsoon rains and support a high percentage of Madrean plants and animals more comfortable in warm temperate zones.

Situated on the east side of the archipelago, the Chiricahuas are rimmed by grasslands (and scattered patches of desert scrub) dominated by eastern-origin Chihuahuan Desert species, which are more abundant here than many of the expected western-origin species described for the Arizona Sonoran Upland habitat of Sky Islands to the west.

Habitat zones of Cave Creek Canyon and the Sky Islands correspond to Earth's major plant and animal communities called biomes. Eight habitat zones or biomes are assigned to Arizona's Sky Islands, and, in the short drive from Rodeo to Rustler Park, one finds examples of these: Desert Grassland and Desert Scrub, Oak-Grassland, Oak Woodland, Pine–Oak Woodland, Pine Forest, and Mixed Coniferous Forest (see sidebar). Riparian habitats are not biomes, but they provide a vital connection between mountain and plain as they follow linear pathways of creeks, rivers, and intermittent waterways. Anyone hiking here notes a strange combination of yuccas and pines as just one hint of the mix of remarkable plant forms enabled by the riparian habitats that cross through our vertically stacked habitat zones. In places like the South Fork and Turkey Creek, one finds Douglas Fir trees at lower elevations than expected, more at home in the Rockies.

An additional aspect of biodiversity in the Sky Islands is that closely related species normally separated geographically may be brought together here or may persist in sheltered pockets over time, supported by the vertically stacked habitat zones. In the Chiricahuas, relict stands of both Colorado and Single-leaf Pinyon, little known south of the Mogollon Rim since Pleistocene times, can be found interspersed with more widespread Border Pinyon, a common borderland Madrean species. Birders are drawn to the Chiricahuas in search of

---

Pioneers of Our Understanding of Sky Islands

In 1889, C. Hart Merriam had been inspired by Northern Arizona's San Francisco Mountains near Flagstaff, where distant views of clear bands of vegetation on the mountain gave rise to his concept of Life Zones. Forrest Shreve, working from Carnegie's Desert Lab in Tucson applied the concept to Southern Arizona, expanding it and sleuthing out its complexities to create a system of vegetation classification published in 1915, still in use today. In 1957, Joe Marshall described the predictable stacking of these biotic communities on the isolated, forested mountain ranges of Arizona, New Mexico, and Texas south into Mexico, in an area he termed the Madrean Archipelago. He set the definition for a mountain island to be an area above 5000 feet, supporting a continuous area of Madrean oak and pine-oak woodland. Weldon Heald coined the term "Sky Island" from his home in Cave Creek Canyon, inspired by the massive walls of welded-tuff and older volcanic layers, all clad with recognizable plant communities.

some 30 or more avian species of Mexican affinity that occur alongside species of the Northern Rockies. More than half the total species of birds in the United States can be found in and around the Chiricahuas. At each level of every taxonomic group, the message of diversity is clear.

The size and complexity of the Chiricahua range helps increase biodiversity. The Chiricahuas are the largest of Arizona's Sky Islands, approximately 40 miles long and extending 4 to 20 miles wide. They are second-highest in elevation of the islands, with Chiricahua Peak standing lower only than Mt. Graham in the Pinaleños. Elevation ranges from 4,124 feet at Rodeo, New Mexico, at the junction of Highway 80 and Portal Road to 9,795 feet atop Chiricahua Peak for a gain of more than 5,000 feet. Within that gradient, with a typical Sky Island gain of 3–4 inches of precipitation for every 1,000-foot increase in elevation, there is a major increase by percentage for life at higher elevations. Net moisture stays available longer as well, with an average decrease in temperature of 3 degrees per 1,000 feet accompanied by shade of forest habitats.

Geologic heritage can also explain Cave Creek Canyon's diversity. As communities reassembled themselves after major events like wetter conditions of glacial epochs and explosions of the Turkey Creek Caldera 27 million years ago, potential reestablishment species poured in from all directions. Plant communities ordered themselves as stacked habitat zones on this mountain platform. Madrean communities are considered young in nature, assembling throughout the Southwest during and after the influence of Pleistocene glaciation to the north, which brought periods of increased moisture followed by arid stages. Desert communities are even younger, with some species finding their way here as recently as 4,000 years ago.

The road and trail systems of Cave Creek Canyon allow the exploration of habitat zones and species mix that change with increasing elevation. Varied rock layers erode to form soils with different chemistry and moisture-holding capacity. This complicates making a neat picture of Nature's organization, and, while there are no clear boundaries, pioneering ecologists like C. Hart Merriam, Forrest Shreve, Joe Marshall, David Brown, Charles Lowe, and Peter Warshall (see sidebar) gave us a framework to understand the tapestry of life here.

Conserving it is now our legacy.

An Olive Warbler's Journey

Imagine the migratory journey of an Olive Warbler, headed north to Cave Creek Canyon from the Sierra Madres to breed in the Chiricahuas. For a less than 1-ounce male, there is little room for error.

While a few Olive Warblers stay in the Chiricahua Mountains each winter, this individual winters in the milder climate of the Mexican Plateau and returns annually to the pine forest habitat that sustains his breeding. This Olive Warbler may make the journey between wintering and breeding terrain four or five times in a lifetime.

Flying over a sea of grasslands, over small mountain islands that hold only sparse oak woodlands, he ignores the lesser islands other than for quick, risky stops to feed. Each night aloft, he keeps focused, keeps flapping wings. Navigating in the easier-flight conditions of night and guided to some degree by stars, after hundreds of miles this male's fuel supply is running out.

In dawn light he descends, knowing he must land. Searching for safe haven, he sees a major canyon that juts deep into its mountain island, through spectacular cliffs.

To this veteran migrant, first light brings clues as a now-familiar drainage helps to point the way. On course, drawing on his last energies, his flight path parallels the green ribbon of vegetation lining Cave Creek's Main

Fork, past where the South Fork comes in, past the Middle Fork branch from Herb Martyr. He continues up the North Fork, ascending the steep terrain of its headwaters, finally landing on a ridge of broad spreading pines. This still-green patch—his patch if he can defend territory and stay dominant—made it through the 2011 Horseshoe 2 Fire that burned 222,954 acres of the Chiricahuas. That year no Olive Warbler nesting was reported. Missing that year, he has work to do. He sings, a first survey of this year's competition.

Finding a clump of mistletoe, the same unusual color as his head, he recognizes nest material. He is home, back at the head of Cave Creek Canyon.

Peg Abbott

7   Trees, Shrubs, and Grasslands
Al Bammann

D riving from Portal to the top of the Cave Creek watershed, there is a remarkable change in the plants seen along the way. The different plant species are responding to changes in moisture, temperature, aspect, soils and historic disturbances. Each plant species has a preferred set of ecological conditions where it does best. Above and below this preferred area, that species will be less common and usually not as tall or as vigorous. For convenience, the Cave Creek watershed can be broken into four elevation zones: mesquite-grassland, lower canyon, upper canyon, and mountain slopes. The two canyon zones, where most visitors spend time, can conveniently be divided into canyon bottom and slope communities.

Mesquite Grasslands

Starting at Portal, the broad upward sloping valley bottom was desert grassland before heavy livestock grazing and fire control allowed shrubs and cactus to invade this area. Fire will never become a welcome disturbance here because of the number of private homes, so shrubs will continue to increase at the expense of grasses. Most of the shrubs that have increased in this area over the last 100 years are more typical of desert communities.

Prickly Pear with fruit.
Photos by Noel Snyder unless otherwise indicated

47

Cave Creek Madrone fruits are a major food source for many bird species through the fall months, including thrushes, woodpeckers, and trogons.

Mesquite is the most conspicuous of the shrubs. Young Mesquites once would have been killed by lightning-caused fires that occurred at an average return interval of about five years. The original grasses, such as Sideoats Grama and Green Sprangletop, are still present but as an inconspicuous understory. Lehmann Lovegrass, brought in from southern Africa during drought years, is present throughout this area and is still increasing. Mesquite is an extremely important species for wildlife. The leaves are heavily browsed by deer. Seed pods are eaten by everything from bears to fox to javelina to people. Because Mesquite is a legume, it fixes nitrogen, and its fallen leaves enrich the soil under the trees.

Prickly Pear Cactus is quite common in the mesquite-grassland, although it also is found at the top of the highest ridges. The pads are an important source of water and food for javelina and woodrats in the dry season. Several bird species prefer to nest between its spiny pads. Cactus fruit, called tunas, are eaten by most of the local birds and mammals.

The Lower Canyon Community

By the time you've driven up the road to the Ranger Station, you will have noticed an increase in dark green Alligator Juniper trees mixed in with the Mesquites. Tall broad-leafed trees such as Sycamore and Cottonwood can be seen along Cave Creek to your left. Major changes in the environment have occurred since leaving the open valley bottom area, resulting in changes in plants. The higher elevation and narrowing canyon have lower average temperatures. Cliffs provide shade during various times of the day and reduce drying winds. More moisture is available to plants here. There has been a gradual shift from plants common in the desert below Portal to those common in forests higher up, but now it is obvious. It will be easiest to consider the plant community found in the canyon bottom near Cave Creek separate from the communities on the steep hillsides above.

Most visitors spend their time in the canyon bottom along the lower reaches of Cave Creek Canyon and its tributaries. The Creek flows year-round in several stretches. Several species of low-growing willows are found where water is present. The smooth white bark of the Sycamores contrasts with the furrowed gray bark of Arizona Cypress and Cottonwood trees near creek banks. Lower terraces are forested with a diverse mix of Arizona Walnut, Madrone, several oak species, and two species of juniper trees. Most of the oak species originated in the Madrean plant community to our south. These oaks keep their leaves through winter to take advantage of rains and mild temperatures and keep growing. Leaves are dropped at the beginning of the dry season in late spring and are regrown before the summer monsoon rains. All these trees produce various types of "fruit" important to the wildlife, but because the environment is quite harsh it might be several years between crops on individual trees. Most of the diverse bird species

found through the lower canyon feed on insects that feed on leaves of these trees. Border Pinyon Pine first becomes common near the Ranger Station.

As you travel up the Canyon, pinyon is first joined by Chihuahua Pine, and by the mouth of South Fork Apache Pine is quite common. The Apache Pine is especially conspicuous because its needles are 10"–12" long and grow at the end of branches in

Apache Pines often reach nearly 100 feet in height and dominate the canyon bottoms at mid elevations.

thick clusters like pompons. Traveling up any of the canyons you'll notice that the pines grow taller and more numerous. Throughout the year, cold air drains off the slopes and into the canyon bottom during the night and early morning. Cooler temperatures favor conifers over broadleaf trees. Beneath the large trees grow a mix of young trees as well as several species of shrubs such as Poison Oak and Birch-leaf Buckthorn. Grass species are especially diverse because this is the mixing zone with both lower and higher elevation species present. The short, thin leaves and tall slender seed stalks of Pinyon Dropseed Grass are conspicuous in shady areas. Thick clumps of Deer Grass become common along stream banks several years after major flood events. Horsetail, a pencil-diameter, unbranched tubular plant is common at water's edge in some stretches. (See Chapter 8 for more about the Horsetail.)

The slopes above the canyon bottom differ by having fewer plant species. The first Alligator Juniper trees you'll see as you enter the lower canyon area are all rather young. They grew from seeds produced by old trees growing on rocky outcrops where they were protected from the wildfires that were once common throughout this mountain range. Several species of oaks, especially Emery, Blue, and White oak are mixed in with Pinyon Pine and two species of juniper. Manzanita shrubs, conspicuous with smooth, red

South-facing slopes above the canyon have far more oak trees and more grasses than the pine-dominated north-facing slopes.   *Jonathan Patt*

bark, are especially common here. Silk Tassel, Mearns Sumac, and Catclaw are other common shrubs. Junipers and Manzanitas are both extremely important to wildlife because, after wet years, they produce large quantities of berries relished by everything from bears to wintering bluebirds. Grasses include several grama grass species, but the tall purple seed heads of Bull Muhly are especially conspicuous after the monsoon rains and into fall. Looking at the south-facing slopes above the canyon, you will notice far more oak trees and more grasses there than on the pine-dominated north-facing slopes directly across. Less direct sun on the north-facing slopes means the soil stays moist longer and temperatures stay cooler here, favoring conifers. Patchy areas of these slopes burned in the recent fires.

The native plant community is well adapted to fire. Individual plants were killed by the 2011 Horseshoe 2 Fire, but overall, the slope community was little affected. Oak and Alligator Junipers readily resprouted from the roots as did the Silk Tassel, Catclaw, and Sumac shrubs. Most perennial grasses regrew with the first summer rains. Manzanita seeds germinated in many locations where old stands were located. Certainly the dead trunks of large trees are conspicuous and will remain so for decades, but the ecological impacts of this fire are rapidly fading in this section of Cave Creek Canyon.

Upper Canyon Zone

An artificial, but useful dividing line between the lower and upper canyon zones is the prevalence of Bigtooth Maple trees on the creek bank and lower terrace. Maples are sensitive to warm night-time temperatures and require moist soil. And, while a few individual trees and small stands are present in the lower canyon zone, they become more numerous as the elevation rises. Maple leaves turn bright yellow or red after the first autumn frost and are quite a sight to see!

With the cooler temperatures, Cottonwoods are now absent. Chihuahua Pines become less numerous. Apache Pines and Arizona Cypress seem to be as common as the oaks, walnuts, and sycamores combined. Trees appear unusually tall and slender as they stretch upward in the narrow canyon, reaching for sunlight. Water is less a limiting factor in the upper canyon area. There is more surface flow in the creek even in the dry season. Between large flood events, Deer Grass grows in continuous stands along the stream banks. Rainfall has increased with elevation. The narrow canyon width increases shade while decreasing wind speed. The cooler temperatures and relatively fewer broad-leafed trees seem to result in reduced numbers of insects available to birds. There still are plenty of Alligator Junipers mixed with Silver leaf Oaks and berry-producing

Maples in autumn after the first frost bring brilliant color to Cave Creek Canyon.

shrubs like California Buckthorn to attract bears and feed Gray Fox, Ringtails, and numerous birds. But the canyon bottom is losing its subtropical feel as the elevation rises. Aspen trees are first found growing in canyon bottoms usually at about 7,000 feet. They indicate that you are truly in environmental conditions typical of the Rocky Mountains.

Many short sections in the upper canyon burned in the Horseshoe 2 Fire. Native plants here are adapted to this natural disturbance. Some, like old-growth Douglas Fir and Apache Pine, have thick bark that protected them from all but the most intense flames. Others, like maple and oak trees, resprouted from root crowns; some even before the summer rains arrived. Still other species have reseeded from nearby surviving trees or from seeds that were deep in the soil. Many burned areas have recovered enough that a casual glance detects no damage after only three years.

The slopes above the canyon bottom have plant groups similar to slopes in the lower canyon area, but there has been a shift in species. Typical temperatures are much lower here, and much more moisture is available to plants. Winter snow is common and will last several months on north-facing slopes. Oak species have shifted from Emery and White Oak to Silverleaf Oak and, at the highest elevations, to Gambel Oak. Pinyon Pine and Alligator Juniper are decreasing in importance and are replaced by more Douglas Firs. Apache Pines, common in Mexican mountains to our south, have been replaced by Ponderosa Pine, common farther north. On the warmer south-facing slopes, shrubs such as Manzanita, Mountain Mahogany, and Three-leaf Sumac are still common. The cooler north-facing slopes have many of the shrub species typical of ridge tops above Rustler and Barfoot Parks. Elderberry, Raspberry, Aspen, and New Mexico Locust grow here.

Mountain Ridge Tops

There are no roads to the upper slopes and ridge tops in the Cave Creek watershed, but what you would find there is the same as what you can drive to near Rustler and Barfoot Parks. Large portions of these areas were severely burned in the Horseshoe 2 Fire. Black trunks of Douglas Fir, Ponderosa Pine, and Gambel Oak immediately catch your attention, but most of the area actually survived largely intact. Trees here are species common in the Rocky Mountains rather than the Sierra Madre. The large pine and fir trees at the junction of Barfoot and Rustler roads seem to be "old growth," but few individuals actually pre-date the logging era, and fewer still were growing before the end of the natural fire era, when the Apache people were removed from their homeland in 1876.

Relatively mild winter temperatures and the two wet seasons (winter rains and summer monsoons) allow conifers to grow rapidly. Gambel Oak, typical of northern forests, loses its leaves in fall unlike the oak species found at lower elevations. Aspen stands are very conspicuous, not only during spring and summer with their bright green leaves and silver bark, but especially in fall when the foliage turns golden. The southernmost stands of Engelmann Spruce in North America are found along the upper-most slopes in the Chiricahua Mountains; another reminder that, at these elevations, the Rocky Mountain plant community prevails.

Dense patches of young Aspens are quickly regrowing wherever the 2011 fire swept through an old stand. This

Aspens in fall color on Flys Peak with leaves ranging from green through yellow to orange.

tree species is fire-adapted, and the entire patch regrows from an extensive, interconnected root system. Actually, fire ecologists consider aspen to be fire-dependent; where fires are prevented, conifer trees come up under the aspens and eventually shade them out.

In places where the fire burned the edges of the meadows, locally called "parks," there are thick patches of re-sprouted Scouler Willow, Mexican Elderberry, and Raspberry. These species would be crowded out if fires didn't periodically kill the taller conifers. Raspberries and Elderberries are as attractive to bears and birds as they are to people when they ripen in July and August. The actual park-like meadows are typically found either where the soils are too shallow to support trees and shrubs, or in low spots where water-logged soils during the growing season prevent survival of woody plants.

With the drying of the climate, some of these unique park communities may be lost if trees are able to survive in drier soils. These forest openings are important feeding areas for bear, deer and many bird species because of the lush low vegetation and abundant insect life.

During monsoons, wildflowers fill the higher elevation meadows, particularly after wildfires.

8   Wildflower Walks in the Canyon
Barbara Miller

C ave Creek Canyon has a great diversity in plant habitats with changes in elevation and topography. It provides opportunities for 'botanizing' with many seasonally different blooming plants. Take a walk along the forest roads, the creeks and trails, and keep a plant list of what you see. Here are three pleasant rambles where you can enjoy the plants and the scenery.

A ramble up South Fork

Start your walk along the road that parallels Cave Creek's South Fork. The creek is a great place to look for flowers—especially after the summer rains have come.

As you near the bridge, go close to the creek itself to

(Top) Beebalm

(Bottom)
Hummingbird
Trumpet
Rose Ann Rowlett

*All photos by
Barbara Miller,
unless otherwise
indicated.*

see the light purple Beebalm, *Monarda fistulosa menthaefolia*, which is in the Mint family (formerly known as Labiateae, now called Lamiaceae), and the deep red-orange *Zauschneria latifolia*, or Hummingbid Trumpet, now renamed *Epilobium canum* in the Evening Primrose family (Onagraceae).

The beautiful Golden Columbine, *Aquilegia chrysantha* (family

Ranunculaceae) also likes the damp and shady creekside location.

Just before the bridge, look carefully into the deep grasses, and you may see one of our milkweeds, *Asclepias tuberosa.*

A member of the Mint family, Lemmon's Sage, or Salvia (*Salvia lemmonii*), has a limited distribution in the Southwest. It can be seen both in South Fork and on top of the mountain. The tubular deep rose-pink flowers, which

(From the top) Golden Columbine, Butterfly Weed, and Lemmon's Sage or Salvia.

bloom in late summer, are hummingbird-pollinated.

Different species of globe mallows, in the Mallow family (Malvaceae) flower all summer. This is one of several species of *Sphaeralcea* in the Chiricahuas. The orange color stands out in the greens of the forest. Look for the five petals.

Scouringrush Horsetail, *Equisetum hyemale,* grows in moist and wet soil along streams as well as along dry trails such as Cave Creek Nature Trail. It produces no flowers but instead has reproductive spores similar to those of ferns, and grows from underground rhizomes. *Equisetum* is the only remaining genus in Equisetaceae, a family of vascular plants and a "living fossil" that dominated the understory of late Paleozoic

Globe Mallow, Scouringrush (also known as Horsetail), and Goldenrod.

forests. The stems are coated with abrasive silicates, giving them a sandpaper texture. Old-timers used them to clean metal cooking pans. Stem sections pulled apart can be made into whistles.

Goldenrod, or *Solidago* sp., (Asteraceae family), is showy in late summer with golden yellow flowers on long spikes. Ray and disk flowers form the flower head.

Stachys coccinea, or Texas Betony, is a perennial herb in the Mint (Lamiaceae) family. Look for the four-sided stem common to this family.

Texas Betony, also known as Scarlet Sage

Monarda citriodora spp., or Lemon Beebalm, and sometimes called Horsemint, is another member of the Mint family. It varies from white to slightly pink. Look for the square stem and flower clusters at intervals on a spike. This *Monarda* does not need to be in wet areas as does the light purple *Monarda menthaefolia.*

The Cave Creek Nature Trail

The Cave Creek Nature Trail begins at the Silver Peak parking area. At this trailhead, take a hard left outside the fence. The trail follows the base of the mountain until it reaches Sunny Flat campground. You will pass two rock-

Lemon Beebalm is also called Horsemint.

walled structures built to store dynamite and blasting powder used by the CCC to build roads in the late 1930s. You can make a loop by crossing the Sunny Flat bridge and walking the road back, or you can just return along the trail to the parking area.

The nature trail traverses through oak, pine, sycamore, and cottonwood with streamside *Salix gooddingii* (Goodding's Willow) as it parallels both the creek and the mountain cliff. In spring and summer *Penstemon pseudospectablis*, *Acourtia wrightii,* or Brownfoot, and the milkweed *Asclepias tuberosa* bloom here and there.

Penstemon is one of our local wildflower rock stars, and these plants have opposite leaves and flowers that are tube-shaped and two-lipped. Formerly they were in the Snapdragon or Figwort family (Scrophulariaceae), but new genetic research has moved them to the family Plantaginaceae. Some species of Penstemon, especially those that are pink and red, are attractive to hummingbirds. Blue and purple Penstemon are bee-pollinated. Pollination ecologists recognize them as attracting large numbers of native bees.

Penstemon pseudospectablis, Desert Penstemon, is one of the very early bloomers with full flowers in April.

The red *Penstemon barbatus* Scarlet Bugler is another canyon Penstemon that begins blooming later. It can also be found at lower elevations and in the high country.

Poison ivy is very common along Cave Creek.

A Claret Cup cactus (*Echinocereus* sp.) hides on top of a large boulder and makes a show in late April.

This route also makes a good fall color walk. But beware of the Poison Ivy (*Toxicodendron rydbergii*)! It's in the Anacardiaceae, the Sumac or Cashew family, and is easy to identify with its three bright green leaflets during the growing season. In the fall, those leaves turn red/orange/yellow just before winter dormancy.

Another autumn treat is the Smooth Sumac (*Rhus glabra*), a thicket-forming small deciduous tree. In summer the yellow cluster of upright blossoms precede the red fruit and scarlet pinnately compound foliage of autumn.

(Top) Those who look up to a boulder along the Cave Creek Canyon Nature Trail are rewarded by seeing a Claret Cup Cactus. (Bottom) In fall the leaves of the Smooth Sumac turn bright red.

60

Conopholis sp. is sometimes called Cancer-root or bear corn, and it has virtually no chlorophyll.

Conopholis sp. (Orobanchaceae family) is a **holoparastic** genus, meaning it is completely parasitic on other plants and has virtually no chlorophyll. In this case, the plant is parasitic on the roots of the forest floor, specifically the oaks. Underground is a vascular system consisting of both parasite and host tissue. When mature, the floral stalks erupt above ground to produce this fascinating inflorescence.

Herb Martyr to Ash Spring along the Basin Trail

The trail from Herb Martyr intersects the Basin Trail just about a quarter of a mile from the parking area. Take a right at the signage, and you will be heading through open oak woodland, then some dark forested area, across a small spring-fed drainage, and then to Ash Spring. There are still

Birds and trees

Near the South Fork Bridge is a tall Siberian Elm—evidence perhaps of early settlers in the area. The migrant Red-naped Sapsuckers are drawn to the tree by its sap and are a common sight in both spring and fall. They drill holes in the tree bark and eat the running sap as well as the insects attracted to it. Later leaf skeletonizer caterpillars will totally defoliate the tree, yet the leaves will re-grow. Also a tall Cottonwood near the bridge is at the species' highest elevation for this drainage.

remnants of an old wooden building here, indicating a long ago residence. An old apple tree and other fruit trees are present.

In the marshy area are two ponds that were added in 2014 for Chiricahua Leopard Frogs. Turn right and take the trail downhill to an old road and return to Herb Martyr, or continue on the Basin Trail to the Greenhouse road, then downhill to the Forest Service road and back to the parking area. That part of the Basin Trail weaves in and out of the drainages with some south and east exposed hills. After the summer rains, the grasses and flowers are in abundance here.

In the late summer, you might also find the spectacular but uncommon Arizona Desert Foxglove, *Brachystigma wrightii*, along this trail. It is in the Snapdragon or Figwort family (Scrophulariaceae) and is also on the New Mexico rare plant list.

(Top) Arizona Desert Foxglove
(Bottom) The Firecracker Bush is pollinated by hummingbirds.

Another mid-summer beauty near Ash Spring is the lovely Firecracker Bush, *Bouvardia ternifolia*, which is in the Rubiaceae (Madder family). Its conspicuous tubular shape and red color are startling to come upon and are excellent for attracting hummingbirds.

Even the grasses are beautiful along the Basin Trail near Ash Spring. The white Mexican Star, *Milla biflora*, is a member of the Amaryllis family, Asparagaceae, and is native to the Southwestern states.

Now you can take the Trans-mountain road and head towards Rustler Park, but make a brief stop at the East Turkey Creek crossing. Here the *Mimulus* grow, both the early yellow *Mimulus guttatus* (bee-pollinated) that begins blooming in April and the orange red *Mimulus cardinalis* (a hummingbird flower) that blooms later in the year. The common name is Monkey Flower, and they are members of Phrymaceae, the Lopseed family (formerly Scrophulariaceae or Figworts).

The yellow *Mimulus* is one of the early spring flowers and blooms continuously through late summer in wet places with *M. cardinalis* joining later on. The *Mimulus* species have very diverse flowers and are being used by the evolutionary biologists to understand how floral diversity evolved.

This is another good area for Golden Columbines with their long spurs to store nectar, making them attractive to hummingbirds, hawk moths, and bumblebees. Research shows Columbines have developed these unusually long nectar spurs to accommodate their pollinators.

(Top) The Mexican Star lurks among the grasses and flowers during monsoons.
Wynne Brown
(Bottom) Both the yellow and red Monkey Flowers are common.

63

Mullein (*Verbascum thapsus*), in the Scrophulariaceae family, is an alien plant that loves to find a place near water where there is disturbed soil. It hosts many insects and is found along with the Monkey Flowers, where East Turkey Creek crosses the Trans-mountain road.

Mullein is a biennial plant living for two years. One Mullein plant may make more than 100,000 seeds in a year, but most birds apparently find the seeds too small to eat. Common Mullein is a pioneer plant, so it is one of the first plants to grow in a place that has burned or otherwise been disturbed. It can also be seen growing along dry trails both in Cave Creek and at the top of the mountains.

Keep in mind that, like people, bears too prefer to walk the easy route. Their droppings are seen often on the trails and roads and are frequently full of juniper berries. Check to see if the droppings are soft and fresh—or maybe even still warm. You may be lucky enough to see the bear! and you can read more about them in Chapter 9.

Now grab your plant identification books, and go take a walk!

(Top and right) Mullein is an introduced biennial.

(Below) Evidence of bears is a frequent sight for hikers.

9 Mammals
Mel Moe

$\mathcal{T}$he Chiricahuas perhaps support the greatest diversity of mammals in the United States. More than 80 species are found in habitats ranging from desert at 4,000 feet to spruce and fir forests at above 9,000 feet.

Bats

Anyone looking up at the sky in the Chiricahuas on a summer night is likely to see bats darting by. This area is home to at least 22 species of bats, the most found in one place anywhere in the United States. Some of these are permanent residents, while others migrate south in winter. Many permanent residents hibernate during the winter, but others are active all year. You can read more about these animals in Chapter 10.

Rodents, rabbits, and hares

The largest group of mammals found here are the rodents, represented by more than 30 species. They range in size from the tiny Pygmy Mouse, weighing less than a third of an ounce, to the Porcupine that can weigh up to 20 pounds. Most rodents are nocturnal, but daytime visitors are likely to see Cliff Chipmunks and Rock Squirrels. You might also

Chiricahua Fox Squirrel
*Photos by Mel Moe
unless otherwise indicated*

65

Merriam's Kangaroo Rat

be fortunate enough to see a Chiricahua Fox Squirrel. This is the only tree squirrel found here, and the Chiricahuas are the only place in the United States where it is found. It is a beautiful large squirrel with a grizzled back, rusty orange sides and belly and a very bushy dark tail, fringed in white.

Unique occupants of the lowlands are Kangaroo Rats. These are long-tailed, round-bodied animals that hop on their hind legs like kangaroos. Of the three species found here, the largest is the Banner-tailed Kangaroo Rat. This animal builds large mounds, 10 feet or more across, and up to 2 feet tall, with numerous burrow openings. Conspicuous in the lowlands, these mounds provide habitat for several species including Burrowing Owls, Kit Fox, and various snakes.

Two kinds of Rabbits are found here. The Desert Cottontail is found in dense vegetation in the lowlands, while Eastern Cottontails are at home in brushy areas in the mountains. One species of hare, the Black-tailed Jackrabbit, prefers open areas, from the lowlands up into the mountains.

Rodents, rabbits, and hares are very important parts of the ecosystem. They consume all kinds of plants, spread seeds, and they aerate the soil with their burrows. These animals are an important food source for many of the area's predators, including hawks, owls, fox, coyotes, badgers, skunks, and snakes.

Hoofed mammals

The Chiricahua region is home to four native species of hoofed mammals. These are Javelina, or Collared Peccary; Pronghorn, or Antelope; Coues White-tailed Deer, and Mule Deer.

Javelina are a new world relative of pigs. Found mostly in tropical and subtropical regions, this area is near the northern extreme of their range. This pig-like animal can weigh up to 50 pounds or more, and roams in herds through the brushy areas of lowlands and canyons.

Pronghorns are a truly American animal. A species of open grasslands, they are the fastest land mammal in America. They differ from deer by having horns instead of antlers. Locally, they are most likely to be seen in the grasslands bordering the southeast portion of the Chiricahuas.

Coues White-tailed Deer, the deer you are likely to see along the road in Cave Creek Canyon, are one of the smallest subspecies of deer in America. Averaging about 65 pounds, they are only about half the size of Mule Deer. They are found in the mountains, while Mule Deer are found in the foothills and lowlands. These deer are the primary prey of the good population of Mountain Lions found in this area.

Predators

Five groups of mammals make up the top of the food chain in the Chiricahuas. These are the Cat, Dog, Weasel, Raccoon, and Bear families.

The Cat family is represented by the Mountain Lion, Bobcat, and Jaguar, the last of which is discussed in Chapter 11.

The Mountain Lion, or Cougar, is a large cat, with males weighing up to 250 pounds, though usually much smaller, and females weigh closer to 100 pounds. These cats are solitary hunters with large territories, mostly

Javelinas are a frequent and sometimes destructive visitor in Portal.

in rugged mountain terrain. Their principal prey is deer, and they will occasionally feed on livestock, creating problems for ranchers. They are fairly common in these mountains but are seldom seen because they are quite secretive and mostly nocturnal. The sign you are most likely to observe is their tracks.

Bobcats are the most common feline in the Chiricahuas. Much smaller than the Mountain Lion (most weigh between 15 and 25 pounds), Bobcats feed mainly on rabbits but also prey on rodents and birds. These cats are also nocturnal, but you will sometimes see them abroad in daylight. They are found from the desert to high mountains. Sightings are rare, but if you're lucky, you can find their tracks.

The Dog family includes the Coyote, Gray Fox, and Kit Fox. The largest is the Coyote, weighing up to 40 pounds or more. They are found throughout the area, feeding primarily on jackrabbits, cottontails, and rodents. Seldom seen, their howls are familiar to anyone spending time outdoors at night.

The Gray Fox (about 8 pounds) is a resident of the foothills and mountains where it feeds on rodents, birds and rabbits. The tiny Kit Fox (4 pounds) finds its home in the lowlands where it feeds mostly on rodents.

The Weasel family includes Skunks, Badgers, and Long-tailed Weasels.

This is the only area in the country where you can find four species of skunks. These are the Striped, Hooded, Western Hog-nosed, and Western Spotted skunks. Mostly nocturnal, the skunks will visit campgrounds and residential areas at night. The Hooded Skunk, with long silky hair, and a dramatic plume-like tail is especially enjoyable to observe.

Bobcat tracks are seen frequently along the damp edges of Cave Creek.

Badgers are large weasels with very long claws adapted for digging out the burrows of their primary prey: ground squirrels and other rodents. The resulting large holes provide shelter for many other creatures, including coyotes, fox, skunks, rabbits, burrowing owls, and desert box turtles.

Long-tailed Weasels are small predators that feed mostly on small mammals and are usually found near water.

The Raccoon family includes Raccoons, Ringtails, and Coatis. Raccoons are the familiar masked resident of wet areas across most of North America. Ringtails and Coatis are both found only in the Southwest.

Ringtails are small cat-like animals found mostly in canyons and foothills. Their preferred den sites are rocky cliffs, caves, and old mines, along with hollow trees and old buildings. They are sometimes called "miners cats" as early miners kept them in their cabins to control mice and rats.

Ringtail   Narca Moore-Craig

The Coati is a tropical and subtropical species not even reported in Arizona by 19th-century naturalists, but fairly common in the Chiricahuas today. Anyone lucky enough to see them is in for a treat. Females and young travel in large groups, and as they move through trees, and over cliffs and rocks, using their long ringed tails for balance, they remind you of monkeys.

Black Bears are the largest wild animal found in the Chiricahuas. They eat all sorts of vegetable matter and insects as well as meat. Quite common here, you are likely to see their tracks and droppings on trails throughout the mountains, though seeing one of these shy creatures is a lucky event.

Former residents

The prevailing philosophy of people in this region until the last part of the twentieth century was that most predators and rodents were vermin that should be exterminated. In this area they managed to get rid of three native species. The last Grizzly Bear was killed in 1901, the last Black-tailed Prairie Dogs were poisoned in 1941, and the last Mexican Wolf was reported around 1971. Fortunately, attitudes have changed. A small population of Mexican wolves has been reestablished about 100 miles north of the Chiricahuas, and attempts are being made to reestablish Black-tailed Prairie Dogs in another area of southern Arizona.

Insectivores

The smallest mammals in the Chiricahuas are Shrews, tiny mouse-like insect-eaters with pointed snouts. They weigh from 1 to 0.3 ounces. Quite secretive, they are seldom seen.

Observing mammals

Visitors to Cave Creek Canyon are likely to see Coues Deer as they drive up the canyon. Chipmunks and Rock Squirrels are often around bird feeders, and sometimes Coatis as well. Quietly walking canyon trails is the best way to see Chiricahua Fox Squirrels, and you may see bear sign as well. Watch a hummingbird feeder on a summer night, and you are likely to see Long-nosed Bats. If you look against the sky while you are outside on a summer evening, you are certain to see bats flitting about. Drive area roads at night, and you should see rabbits, skunks, and various rodents. Javelinas might be seen at any time, especially in the vicinity of Portal. Although many animals won't be seen, you can often find their tracks, droppings, and burrows.

A fun way to indirectly observe mammals is with a trail camera. These digital devices will capture still pictures or video, either day or night, if you set them up where wildlife is likely to be found. They can be purchased at most outdoor sporting goods outlets for about $100 on up.

This female Mountain Lion spent several weeks hanging out in various yards and gardens around Portal. *Terrie Gates*

10 Bats

Janet Tyburec

as dusk settles in the narrow canyon and most wildlife-watchers are enjoying after-dinner drinks, the skies come alive with some of the 20-odd species of bats known from Cave Creek Canyon.

These winged mammals perform by night what many of their bird counterparts accomplish by day: foraging on the vast array of insect biomass and rich nectar resources found here. As the only mammals capable of true, powered flight, bats fill important, mostly nocturnal niches, in every habitat where they occur. Cave Creek Canyon is no exception,

Cave Creek Canyon is Nirvana for bats, with an incredible diversity of roosts (caves, cliffs, talus, deciduous and coniferous foliage), prey (insects, arachnids, nectar), and most importantly, water. *All photos by John Chenger, www.batmanagement.com*

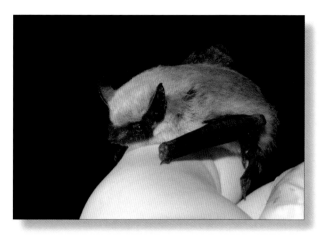

The Western Pipistrelle has pale brown, suede-like fur and a dark Lone Ranger-style face mask formed by its black muzzle and ears.

where our bats feed on and roost in every available resource. Some species live in traditional cave roosts, but others find homes high up on rocky **talus** slopes, in tree cavities created by other animals and in natural crevices.

Other bats roost within dense deciduous or coniferous vegetation, and many have adapted to live in man-made structures such as attics and barns or in some of the myriad hard rock mines excavated (and quickly abandoned) after the Civil War.

Different bats forage on their favorite insect prey. Some are attracted to insects that visit night-blooming plants. Others simply sip the nectar from the plants instead.

Bats are a truly diverse order of mammals, with an impressive variety of body sizes, behaviors, diets, and home ranges. The smallest bat in Cave Creek Canyon is the tiny Canyon Bat (*Parastrellus hesperus*, formerly referred to as the Western Pipistrelle, *Pipistrellus hesperus*). Just 2-4 grams in weight (a single plain M&M weighs about 1 gram) and with a wingspan of about 7 inches, these thumb-sized bats with pale brown fur and dark black wings are among the first bats to emerge each night. Their erratic, slow, fluttery flight can be observed against the darkening sky as they forage on insects and make regular forays down to quiet pools of water for a drink.

Our largest bat is the Western Mastiff Bat (*Eumops perotis*), weighing 65-grams and sporting a wingspan of nearly 2 feet. These bats live high in cliff crevices where they often drop 10-20 feet just to gain flight. They are the B-2 bomber of the bat world, with fast direct flight, specialized for open-air maneuvers. They feed at high altitudes on large moths. These giants are rarely seen, but unlike most bats, they have echolocation calls that fall into the humanly audible range of around 10-kilohertz. On quiet nights,

Townsend's Big-eared Bat has ears almost as long as its body. It is a "whispering" bat, producing very quiet echolocation calls so as not to warn its prey (mostly moths) that it is on the hunt.

their piercingly loud, pinging calls can be heard high amongst the canyon walls.

In fact, most bats produce very intense echolocation calls, around 110 decibels, so if we could hear them, they would be as loud as a triggered smoke alarm. In many ways it's good that bat vocalizations are well out of range of our ears. Humans can hear sounds from 1kHz up to about 20

A bat, outfitted with a small LED light tag, leaves a trail captured by a 10-second time-exposure photo as it is released and re-orients itself over the Southwestern Research Station.

Big Brown Bats are common throughout the U.S. They appear to be especially dependent upon people, roosting almost exclusively in man-made structures like houses, barns, bridges, and hard-rock mines.

kHz and most bats begin vocalizing around 20 kHz, sometimes exceeding 120 kHz. With high-frequency sound, bats are capable of not only locating objects in three-dimensional space, but also discerning important information about the texture and speed of an object. It is a truly masterful use of sound, towards which we humans are largely deaf.

In between the largest and smallest bats, Cave Creek Canyon has a wide array of species. Some are year-round residents, and others enjoy seasonal layovers in the canyon during their spring and fall migrations. Townsend's Big-eared Bats (*Corynorhinus townsendii*) form summer colonies in warm locations, like the gated Chiricahua Crystal Cave. Then they retreat to cold hibernation caves at higher elevations to sleep away the winter. Other bats like the Southwestern Myotis (*Myotis auriculus*) form colonies and rear young in Sycamores along Cave Creek. Forty or more bats can fit in a single cavity. Nobody knows where these little bats spend the winter, but they return to the creek each summer and probably don't make long-distance migrations.

The heavily furred Hoary Bat (*Lasiurus cinereus*) does make long-distance migrations, often traveling right through Cave Creek Canyon. Sometimes it is the most commonly captured species on spring surveys. But in the winter, Hoary Bats from other populations come to the Canyon to hibernate.

Unlike most hibernating bats or other animals, Hoary Bats sleep right out in the open on Apache Pine tree trunks, where their heavily furred bodies keep them from freezing, but also blend in nicely with the speckled bark of the trees, camouflaging them from predators.

Looking more like fast-moving wind-blown leaves as darkness falls, most bats garner little more than a casual observation out of the corner of one's eye. But, human residents of Cave Creek Canyon are often privy to some of North America's most interesting and watchable bat species: the nectar-feeding Mexican Long-tongued Bat (*Choeronycteris mexicana*) and federally endangered Lesser Long-nosed Bat (*Leptonycteris yerbabuenae*). Rare amongst U.S. and Canadian bats, these two species subsist almost entirely upon flower nectar, just like their hummingbird counterparts. And like the speedy birds, nectar bats enjoy the backyard abundance of feeders up and down Cave Creek Canyon.

The Mexican Long-tongued Bat is present in small, dispersed populations throughout the southwestern United States and northwestern Mexico. In Cave Creek Canyon, females roost in cliff crevices high along the canyon walls where they give birth to a single young referred to as a "pup." Larger than hummingbirds, Mexican Long-tongued Bats have strong direct flight, and dart in to sip from feeders, barely pausing as they extend their long, sponge-like tongues into the nectar reservoirs, before falling away in controlled dives as they circle for another approach. Hardly shy, these bats can become acclimated to porch lights or other nighttime

A Hoary Bat (top) and Silver-haired Bat (bottom) are known as "tree bats." They do not roost in caves or underground. They are solitary animals, roosting alone amongst the vegetation of coniferous or deciduous foliage in woodland habitats.

illumination, allowing their nectar-visiting habits to be easily observed and photographed.

The Lesser Long-nosed Bat forms much larger colonies and is a migratory species that spends its winters in southern Sonora and northern Sinaloa. In spring females migrate to northern Baja and southwestern Arizona where they rear young in caves. After the pups are **volant** (able to fly), the populations disperse into central and eastern Arizona, capitalizing on the diverse blooming patterns of numerous agave species.

In early summer, a small population of mostly bachelor male Lesser Long-nosed Bats take up residence in Cave Creek Canyon. When they are joined by the females and pups, this migrant population dwarfs that of the resident Mexican Long-tongued Bats. With both species competing for nectar, area feeders take a serious hit.

Some canyon homeowners enjoy close encounters with otherwise seldom-seen animal neighbors and leave their feeders out as a welcome mat for the bats. Others bring their feeders in at night to avoid marauding bears.

Some of the area's most fascinating bats are the "hummingbird bats," nectar-feeding bats that are attracted to backyard feeders. They can easily become habituated to people and porch-lights, providing enviable photo opportunities for wildlife enthusiasts.

11   Jaguars
Diana Hadley and Peter Warshall

The subject of legend and the core of Mexican and Central American religious beliefs for millennia, the Jaguar (*Panthera onca*) continues to capture our imaginations today. These dramatic spotted cats are the largest **felids** in the Western hemisphere and the only ones that roar. Powerful, secretive, and largely nocturnal, the elusive cats rarely allow themselves to be seen by humans. Yet history has recorded at least four observed Jaguars in the Chiricahua Mountains during the 20th century.

Arizona Jaguars: Historic Record and Changing Attitudes

Only a little more than a century ago, Jaguar territory within the United States extended along the entire southern tier of states from California to Louisiana. Records from the 19th century show that Jaguars ventured as far north as southern Colorado and the Grand Canyon.

Never abundant in the U.S., they are now listed as critically endangered in this country and either endangered, threatened, or near threatened throughout their entire range from Argentina to the American Southwest.

Today, we know of only one Jaguar in our country—a lone male roaming through the canyons and foothills of the Santa Rita Mountains in southern Arizona. The closest female to this bachelor is likely part of the well-documented breeding population some 125 miles south of the US-Mexico border, where an estimated 80-100 Jaguars maintain a fragile existence in the remote, mountainous *municipios* near the border of Sonora and Chihuahua.

In Arizona, during the past two decades, several projects have employed remote camera-trapping and track identification to increase knowledge of Jaguar habits, habitat, and needs. This interest in Jaguars was undoubtedly spurred by the experience of two professional mountain lions hunters who both encountered Jaguars in 1996 in southern Arizona. In March, hunting in the Peloncillo Mountains about 40 miles southeast of the Chiricahuas, Warner Glenn heard his hounds begin an unusually intense baying and yapping. Assuming the dogs were on the trail of a large tom lion, Warner chased after the agitated pack for several miles.

When he reached them, Warner was astounded to see a Jaguar, not treed, but clambering over bluffs with the hounds still in pursuit.

Realizing his lifelong dream to see a Jaguar in the wild, Warner sheathed his rifle, grabbed his camera, and pulled the frenzied hounds away from the cat as best he could. A few photos later, the Jaguar scrambled off toward Mexico, leaving several of the hounds with minor wounds and Warner with the thrill of his lifetime of hunting. Warner went home and began writing *Eyes of Fire*, an amply illustrated account of the encounter. The book promptly appeared in bookstores and ranch houses throughout Arizona.

Warner Glenn captured this image of a Jaguar in the Peloncillo Mountains in 1996—the closest sighting to the Chiricahuas in recent years.   *Warner Glenn*

A few months later in August, fellow lion hunter Jack Childs photographed a different Jaguar some 150 miles to the west in the Baboquivari Mountains, where there are several sites held sacred by members of the Tohono O'odham Nation. This time the Jaguar treed, enabling Jack to take beautiful photographs. Also inspired by the experience, Jack and his wife Anna initiated the Borderlands Jaguar Detection Project and began setting dozens of motion-triggered cameras to gather information. Their book, *Ambushed on the Jaguar Trail*, details the Baboquivari encounter and presents information collected from years of camera monitoring, which successfully captured animal behavior across the entire ecosystem.

Both the Peloncillo and the Baboquivari Jaguars were thought to be males, and both were photographed near the Mexican border. These two sightings stimulated widespread interest in Arizona Jaguars. Attitudes toward the species began to alter, with some members of the public recognizing the benefits that top predators bring to an ecosystem. Others questioned whether these two Jaguars were transient immigrants from Mexico or possibly part of a remnant breeding population in Arizona.

Prior to the 1990s, knowledge of Jaguar distribution came from sporadic, incomplete wildlife records, largely supplied by hunters, ranchers, and rural residents. A list compiled by the Arizona Game and Fish Department (AZGFD) documents 69 sightings within the state between 1848 and 1988. Although the list is incomplete, randomly recorded, and does not give exact locations, it nevertheless provides information about Jaguar presence and distribution. Prior to 1988 the majority of confirmed AZGFD sightings were mortalities, substantiated through body parts or carcasses.

Although locations were given by county only, the list indicates a thin but widespread distribution throughout the state. The majority of sightings occurred near the border, with 11 in Santa Cruz County, and 10 each in Cochise and Pima counties.

The issue of historical breeding populations of Jaguars in Arizona, or in the Southwest, is now widely debated and has great significance for protection and legislation. Male-female ratio is important in determining the best approach. In the AZGFD records, it is clear that males, presumably young wide-ranging males in search of females, comprised the majority of sightings.

Nevertheless, a female and two cubs were killed at the Grand Canyon in 1889 and a female and young were killed in Coconino County in 1900. In September 1963, a hunter shot and photographed the state's last confirmed female in the White Mountains at an elevation of 9,000 feet, belying the notion that Jaguars are a predominantly tropical animal. Some specialists interpret these records to indicate that most of the Jaguars in Arizona were transient. Others believe that the records, particularly those documenting the presence of cubs, indicate an over-exploited resident Jaguar population, rather than random individuals from Mexico.

Chiricahua Jaguars

The Chiricahua Mountains had at least four sightings during the 20th century, although not all were reliable enough to be included on the AZGFD list. In 1906, the Arizona Daily Star (6/1/1906) reported that two "unknown Mexicans" had trapped and killed a female Jaguar in the Chiricahuas and were offering her two cubs for sale in Bisbee—most likely in one of the town's many cantinas. In 1910, an "unknown cowboy" reported a Jaguar on Flys Peak in montane conifer

John Hands' grave in Portal with the pelt of the Jaguar he helped kill in 1912.
David E. Brown, author of Borderland Jaguars: Tigre de la Frontera

forest, but made no mention of whether he had killed the animal or not. This report, however, was reliable enough to have been accepted by game warden, Ralph Morrow, and it subsequently appeared in Ernest Thompson Seton's *Lives of Game Animals* (1929). Another poorly documented Jaguar was sighted some time between 1926 and 1930 in Madrean evergreen woodland and is included in the list published by Brown and López in *Borderland Jaguars*.

For the Chiricahuas, the most thoroughly described Jaguar encounter took place in January 1912, when a Jaguar was trapped and later shot in what is now the Chiricahua National Monument. Although several versions of the story exist, the one that seems most likely is repeated here. When rancher Jay Hugh Stafford found a cow and calf killed and partially eaten, he set a heavy leg-hold trap on a long chain at the site of the depredation. A large animal was caught in the trap but was strong enough to escape, dragging along the trap and chain. Stafford evidently went first to the Erickson's Faraway Ranch to report the loss of the trap.

Unable to track the animal himself, he then went on to the Hilltop Mine to enlist help from John Hands and his dogs. The dogs, trained to run off coyotes, were little help in following the scent. After three days and a snowfall, John Hands, now accompanied by his brothers Percy and Frank, tracked the wounded prey to "the Pinnacles," where one of the brothers peered into a dark, cave-like break in the rock pillars, and saw a full-grown Jaguar only a few feet away. He yelled to Frank to bring his rifle, and with it Frank ended the Jaguar's four-day ordeal.

The brothers took the carcass to the Riggs Settlement in the Sulphur Springs Valley, where neighbors came from miles around to view and photograph it. Although the event was reported in a local newspaper, mentioned in John Hands' diary, and recounted in Riggs family memoirs, no one gave the animal's sex or weight. Hands had the animal mounted, incorporating the Jaguar's skull and teeth, which gave indications of old age. In 1932, Hands donated the mount to the Arizona State Museum, which later donated the mount to the small museum in Portal. After thieves made off with many of the Portal museum's artifacts, a sheriff's deputy spotted the Jaguar pelt in a landfill and returned it to Portal resident rancher, Ted Troller.

Natural History of Jaguars and their Suitability to Chiricahua Habitat
Jaguars near the international border with Mexico weigh an average of 90-110 pounds for females and 100-130 pounds for males, making them considerably smaller than those of southern Mexico and Central America.

Jaguars lead a solitary existence, avoiding each other except during estrus. Females reach sexual maturity at age 2, males a year or two later. Gestation lasts approximately 100 days, and litter size can vary from one to four cubs, with cubs remaining in the den for up to six months. Jaguar rosettes provide effective camouflage, and their short, stocky builds enable them to stalk their prey effectively by creeping through underbrush and pouncing for the kill. In the northern reaches of their territory, the preferred prey are White-tailed Deer and Javelina, although Jaguars will consume any small mammal, fish, turtle, and, unfortunately, domestic livestock.

Not adverse to water, Jaguars willingly swim rivers, and will swim to reach prey. With the strongest bite of any felid, Jaguars' teeth can penetrate the skulls of their prey and the shells of turtles. They normally consume the neck and chest portions of the prey first, a practice that makes it possible to distinguish Jaguar kills from those of mountain lions, who consume the stomach area first.

Home ranges vary widely depending on habitat, water supply, and abundance of prey, with male home ranges being roughly twice the size of a female range. Recent studies have revised the estimated home range to 90 square miles for females and 270 for males. Home ranges occasionally overlap, with male home ranges incorporating those of one or more females, and females occasionally sharing home ranges with their female offspring.

Jaguars are found in a wide variety of habitats, although among these various habitats, they seem to favor areas with closed canopies and vegetative structures that would likely facilitate their stealthy stalk and pounce hunting technique. In northern Mexico and the southwestern U.S., their territories extend over a variety of elevations and include foothills thornscrub, semi-deciduous forest, pine-oak woodland, piñon-juniper woodland, and evergreen forest.

That the Chiricahua Mountains have suitable Jaguar habitat is unquestionable. That the mountains may have supported a resident population of Jaguars in past centuries is a matter of speculation. Although more densely populated by humans, the Chiricahuas have large areas of terrain very similar to that found in the Jaguar homeland of Sonora.

With new appreciation for the ecological importance of apex predators, it might be possible that human residents of the Chiricahua Mountains would tolerate—or even welcome—the return of Jaguars.

12   Introduction to the Canyon Birds
Richard E. Webster

For birds, the Chiricahua Mountains are one of the three richest "Sky Islands," the Huachuca and Santa Rita mountains being the others. The special attraction of the Chiricahua Mountains is being able to bird in national-park-quality scenery such as Cave Creek Canyon and Chiricahua National Monument. A logistical advantage is the ready road access (winter snow aside) to all the habitats. One species, Mexican Chickadee, is readily accessible nowhere else in the U.S. Missing from the portfolio is nearby lowland riparian habitat, exemplified by the San Pedro River and Sonoita Creek. While many specialties are resident and each season brings its own appeal, striking migratory breeders are the foremost attractions of May to August.

For most visiting birders, the "must-see" habitat is the Encinal (Oak) Woodland, part of the Madrean Evergreen Woodland. Whereas the premier destination is Cave Creek Canyon—especially South Fork, with the most consistent territories of Elegant Trogon (see Chapter 16)—other canyons in the range such as Rucker, West Turkey Creek, Pinery, and Price offer a very similar selection of species in what may be a nearly

Mexican Chickadee is a fairly common resident in conifers above 6,500 feet.
All photos by Richard E. Webster

An Elegant Trogon carrying a moth, the showy Painted Redstart, and a Sulphur-bellied Flycatcher

private birding spot. Residents of the Oak Woodland (with its Sycamore riparian areas) include Whiskered Screech-Owl, Arizona Woodpecker, Mexican Jay, and Bridled Titmouse, supplemented in the summer by Blue-throated Hummingbird, Elegant Trogon, Sulphur-bellied Flycatcher, and Painted Redstart, all centered in this relatively narrow zone (5,000-6,000 feet).

The Encinal Woodland grades into another part of the Madrean Evergreen Woodland, the Mexican Pine-Oak community. This more even mixture of conifers and oaks encompasses the zone of maximum abundance for Mexican Whip-poor-will, Magnificent Hummingbird, Greater Pewee, Plumbeous Vireo, and Hepatic Tanager.

Although the Madrean Evergreen Woodland may have the greatest appeal, birders are likely to allocate just as much time to the Petran Montane Conifer Forest at upper elevations. The "star," in terms of its status in relation to the International Border, is the Mexican

Chickadee, widespread in the Chiricahua Mountains, although often quiet and inconspicuous. The "star" in terms of biological distinctiveness in the Madrean avifauna is the Olive Warbler (also see Chapter 6), a member of a monotypic family and a fairly common breeder in the conifers (a few winter lower in the Encinal); it is most closely related to the Old World **accentors**.

Other special breeders include Grace's and Red-faced Warblers and Yellow-eyed Junco. Future taxonomic work may reveal species-level distinctions involving the local-breeding House (Brown-throated) Wrens and Brown (*albescens*) Creepers, just as it has for Cordilleran Flycatcher.

Although it is useful to draw lines and delineate communities, for the birds those lines are fuzzy, just as they are for the plants, as the pines increase gradually in frequency up the mountain and the oaks decrease. This gradation occurs for each species of oak and conifer. In general, the lower-elevation birds occur at their highest points on dry, south-facing slopes, and the upper-

Olive Warbler (top) and Yellow-eyed Junco both breed at upper elevations.

elevation species occur at their lowest points in narrow, shaded canyons. In the conifer zones, the specialty birds occur reliably from top to bottom, and a few pairs of most extend down into the intersection with the Madrean Evergreen Woodland (e.g., South Fork at the level of Maple Camp, East Turkey Creek near FR 42/Trans-Mountain Road). What extends the range of some species (Red-faced Warbler as a prime example) to the higher peaks is the presence within the conifers of some broad-leafed trees such as Emory (Western Black) Oak, Rocky Mountain Maple, and Quaking Aspen.

In summary, while all of the conifer-related specialties mentioned so far can be found either below Onion Saddle (6,500-7,300 feet) or above Rustler Park (8,500 feet), the easiest way to see them all is to bird your way steadily through the continuum. The uppermost Petran Subalpine Conifer Forest hosts a small set of scarce breeding species that are more limited within the Chiricahuas, and which we think of as "boreal," e.g., Red-breasted Nuthatch and Golden-crowned Kinglet, and sporadic visitors or breeders, e.g., Clark's Nutcracker, Townsend's Solitaire, and Evening Grosbeak. (A couple of these breed well into Mexico, one reason the old life zones "Canadian" and "Hudsonian" seem inappropriate.)

Bracketing the mixed-conifer forest and Madrean Evergreen Woodland, and outside the drainage lines and cooler canyons, are several types of short-stature, open woodland featuring species of oaks, junipers, and pinyons that thrive on the dry slopes. Vast in extent, these communities are important for the large populations supported, but hold few species unique to them. Montezuma Quail is an example: Though found in

Red-faced Warblers are here from April to August.

Scott's Oriole and Black-throated Sparrow prefer drier habitats.

other habitats with the requisite grassy understory, most of its Chiricahua population is found on these extensive woodland slopes (as is the case with Blue-gray Gnatcatcher, Black-throated Gray Warbler, Rufous-crowned and Black-chinned Sparrows, and Scott's Oriole). Two species of these habitats often sought by visitors are "Great Basin" species near their southern limit: Juniper Titmouse (lower slopes, e.g., Paradise and Portal) and Virginia's Warbler (upper-elevation Interior Chaparral).

The desert surrounding this Sky Island reflects the ill-defined border of the Chihuahuan and Sonoran Deserts. With regard to birds, most of the characteristic desert species occur in both deserts: Gambel's Quail, Cactus Wren, Verdin, and Black-tailed Gnatcatcher, for instance. But the desert here is perhaps more Sonoran ornithologically than Chihuahuan because although several species typical of the Sonoran Desert (Common Ground-Dove, Abert's Towhee, Rufous-winged and Botteri's Sparrows), which are uncommon and local in eastern Cochise County, barely extend into New Mexico, yet the converse applies less (Lucifer Hummingbird and the extirpated Aplomado Falcon). While some desert birds are common (the Portal Christmas Count has achieved national highs of Curve-billed and Crissal Thrashers), the desert around here "feels" more Chihuahuan because most species are at lower density than in the cactus-rich portions of the Sonoran Desert near Tucson. At the level of subspecies and populations, much remains to be studied, but the Chiricahuas appear to be near a boundary between the deserts (as with reptiles; cf. the "Deming Divide"). For instance, within Curve-billed Thrasher, the subspecies divide is right around here, while the genetic divide may be in eastern New Mexico.

Although extensive riparian habitat is missing from the area covered by this guide, Hackberry and Mesquite thickets and Sycamores along canyon outflows do provide habitat for some lowland riparian breeders, including Violet-crowned Hummingbird (scarce), Brown-crested Flycatcher, Bell's Vireo, Yellow-breasted Chat, and Summer Tanager.

Fire has extensively altered the landscape, most notably the 2011 Horseshoe 2 Fire, which affected around 225,000 acres. Beyond the portions severely burned, fragmentation affects much of the rest; certainly there have been substantial reductions in the populations of many species. Fortunately, there are intact sections of all habitats, and no known losses of species thus far. The results of the fire have been little studied, and any study is confounded by other variables, such as an ongoing drought. There will certainly be winners and losers; impressions at this early date are that some species (e.g., insectivores like warblers) are not doing well, while others (woodpeckers; understory species like House Wren and Spotted Towhee) are increasing.

Little is to be said about aquatic species. Taylor's list includes about 80 species of waterbirds, most of which are low-volume or casual migrants encountered occasionally at the few small ponds in the region. Excellent habitat is to be found to the west in the Sulphur Springs Valley at Whitewater Draw and Willcox, but migrant waterbirds have few reasons to stop in the Chiricahua region.

About 400 species are known from the region. Subtracting 80 waterbirds and another 80 casual to accidental landbirds leaves about 240 species of regularly occurring landbirds. Of that 240, about 65 are resident (not as simple a categorization as it might

Arizona Woodpecker is widespread in oaks.

Curve-billed Thrasher (left) and Crissal Thrasher are fairly common residents.

seem). So roughly three-fourths of the basic landbirds are migratory, and, if you include the waterbirds and accidentals, it truly is a mobile avifauna.

Winter is a slow time. The average low temperatures are a little below freezing, and perhaps more importantly, most winters bring a couple of several-day periods of low temperatures in the teens or even lower. The result is that only a limited number of insectivores winter in numbers (e.g., Ruby-crowned Kinglet) and even semi-hardy species such as Yellow-rumped Warbler are scarce. Still, there is good diversity, with the Portal Christmas Bird Count averaging around 130 species of landbirds. A particularly strong suite of towhees, sparrows, and juncos, many originating in the Great Basin or western Plains, are present, their numbers fluctuating depending on the seed crop after the summer rains.

Spring can be a windy period, but migration is often good, and the combination of passage migrants, arriving breeders (many specialties listed above), and residents makes May perhaps the prime month of the year. There are no real fallouts of migrants, but frontal passage can slow birds down, and dozens of Black-headed Grosbeaks, Lazuli Buntings, and Western Tanagers may congregate at feeding stations or water features, while a good mix of flycatchers, vireos, and warblers are found in riparian and woodland habitats. Some migratory breeders arrive early (even by mid-

March, e.g. Painted Redstart and Olive Warbler), but migration is generally slow until the second half of April.

If migrants are not a major interest, then summer is just as good as spring. June may be hot and dry, although any sources of water are magnets for birds, and nesting activity is around its peak. A few species, such as Elegant Trogon and Sulphur-bellied Flycatcher, do not reach peak abundance until June. July and August are the "monsoon" months, with the periodic thunderstorms transforming the landscape. Much of the breeding activity is winding down, but for species like Cassin's and Botteri's Sparrows, the summer rainy season is their primary breeding period in the Semidesert Grasslands, and for visitors the climate is more pleasant and the scenery more dramatic under the thunderheads. Hummingbird diversity peaks during the summer with the addition of casual visitors, such as White-eared and Berylline, and the gradual arrival of fall migrants, such as Rufous and Calliope (see Chapter 15).

The Bridled Titmouse thrives in the oak woodlands, rarely venturing higher or lower in elevation, but happily uses feeders near good habitat.
Narca Moore-Craig

Fall brings glorious weather for birding (calm days and deep blue skies), but migration is less evident than in spring, with very few obvious pulses. For some species, there is a shift in route and habitat usage, from a more lowland and Pacific route in spring to an interior and montane path in fall; birding the coniferous zones in fall can produce good numbers of Hammond's Flycatchers and Townsend's and Hermit Warblers. Southbound migration in the West is generally earlier than in the East, and many species are on the move in August and early September, and greatly reduced in number by even late September.

Birding is easy in this region: Almost all species can be found from roads passable in passenger cars, and many additional opportunities are available on a network of Forest Service trails. The American Birding Association's birding ethics should govern vistor behavior, with the added note that the U.S. Forest Service prohibits playback of bird calls in South Fork from April through September.

13   Raptors
Helen Snyder

ave Creek Canyon has a claim to biological fame unmatched anywhere in North America: It's home to the densest nesting population of birds of prey ever measured. Twenty-four species of raptors occur here in astounding numbers, and 11 of them are owls.

To appreciate this, let's spend 24 hours in the canyon, starting out on an imaginary April evening when the moon is waxing as twilight deepens.

The Owl Nebula is nearly overhead in the night sky, and the owl breeding season gets into full swing.

At Idlewilde Campground, a male Whiskered Screech Owl arrives at his nest with a moth for his incubating mate. He toots his arrival in Morse code: *dash, dash, dot-dot-dot-dot*. Down by the Visitor

Not much larger than the tiny Elf Owl, the Northern Pygmy Owl is much less abundant and is partially diurnal in its foraging habits. Its diet consists largely of small vertebrates such as this Tree Lizard.   *Noel Snyder*

Information Center, the resident Northern Pygmy Owl announces his evening hunt with a few double-note calls from a dead treetop.

In lower South Fork, the Spotted Owl pair flies silently to the "Rabbit Ears" spires to await deeper dark and brighter moonlight, when they will suddenly erupt into an unearthly caterwaul of shrieks and hoots that echoes off the moonlit canyon walls and startles unsuspecting campers in nearby Sunny Flat.

The Elf Owl is the smallest owl in the world. Weighing in at under 2 ounces, dozens of them are chortling a chorus up and down the canyon. Two weeks ago, the males returned to their canyon home and have each claimed an Acorn Woodpecker cavity, smoothly evicting the owner and spacing themselves about 100 yards from the nearest Elf Owl neighbor. Down at the Portal library, one male in particular has returned to his well-known nest and awaits his mate. Hundreds of birders have seen their first Elf Owl here. Tonight a hushed crowd awaits the owl—and he does not disappoint.

This is a special night for the male Elf Owls because right now, the female half of the canyon's population is still off to the south, waiting for dark to fly the last homeward leg of their spring

Dozing during much of the daylight hours, a fledgling Spotted Owl stretches its left wing and leg. A resident of middle and high elevation forested canyons, this relatively large and threatened species often nests in the tops of broken-off snags.
N. Snyder

The world's smallest owl, the Elf Owl is one of the most abundant raptors in Cave Creek Canyon. It is no bigger than a large sparrow and commonly nests in streamside sycamores in holes originally created by Acorn Woodpeckers. Its diet is confined almost entirely to insects and other arthropods.   *Helen Snyder*

migration journey. In a matter of hours they'll be homing in on the calls of mates sitting in the entrance of their cavities. After the human crowd has left, our Portal library male hears his partner as she flies in and lands almost on his face, shoving roughly past him to dive to the bottom of the nest. It's time to get nesting!

Meanwhile, up in the forest, the first wave of another forest-nesting owl arrives sometime during the night: The Flammulated Owls are here and fill the oak woodlands with their deep soft *BOO* calls as they forage for Noctuid moths. Some will remain to nest in South Fork and in the mixed conifer forests at higher elevations. The rest will launch northward again tonight.

By April in the lower reaches of Cave Creek, the non-migratory Great Horned Owls and Western Screech Owls are already on eggs or feeding young, as are Barn, Burrowing, and Long-eared Owls. From high montane

The Goshawks of southern Arizona belong to a distinctive dark race called the Apache Goshawk, found mostly in the Sierra Madre of Mexico. This male of 1969 is perched near his nest in an Apache Pine, his belly feathers stained with the blood of his prey, which were mostly medium-sized birds. *H. Snyder*

conifer glades, the Saw-whet Owls' delicate bell tones remind us of a car's repetitive hint to put our seat belts on.

Now that it's getting light, what about the other raptors? the hawks, falcons, and eagles?

As Orion fades with dawn, the first morning color returns to the cliffs, and, with sunrise still a half-hour away, the Peregrine and Prairie Falcons sail off to begin the daily hunt for food. Peregrines were **extirpated** here and over much of North America during the DDT era, but they began to return in the early 1980s. Now they are at healthy population levels again, nesting about 3 miles apart all over the Chiricahuas on vertical expanses of cliffs. Prairie Falcons moved in when the Peregrines disappeared but have now moved back to cliffs closer to their favored grassland hunting grounds. The third nesting falcon, the American Kestrel, occurs here in low but stable numbers, nesting in tree hollows, nest boxes, and holes in cliffs.

Our canyon Red-tailed Hawks are cliff-nesters, spacing themselves every 3 miles like the Peregrine Falcons. Other hawks like the Zone-tailed, the Short-tailed and the three Accipiters (Cooper's and Sharp-shinned Hawks, and Northern Goshawk) build their stick nests in trees, either in the canyon bottoms or where the conifers grow tall against north-facing slopes or cliffs.

We include vultures and ravens in the raptor tribe here. Turkey Vultures are an important part of the Chiricahua sky-scape, and if you're up just before sunrise in late summer, watch for the 20 or so residents to come gliding out of the canyon mouth, flying in formation like squadrons of bombers on D-Day, on their way to forage in the valley below. They are most easily enjoyed in late afternoon back in the canyon, in their nightly pre-roost flight spectacle. Watch from Sunny Flat or at the Vista Point overlook as they circle in the thermals rising from the sun-warmed cliffs, often staying aloft till they're soaring against a backdrop of early stars winking into view.

You can find their nests by smell alone in crevices, caves, and boulder piles high above Sunny Flat.

Vultures migrate south in October and return in mid-March. During migration, compact flocks of up to 80 arrive and depart in commuter fashion, coming in high and roosting overnight on the highest rimrocks, then ascending at first light to beam off in a purposeful group, behaving very differently from the resident vultures joyriding the air currents below.

Ravens round out the scavenger niche and do a fair amount of preying upon other creatures such as nestling birds and small reptiles. The Common

This female Short-tailed Hawk of 2007 is resting on her nest at the top of an Arizona Pine at about 8,000 feet in the Chiricahuas. This was the first nest known for this recently invading species in the western United States, and it produced two fledglings.   *N. Snyder*

Raven is a cliff-nester and the smaller, crow-like Chihuahuan Raven builds stick nests in low trees in flatter terrain.

Rarely glimpsed, our resident Golden Eagle pair nonetheless has us under surveillance from their nest on Silver Peak. In spring, you may actually hear the eagles before you see them when the female chirps to her incoming mate as he circles down with a dangling rabbit.

By evening both eagles have settled into rocky roosts. Orion winks into view star by star in the western sky as our 24-hour adventure ends and owl calls float up once again from the canyon below.

Flammulated Owl   *Narca Moore-Craig*

14 Extirpations and Introductions: Thick-billed Parrots and Wild Turkeys

Noel Snyder

The creatures living on small islands, whether classic islands in the midst of vast oceans or isolated mountainous islands rising from our southwestern deserts, face a heightened chance of local extinction. This is because they can only have relatively small and local populations at best, and such populations have a greater chance than widespread large populations of winking out during the fluctuations that all populations experience. A number of species are known to have disappeared from the Sky Islands in historical times, and efforts have been made to restore some of these populations by deliberate reintroductions.

Among the birds, two especially charismatic species have had

A Thick-billed Parrot uses its massive bill to tear apart a pine cone for its seeds. Learning how to properly rip apart cones takes many months for young parrots, and most Thick-bills hold cones in their left foot for processing. *All photos by Noel Snyder*

An adult Thick-billed Parrot approaches its nest and nestling in a natural cavity of a Southwestern White Pine snag in the Sierra Madres of Chihuahua, Mexico, in 1996. Seeds of living Southwestern White Pines are an important food for this parrot.

fluctuating residences in the Chiricahuas—the endangered Thick-billed Parrot and the Wild Turkey. Both species have been stressed by overhunting and apparently can persist only when provided some protection from gunfire. But both have also shown sensitivity to other environmental stresses, especially those influencing food supplies.

A brilliant green species with yellow patches on the wings and red on its forehead, the Thick-billed Parrot is one of only two species of parrot native to the U.S., the other being the now extinct Carolina Parakeet of the eastern states. Both are, or were, species capable of tolerating snowy winter weather, and indeed the thick-bill inhabits high elevation pine forests year-round, where it feeds mostly on pine seeds and occasional acorns. Like most other parrots, it nests in natural cavities in trees, but unlike most other bird species, it nests very late in the year, often fledging young in September or October, the season of peak abundance of pine seeds. Springtime is the season of lowest food availability for this species, at which time it sometimes resorts to feeding on the buds of trees. Highly social, the thick-bill is almost always seen in flocks, which often fly in the V formations we normally expect to see with waterfowl.

A small population of thick-bills existed naturally in the Chiricahuas around the turn of the 20th century, at least during the summer months, and the species was also known as an **irruptive** (an atypical migrant) visitor from the south, apparently when pine seed crops failed in its primary range in the Sierra Madres of Mexico. During 1917-1918 thousands of individuals from Mexico took up residence in the region. The species is large, noisy, gregarious, and approachable—characteristics that make it especially vulnerable to shooting. Indeed the vocalizations of this species can sometimes be heard from more than a mile distant. The Chiricahua population was heavily impacted by shooting in the early 20th century, and may have disappeared largely because of such pressure.

The Thick-billed Parrot is currently absent from the Chiricahuas. A reintroduction effort in the late 1980s and early 1990s, successful at first, ultimately failed to achieve a lasting population. Failure of this reintroduction attempt appears to have been mostly due to an extended drought that began at that time and has continued until 2014, seriously impacting the species' principal food supply of pine seeds. This drought has also greatly reduced the extent of the pine forests of the region, especially through massive recent fires. The Chiricahuas apparently represent the northernmost extent of the historical regular range of the thick-bill, likely because the diversity of pine species drops off conspicuously farther north. But to the extent that the current drought represents a long-term climate change, we may now be entering a period when the species' potential range is limited to regions farther south.

Even by the time of Alexander Wilson and John James Audubon in the early 19th century, the Wild Turkey had been largely exterminated for the

A male Wild Turkey of the race *merriami* displays to members of his harem on the grounds of the Southwestern Research Station in 1969. This reintroduced population of turkeys disappeared by the end of the 20th century.

dinner table throughout the eastern states, and most wild populations of today represent the fruits of deliberate reintroductions. The species virtually disappeared from southern Arizona by the turn of the 20th century but was reintroduced to the Chiricahuas in the late 1930s and early 1940s from sources farther north. This population was vigorous for several decades, but crashed by the end of the 20th century, this time not to shooting but to factors that are not completely understood.

Currently these mountains again harbor a population of turkeys, although this time the birds introduced came from Mexico, not from other populations in Arizona, in the hopes that they might be better adapted to local conditions. The original turkeys in the Chiricahuas may well have belonged to the Mexican subspecies *gouldi,* as this is the kind of turkey that still occurs naturally just to the east in the nearby Peloncillo Mountains. The *gouldi* turkeys presently in the Chiricahuas all stem from releases that started along West Turkey Creek in 2003, but the birds also spread to Cave Creek Canyon almost immediately.

Wild Turkeys surely need no description as they belong to the same species as the familiar domesticated turkey that we celebrate each Thanksgiving. Largely terrestrial, turkeys nevertheless fly up to roosts high in trees every night, presumably for protection from capable nocturnal predators, such as mountain lions and bobcats. This tendency has made the species especially vulnerable to shooting, as the birds often return to the same roost trees repeatedly, where they can be readily killed by waiting hunters.

Foods of the Wild Turkey include diverse plants and animals that are found on the ground, and indeed the turkey, like the Thick-billed Parrot and various squirrel species, commonly focuses on the seeds of pines. Males acquire harems of females and travel together with females during the early breeding season at which time their strutting visual displays and gobbling vocalizations are highly conspicuous. During the nonbreeding season the birds are less obvious, and flocks of both males and females are normally unisexual. Nests are built in sheltered locations on the ground. Most clutches consist of about a dozen eggs incubated solely by the females who also care for the young hatchlings without the help of males.

Adult turkeys are too large to be common prey of hawks and owls, but the hatchlings are vulnerable to many predators and frequently suffer heavy losses before they reach adult size.

15   Hummingbirds

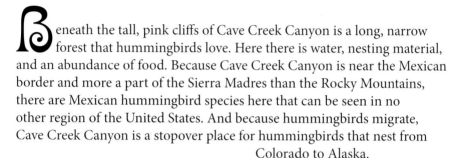

Larry and Terrie Gates

B eneath the tall, pink cliffs of Cave Creek Canyon is a long, narrow forest that hummingbirds love. Here there is water, nesting material, and an abundance of food. Because Cave Creek Canyon is near the Mexican border and more a part of the Sierra Madres than the Rocky Mountains, there are Mexican hummingbird species here that can be seen in no other region of the United States. And because hummingbirds migrate, Cave Creek Canyon is a stopover place for hummingbirds that nest from Colorado to Alaska.

Cave Creek Canyon is the best place in the United States, perhaps the best place in the world, to see the Blue-throated Hummingbird. From spring to fall, birders hiking in the canyon repeatedly hear the monotonous peep of this surprisingly large hummingbird. Anywhere in the canyon there is a very real chance of seeing a Blue-throat either perched or hovering in front of a flower.

The best time to see these and other hummingbirds in Cave

Male Blue-throated Hummingbird
All photos by Richard E. Webster

Creek Canyon is in late summer when migrating hummers join locally nesting hummers. Usually there is a surge that lasts a few weeks. The surge can begin as early as late July or as late as early September. August is always a good month for hummingbird viewing.

During peak migration the most common hummingbirds are Black-Chinned, Rufous, Broad-billed, Broad-tailed, Blue-throated, Magnificent, and Calliope. The mix often includes Costa's, Anna's, Violet-crowned, and Lucifer. Less common and not as regular are White-eared, and Berylline. Allen's are possible, but in the field they are, for all practical purposes,

impossible to distinguish from the far-more-common Rufous Hummingbirds.

Plain-capped Starthroats have been seen during this period, but they are quite rare.

In early fall Anna's Hummingbirds become common, sometimes outnumbering all other species. Hummingbird activity remains good until early or mid-October.

When cold weather arrives, only the two largest species, Blue-throated and Magnificent, can be reliably seen—usually just at feeders in Portal.

Male Broad-billed Hummingbird (top) and male Broad-tailed Hummingbird (bottom)

Locals and visitors see them all winter—even when it is snowing. During some winters, one or two members of some other species (most likely the Violet-crowned) manage to survive at feeders.

Male Calliope Hummingbird

Spring migration begins in March and by late April many hummingbird species have arrived. The Broad-tailed is usually the first. Broad-tails are common in the lower canyon in spring as well as late summer and early fall. In late spring they fly up to the highest peaks, where they nest.

From spring until their departure in October several other hummingbird species are easy to see in Portal. These include Black-chinned, Broad-billed, Blue-throated, and Magnificent.

In spring and early summer, a hike through the canyon will almost always give birdwatchers an opportunity to see Black-chinned, Blue-throated, and Magnificent Hummingbirds. Broad-billed, Black-chinned, and Blue-throated Hummingbird nests are often found both in Portal and in the canyon.

Occasionally a Violet-crowned nest is found. Blue-throated Hummingbird nests are almost always found on human-built structures such as carports.

Female Magnificent Hummingbird with bee.

Male Rufous Hummingbird (top), male Black-chinned Hummingbird, and the nest of a Black-chinned Hummingbird (bottom)

Since hummingbirds like water, they are often seen in pools or at small waterfalls in the canyon.

Above all they like flowers, especially red ones. Sometimes a hummingbird will buzz at a red hat or T-shirt. They might even buzz at a red tail light on a parked car.

In early summer it can be fun to sit or stand quietly while a mother hummingbird gathers nesting material. Watch where she goes, and you might actually see her building a nest. You also could spot a nest with a female sitting quietly on her eggs. Always watch from a distance. This is especially true if you find a mother feeding nestlings. If she doesn't come and go at regular intervals, you should go away and leave her alone.

Another interesting thing to watch is hummingbirds fighting. They can be belligerent. Sometimes two male Blue-throats will collide in mid-air, and then flutter to the ground swirling and pecking at each other. The stronger one will force the other to lie on the ground and endure a pecking. Eventually the loser will break loose and fly away.

Male Lucifer Hummingbird (top)
Male Anna's Hummingbird (bottom)

The easiest way to see the hummingbirds of Cave Creek Canyon is at sugar-water feeders. There are feeders at the Southwestern Research Station, Cave Creek Ranch, the Portal Store, the George Walker house, and campsites in Sunny Flat or Stewart campgrounds.

Sometimes visiting birders are allowed to visit feeders at private residences in the village. At the peak of migration persistent birders have been known to see as many as fourteen different species in a single day.

Another interesting way to see hummingbirds is to drive out of the canyon and up the trans-mountain road to the high country above the canyon.

This can be especially rewarding in late summer when migrating hummingbirds dart through flower-covered meadows.

There are many places in the United States where greater numbers of hummingbirds can be seen on a good migration day, but—in terms of variety—the only places that rival Cave Creek Canyon are a few similar canyons in the "sky island" mountain ranges south and east of Tucson.

Sally and Spoff

In Cave Creek Canyon, hummingbird feeding began with the migration of Sally and Walter Spofford in 1972 from Etna, New York, to the tiny village of Portal. Immediately after arriving, even before purchasing furniture for the house, Sally began setting up feeders for hummers as well as other birds. She wrote, "I was well on the way to being addicted to feeding birds when I lived in New York State, but I didn't know the meaning of true dedication until a few years after acquiring our small ranch in the Chiricahua Mountains of southeast Arizona."

Sally and Spoff opened their yard to birders 365 days a year from dawn 'til dusk for the rest of their lives. Sadly, Spoff passed away in 1995, but Sally continued to feed her beloved birds until she died at

the age of 88 in 2002. During those 30 years, thousands of birders from all over the globe visited the Spoffords' backyard each year. Twelve species of hummingbirds visited this avian mecca. It was often referred to in print as "The most famous birding backyard in the country, if not the world."

We learned so much from Sally and Spoff. We first met them in 1982 and became neighbors in 1999. Spoff held a degree in neuroanatomy, but he knew everything there was to know about raptors. Sally was an ornithologist at Cornell with a special love for hummingbirds, songbirds, and owls. Both shared their knowledge freely and with joy.

Many a birder had the pleasure of being introduced to Sally's "friends": Rhoda, the roadrunner catching Sally's hamburger balls, Smokey, the coati munching on peanut butter and jelly sandwiches, and Tink, the canyon wren scurrying through the screen door hunting for mealworms.

But it's the hummingbirds that remind us of Sally most. Whenever we see a blue-throated hummer, we can still hear Sally laughing with glee as it darts by her face.

— Terrie and Larry Gates

16   Elegant Trogons
Richard Cachor Taylor

g was 21 when I saw my first Elegant Trogon.

On a day off as the lookout in Chiricahua National Monument, the Park Naturalist and I drove across the top of the mountains to hike up the South Fork of Cave Creek. Probably it was the context of the experience as much as the intrinsic beauty of the bird. With red cliffs towering thousands of feet above the pastel green floor of the canyon, the morning light seemed

Male Elegant Trogons are about 11 1/2" long. After their second summer adult males have very fine bands of dots on the white outer rectrices (the undertail feathers).   *All photos by Richard Cachor Taylor unless otherwise indicated.*

to envelop every Sycamore leaf in a film of incandescence. The songs of Canyon Wrens spooled down the rhyolite walls, and the silvery harmonics of Hermit Thrushes filled the winding aisles of the gallery forest like a cathedral. Even the air we were breathing was redolent with the delicious smells of new growth.

There were not many trogons in those days. In spite of decades of collecting by early scientists, the first actual trogon sighting in Arizona—and the United States—did not occur until 1884. It wasn't until 1942 that Portal resident Alden Hayes (see Chapter 45) reported an Elegant Trogon from the "old orchard" in the Main Fork of Cave Creek. Expert birders thought there were perhaps 20 in Arizona, two or three pairs in the Chiricahuas. We were thrilled to hear one vocalizing just a mile above the roadhead in South Fork.

I was blown away when we finally saw the bird.

It was a male. Almost 12 inches long with a shimmering emerald-green back and a crimson red breast, it seemed to condense all of the glory of that South Fork day into one dynamic package. It challenged our coming with a series of loud calls that it repeated from its perch high in a pine for what felt like hours—but what was probably just a few minutes.

Eventually the trogon retreated from view. Eventually even the croaking calls dissolved, leaving nothing behind but

Female Elegant Trogon. Nearly 12 inches long, female Elegant Trogons are slightly larger than males but lack the iridescent upperpart plumage of their mates. Neutral colors probably make them less conspicuous when nesting.

Fledgling Elegant Trogon. Both genders of bob-tailed young Elegant Trogons leave the nest with the same white "teardrops" below and behind the eyes as adult females. Their wings also have rows of white spots that remain well into their first winter. A fledgling's tail grows to full length within two months after it leaves the nest.

the subdued burbling of the stream. We hiked up the canyon miles farther until the South Fork Trail climbed up the dry Sentinel Fork, but if we saw any other birds that day I've forgotten.

Numbers of Elegant Trogons in the Chiricahua Mountains have waxed and waned. Presently they're at low ebb. The annual summer census in 2013 turned up 12 birds altogether: nine in the Cave Creek–South Fork area and three in Rucker Canyon at the south end of the mountains.

In 1994 a pattern of lower-than-normal summer precipitation began to dominate the Southwest. Inexorably the Chiricahua population of Elegant Trogons began to slide. In 2011 the Horseshoe 2 Fire swept over 223,000 acres of the Chiricahuas. Subsequent flashfloods have temporarily impacted some of the stream bottom habitat, especially the understory where trogons typically forage. Short-term or long-term, Elegant Trogons seem to have survived the recent environmental cataclysms.

In 1980 I was half-way through an eight-year research project to determine the population, distribution, and ecology of Arizona's Elegant Trogon. By 1980 eight to 10 pairs were breeding in South Fork, where I focused most of my study time, and a handful of different pairs were pioneering other tributaries of the Cave Creek complex. Conservatively, in 1980 there were 25 adult Elegant Trogons summering in the Chiricahua Mountains.

Determining habitat requirements for trogons was the first step in developing a population estimate for Arizona. Elegant Trogons are confined to Sierra Madrean pine-oak woodland in the southeast corner of Arizona. Although they forage upslope, nests are almost invariably in the shady timber growing along streambeds.

Male Elegant Trogon. The rich red underparts are derived from true pigment, and the hue varies from soft rose to fiery orange with the age and condition of the bird, and from season to season during the year.

Over the years I found more than 80 trogon nests. Nests are usually located in canyons more than 1,000 feet deep, well-protected from desiccating winds and long periods of direct summer sunlight. Canyons facilitate cold air drainage in the spring and are often 5 or more degrees warmer than the valleys below where the cold air pools up on chilly spring nights. Conversely, canyons may be 5 degrees cooler in mid-summer. From a climate perspective, the border canyon habitat used by Arizona Elegant Trogons is probably the most stable environment available in the entire American Southwest.

Most trogon nests are at canyon confluences where side drainages contribute to deeper soils, replenish nutrients, and deliver additional underground moisture. Sycamores flourish in these circumstances.

Sycamores are a critical component in the U.S. distribution of Elegant Trogons because they are riddled with potential nest cavities. Undoubtedly some cavities occur naturally as the result of normal decay. But the soft heartwood of sycamore can easily be carved into a nest chamber by an Acorn Woodpecker, the primary cavity excavator in the border ranges.

Northern Flickers, in turn, enlarge those holes to suit their needs. Flickers and Elegant Trogons are almost the exact same length, so used flicker nest cavities make perfect trogon nurseries, too.

Less often, both Acorn Woodpeckers and Northern Flickers also chisel nest holes into oaks and pines, typically where a limb has broken off affording the bird ready access to the interior tree. Because the diet of an Acorn Woodpecker is, of course, primarily acorns which it harvests still green from leaf clusters, and because a flicker is primarily consuming ants that it gathers from the ground or rotten wood, neither species is particularly well-equipped to drill hard substrates. On average, Sycamores are the biggest trees and have the softest wood of any tree species in the mountain canyons used by trogons. They acquire the most nest holes.

Even with many holes available, there is a lot of competition for cavity homes. Aside from snakes and squirrels, there are returning Northern Flickers as well as Brown-crested and Sulphur-bellied Flycatchers. In 1981, watching a potential Sycamore nest in Cave Creek, long-time birder Burdette White counted more than 200 hostile encounters between a pair of Elegant Trogons and a pair of Sulphur-bellied Flycatchers. Feathers literally flew for several weeks, but—in this instance—the trogons triumphed over the flycatchers.

Small owls potentially represent more serious competition. Surveying the eastern flank of the Chiricahua Mountains from 2002 through 2008, biologist Helen Snyder recorded 11 pairs of Flammulated Owls, 75 pairs of Whiskered Screech-Owls, and 24 pairs of Northern Pygmy-Owls. Trogons are unlikely to appear in the diet of any of these small nocturnal raptors. However, when it comes to a

Male Elegant Trogon bringing a lizard to a nest. While many trogon nests appear to be natural cavities, usually a closer inspection shows that Acorn Woodpeckers probably created the original hole.

Noel Snyder

111

possible nest hole, they are likely to be displaced by them.

Obviously, not all trogon pairs obtain optimum nest sites. During my study I found the average trogon nest was fractionally over 25 feet high and averaged about 19 inches deep. But I also found a few nests less than 10 feet high, which were far more accessible to snakes and raccoons. Similarly, some nests, usually in oaks or pines, were less than 12 inches deep, and one in an Arizona White Oak was only 5 1/2 inches deep. Shallow cavities almost certainly facilitate predator access.

Elegant Trogons are probably the most sought-after species in the Chiricahuas. While trogons have occurred in most of the major canyons, only the Cave Creek-South Fork complex and Rucker Canyon were known to harbor breeding Elegant Trogons in 2014.

Nesting success hovered just below 50 percent during my study. While Elegant Trogons may lay three or four eggs, usually only two young survive to fledge. Trogons ordinarily do not re-nest unless a nest fails completely. Although indirect evidence suggests that these birds may live up to 10 years or longer if they survive their first winter, it takes years to build a trogon population.

Rainfall was generous in the 1980s. The Canyon Grape, Birchleaf Buckthorn, and Southwest Chokecherry crops never failed, nor did the katydids, mantids, or the spring birth of baby Yarrow's Spiny Lizards. In the 1980s, food was probably not a limiting factor for Chiricahua Elegant Trogons. Anecdotally, in the early 1990s Portal birding guide Dave Jasper once told me he thought there were approximately 40 adult Elegant Trogons in the Cave Creek Canyon complex.

Like all who love the Chiricahua Mountains, every summer I hope life-giving summer rains re-visit its zig-zag canyons, that the ivory boughs of sycamores arch over running water, and that the calls of Elegant Trogons reverberate up and down those red-walled corridors without breaks between territories. Trogons reflect the ecological health of the Chiricahuas. Selfishly, I recall a time when trogons were just as rare as they are beautiful, and relive again the raw joy I had that long-ago day in South Fork.

17 Snakes
Bob Ashley

The Chiricahua Mountains, a Sky Island rich in diversity, are home to more than 30 different species of snakes.

The range contains a wide variety of habitats and climates with peaks as high as 9,700 feet with pine- and aspen-forested rocky outcroppings where snakes such as the Western Twin-spotted Rattlesnake (*Crotalus pricei pricei*) and Black-tailed Rattlesnake (*Crotalus molossus*) can be found. The temperatures here can be very cool to cold even in the summer months, and these areas accumulate snow that can last well into May after a good winter's precipitation.

Most people assume that snakes that occupy these high elevations hibernate during the colder months. They do become extremely inactive and **brumate** much of the winter, but they can be seen in every month of the year, basking in the sun on warm winter days in small amphitheaters of rocky habitat. Snakes at these elevations are almost entirely diurnal.

Young Black-tailed Rattlesnake on the horn of a Western saddle. This snake has the largest range in the Chiricahuas.
©Ray A. Mendez 2014

Below 7,500 feet, the pine and aspen forest gives way to more open rocky scrub terrain with agave, prickly pear cactus, junipers, and sycamores. Here you'll see species like

- Arizona Mountain Kingsnake *(Lampropeltis pyromelana)*
- Banded Rock Rattlesnake *(Crotalus lepidus klauberi)*
- Black-tailed Rattlesnake *(Crotalus molossus)*
- Sonoran Whipsnake *(Masticophis bilineatus)*
- Mountain Patch-nosed Snake *(Salvadora grahamiae grahamiae)*
- Black-necked Gartersnake *(Thamnophis cyrtopsis cyrtopsis)*
- Sonoran Lyresnake *(Trimorphodon biscutatus lambda)*
- Green Ratsnake *(Senticolis triaspis)*

These snakes share many of the same habitats of exposed rocky outcroppings in grassy areas usually near washes and heavier vegetation. When trying to locate some of these species, I typically look for rocky outcroppings near the greenest vegetation. This tells me there is better

(Top) A yearling Green Ratsnake
(Bottom) A large female Green Ratsnake from the Santa Ritas *All photos by Bill Love Photography unless otherwise indicated.*

This Gophersnake is often called a Bull Snake, to which it is closely related. It does the same show of open mouth, loud hissing, and even rattling of its tail. This animal looks dangerous but is totally harmless and rarely even bites.

drainage/more water in these areas and the most likely place to view these mountain dwellers. Sonoran Whipsnakes, Mountain Patch-nosed, and Black-necked Gartersnakes are diurnal and rarely encountered after dusk. Arizona Mountain Kingsnakes, Green Ratsnakes, and Banded Rock Rattlesnakes are active during the day, most typically mid- to late mornings. They are also active at night.

Sonoran Lyresnakes are strictly nocturnal but can be seen during the day deep inside crevices in rocks. These snakes are rarely encountered below 4,700 feet in elevation.

Below 5,000 feet, the species encountered become increasingly nocturnal, mainly because of the increase in daytime temperatures at lower elevations. The lack of rocky outcroppings, logs, and other vegetation that help shelter snakes from the heat of the sun and from daytime predators, like birds of prey, is also a factor.

Snakes found at these lower elevations include:

- Texas Threadsnake (*Leptotyphlops dulcis*)
- Western Threadsnake (*Leptotyphlops humilis*)
- Painted Desert Glossy Snake (*Arizona elegans philipi*)
- Lined Coachwhip (*Masticophis flagellum lineatulus*)
- Sonoran Ring-necked Snake (*Diadophis punctatus*)
- Chihuahuan Hook-nosed Snake (*Gyalopion canum*)
- Mexican Hog-nosed Snake (*Heterodon nasicus kennerlyi*)
- Texas Nightsnake (*Hypsiglena torquata jani*)
- Desert Kingsnake (*Lampropeltis getula splendida*)
- Sonoran Gophersnake (*Pituophis catenifer affinis*)

Rare in the Chiricahuas, the Sonoran Ring-necked Snake, with its bright orange ventral side, is most active near dawn and dusk. It has a mild venom, not dangerous to humans, that immobilizes its prey, mostly small snakes.

- Long-nosed Snake (*Rhinocheilus lecontei*)
- Big Bend Patch-nosed Snake (*Salvadora hexalepis deserticola*)
- Variable Ground Snake (*Sonora semiannulata semiannulata*)
- Smith's Black-headed Snake (*Tantilla hobartsmithi*)
- Plains Black-headed Snake (*Tantilla nigriceps*)
- Yaqui Black-headed Snake (*Tantilla yaquia*)
- Checkered Gartersnake (*Thamnophis marcianus marcianus*)
- Western Diamondback Rattlesnake (*Crotalus atrox*)
- Mojave Rattlesnake (*Crotalus scutulatus*)
- Desert Massasauga (*Sistrurus catenatus edwardsii*)
- Arizona Coral Snake (*Micruroides euryxanthus euryxanthus*)

The snake with by far the largest range throughout the Chiricahuas is the Black-tailed Rattlesnake. These snakes range from the highest peaks to as low at 4,500 feet. The valley floor between the Chiricahua and the Peloncillo mountains drops to a similar elevation at Silver Creek, so some gene flow is likely between the different mountain ranges for this species.

As the American Southwest, including the Chiricahuas, has become a drier environment over the past century, we have seen many species of snakes slowly move their ranges farther and farther up in elevation. This is because of their need mainly for water. Their prey species are making the same migrations to higher elevations for the very same reasons. Formerly, Western Diamondback Rattlesnakes were rarely seen above 4,700 feet, near the Portal Peak Lodge. Recently they have been seen as high as 5,300 feet near Sunny Flat Campground.

The Coral Snake is the only member of the Elapidae family found in the U.S. and has neurotoxic venom. Although their venom is very toxic, this snake delivers only a tiny amount. Many people say that a bite from a Coral Snake is almost impossible because of the size of the snake's head. This statement is untrue, as this snake has the ability to open its mouth very wide and can bite something almost flat like an arm. The Coral Snake's bite is typically not as bad as a bite from a rattlesnake but should still be treated as serious. Medical attention should be sought immediately.

A well-known rhyme that helps to distinguish this snake from the harmless kingsnakes also found in this area is "Red Touch Black—A Poison Lack, Red Touch Yellow—Kill a fellow." This rhyme refers to the bands of color on the snake's body. This rhyme works well in the Chiricahuas but as you go south of the Mexican border, there are some exceptions to it.

The Mojave Rattlesnakes found in this valley have the distinction of having the most potent venom with the highest amount of neurotoxic properties. This is the deadliest snake in North America and should be avoided. Mojave Rattlesnakes, like all snakes, try to flee if they have a chance, but be very careful of where you step.

A very few Prairie Rattlesnakes (*Crotalus viridis*) are rumored to have been found on Foothills Road in the past and a handful of the undescribed Arizona

Arizona Mountain Kingsnakes (top) and Arizona Coral Snakes (bottom) live in similar areas. When encountered, a Coral Snake sometimes buries its head under its coils and raises its tail, forcing air from its anus in a popping sound.

Milk Snakes have been found 10 miles south of Apache in the lowlands of the Chiricahuas. There have been rumors in the past of Ridge-nosed Rattlesnakes being found in the Chiricahuas as well, but nothing has ever been substantiated or supported by any reputable source. If this were true, it would most likely be the New Mexico Ridge-nosed Rattlesnake (*Crotalus willardi obscurus*) that is found in the adjacent Peloncillo Mountains. This rattlesnake has the distinction of being the only federally protected rattlesnake in the United States.

The Chiricahuas are an iconic place for natural history for a myriad of reasons and especially for people that love to see snakes in the field. People come to the Chiricahuas from all over the world to have a chance to see the vast number of species of snakes that can be found here.

Mojave Rattlesnake

Banded Rock Rattlesnake

Snake bite!

Most people bitten by venomous snakes are attempting to interact with them—much better to leave them alone!

If you are bitten, try to remain calm and still. Contact Portal Rescue by calling 911, or send someone to get help if there is no phone service.

All snake bite kits or remedies in the field are useless.

Immediate medical attention should be sought, including a helicopter ride to a hospital with the proper staff and antivenin, especially in the event of a Mojave Rattlesnake bite.

18 Lizards
Carol A. Simon

Welcome to the American Southwest! The highest diversity of lizards anywhere in the country is here. If you are alert, it won't be hard to find these captivating creatures in Cave Creek Canyon.

Lizards are vertebrates that usually have four legs, long tails, and scales. Since they are reptiles they are said to be cold-blooded. All this means is that they cannot produce their own body heat as we do, and instead must gain heat from the sun. Scientists don't like this term because some of the time lizard blood is as warm, or warmer, than yours. If you watch a lizard carefully, you'll see that it thermoregulates all day long: It moves out of the

Male Yarrow's, or Mountain Spiny Lizards, tend to have a more uniform and darker coloration than females.   *Howard Topoff*

The Sonoran Spotted Whiptail has no males! The all-female populations reproduce asexually.

Stephen J. Mullin

sun when it is too hot, changes its body position to get more or less heat, flattens itself on warm rocks when the sun goes down, and may have a darker color early in the morning so it warms up faster. If lizards get too hot, they die—just like humans.

It is a lot of fun to identify lizards and to simply know their names. But the more you learn about their behavior and ecology, the more interesting these animals become. Let's start with the most common lizard in the canyon, the

The Madrean Alligator Lizard is long and snake-like with very short legs. This ground-dweller can be found scurrying in leaf litter and under rocks, logs, and plants. The photo below shows the position that alligator lizards are reputed to take when confronted by a snake predator.
Stephen J. Mullin

120

Yarrow's or Mountain Spiny Lizard (*Sceloporus jarrovii*). Adult males are dark with a collar around their neck. Females and young also have collars but appear brown with splotches.

You can find these reptiles scrambling about on rocks in South Fork, sitting on the walls of the buildings at the Southwestern Research Station or even at the very top of the Chiricahuas, as these are high-elevation lizards. Yarrow's Spiny Lizard is primarily a Mexican species that barely gets into southern Arizona and New Mexico. One of the reasons that the Chiricahuas have such high biodiversity is because the ranges of quite a few Mexican plant and animal species extend here.

A little patience will reveal feeding behavior. Yarrow's Spiny Lizard often sits still while looking for its prey, which consists of insects and other arthropods such as spiders and even scorpions. A hungry animal will dart out, grab a prey item and return to its perch. Like many lizards, this species effectively shares its food and habitat with other individuals. Larger lizards eat larger prey, and females eat bigger prey than males. Not all lizards are active at the same time of day, and not all sit and wait for prey in the same exact portions of the habitat. There is a lot going on here!

You may also see a fair amount of social behavior. Both males and females are territorial and use head bobs and push-ups to help declare their space. The size of their territories can depend upon how much food is available, how many other lizards are present, and even the time of year. In the fall, when the males are searching for mates, they increase their territory sizes. At this time you might even see males fighting with each other.

Almost all the lizard species you will see in the canyon lay eggs. Yarrow's Spiny Lizards is an exception. They mate in the fall and give birth to live young in the spring or early summer. This is apparently an adaptation for living at high elevations. Lizards and snakes that live in colder climates have a tendency to retain their developing young

The Ornate Tree Lizard is one of the most common in the Canyon. It is found on many surfaces other than trees.
Stephen J. Mullin

within their bodies. If they laid eggs, temperatures might get so low that the eggs would freeze or fail to develop. Instead, pregnant females can move their bodies into the sun on cold days and raise the temperatures for the developing young.

The white dot in the center of the head of this Yarrow's or Mountain Spiny Lizard is the parietal eye. It sits on an enlarged parietal scale, for which it is named.

Carol A. Simon

Take a good look at the head of a Yarrow's Spiny Lizard, or almost any lizard, and you will see a third eye on top! This parietal "eye" doesn't focus an image the way your eyes do, but it does receive light. When spiny lizards are moved outside of their home ranges they can usually return to their homes easily. But if the parietal eye is covered, the lizard just wanders about and is unable to find its way home. Clearly that parietal eye is important. Even more amazing, in order to use the parietal eye to return home, the lizard has to know the time of day and the sun's position at that time. Wow!

Cave Creek Canyon boasts other lizards with equally riveting stories. How about species where there are no males, just females? That's right, no males at all—ever. Whiptail lizards are long and thin, with lengthy tails and tongues that flick out often. The tongue is bringing chemicals into the mouth, delivering them through two slits in the roof of the mouth to paired **vomeronasal organs**. Here nerves connect to the brain and the lizard is able to interpret the chemical information. Is food nearby? Other lizards? Lizard ready to mate? Whiptails actively pursue their prey and rely upon tongue-flicking to direct them to food. You can see the tongue of a Yarrow's Spiny Lizard flick out every once in a while, but this behavior is not so important for a sit-and-wait predator that is not actively searching for food.

But what about this business of no males?

Some species of whiptail lizards, including two in Cave Creek Canyon, the Sonoran Spotted Whiptail (*Aspidoscelis sonorae*) and the Chihuahuan Whiptail (*Aspidoscelis exsanguis*) are parthenogenetic. That means that females give birth to clones of themselves without sperm from males because there are no males. The advantage of this is that ALL individuals directly produce offspring, and, if the mother is well adapted to her environment, her offspring will be also. The disadvantage is that if there is a harmful change in the environment, such as a new disease, there is a danger

This secretive lizard is hard to see even though it is active during the day. The Great Plains Skink spends most of its time under cover.
Stephen J. Mullin

that an entire population will be lost because all individuals share exactly the same genes.

The canyon also has Ornate Tree Lizards (*Urosaurus ornatus*) and Striped Plateau Lizards (*Sceloporus virgatus*), which are easy to spot. The heavy-bodied, fast moving Clark's Spiny Lizard (*Sceloporus clarkii*) is not as common as Yarrow's Spiny Lizard but can often be seen on tree trunks or building walls.

The shiny Great Plains Skinks (*Eumeces obsoletus*) and Madrean Alligator Lizards (*Elgaria kingii*) are more secretive. The flat bodied horned lizards (*Phrynosoma* spp.) have astonishing adaptations and command an entire chapter in this book (Chapter 19).

The young Great Plains Skinks are very colorful.
Stephen J. Mullin

Gila Monsters (*Heloderma suspectum*), the only venomous lizards in the U.S., are typically found at lower elevations just outside the canyon but occasionally an individual is spotted in Portal; one was seen at the Portal Ranger Station.

Other lizards are also found just outside the canyon and it is worth exploring the lower elevations as well as the high country.

Cave Creek Canyon and adjacent areas are truly a herpetologist's dream come true. And the more you learn about these intriguing animals, the more you want to know!

You might get lucky and see a Gila Monster if you patrol our roads early in the mornings and afternoons. Although easy to approach, do not attempt to handle one. Gila Monsters, especially those that have been in direct sunlight, can become quite aggressive and, literally, with mouth agape, will launch the front of their bodies into the air to defend themselves. These giant beautifully patterned animals have been used through time as models for artwork, bead work, and pottery.
©Ray A. Mendez 2014

19   Horned Lizards
Wade C. Sherbrooke

elow Portal, descending the Chiricahua **bajada**, Cave Creek has cut **dendritic** paths to the usually dry San Simon River. Two species of horned lizards live here and throughout the surrounding valleys: the larger Texas Horned Lizard (*Phrynosoma cornutum*) and the Round-tailed Horned Lizard (*Phrynosoma modestum*).

Both camouflage specialists, the Texas sports a bright white line down the middle of its back (resembling a stem of plant litter under a shrub) whereas the Round-tailed resembles a small stone (complete with appropriately darkened shadow-patterns along its sides). These wide, flat-bodied lizards are always difficult to see as they habitually sit motionless on natural backgrounds. Like other members of their 17-species rich genus (nine found in the U.S., 15 in Mexico), their skulls support sharp extending horns projecting backwards.

Leaving the valley and heading up Cave Creek into the mountains, one may encounter the Greater Short-horned Lizard

Texas Horned Lizard

All photos by Wade C. Sherbrooke

(*Phrynosoma hernandesi*, formerly *douglasii*), with stout short horns, or if traveling not far south into the Douglas area, one can run across a fourth species, the Regal Horned Lizard (*Phrynosoma solare*) whose impressive horns form a complete whorl around the back of its head.

These four horned lizard species, whose wider distributions overlap here, help tie the landscape together into one of rich local biodiversity: Texas Horned Lizards range from the western U.S. short-grass plains of Oklahoma,Texas, New Mexico, and south into Mexico. Round-taileds are found in southeastern Arizona, New Mexico, west Texas, and south into Mexico (both are Chihuahuan Desert inhabitants). The Greater Short-horneds' range extends from the northern Rocky Mountains of the southwestern Canadian border southward into Rocky Mountain areas of the western U.S. and through the Sky Islands, then on into the Sierra Madre Occidental mountains and plateaus of northwest Mexico. The Regal enters our area, its farthest extent east, from the dry and warm Sonoran Desert typical of Tucson and southward into Sonora, Mexico.

What do they eat?

In a word, ants! But, as you might suspect, not all kinds of ants. Within ant species, communal and chemical defenses vary widely. Horned lizards eat other insects and invertebrates too (some toxic to mammals), and their diets vary between species, age groups, and local availability of prey. Texas and Regal horned lizards in particular have the tools to deal with the large colonies of fearsome (to us) stinging and biting seed-harvester ants (*Pogonomyrmex* sp.).

Alerted groups of seed-harvester ants can organize defensive biting-attacks, so these horned lizards are most comfortable at the edges of ant gatherings, picking off individuals one by one, eating tens or hundreds at a sitting—and retreating

Greater Short-horned Horned Lizard (top) and Round-tailed Horned Lizard

if necessary. Leaning forward toward an unsuspecting ant, each lizard can visually determine the exact distance and, in milli-seconds, flip out its tongue so that the sticky tip holds the ant by the back of its head or thorax. Just as quickly the lizard pulls it back, passing the struggling ant between its teeth without a bite, into the rear of its throat where copious amounts of mucus bathe and encase the ant, thus preventing defensive use of its jaws or stinger. As the encumbered ant proceeds down the lizard's esophagus, it's coated with more mucus till it reaches the stomach, immobilized.

When do they drink?
Not at streams or the puddles that quickly disappear during infrequent rains. They use their backs and their waterproof reptilian scales to "rain-harvest" droplets before they hit the ground. Alerted by the first drops, even when under the sand at night, Texas horned lizards emerge to spread and arch their backs, maximizing the rain-capturing surface area.

Surface tension then takes droplets to the hinges between scales, where capillary adhesion pulls the water in all directions, including deeply into the scale hinges. Here the moisture feeds into a semi-tubular water-transport system and spreads throughout the lizard's scaly outer surfaces, including to the rear edges of the mouth. Slowly opening and closing their jaws, with a 1-per-second rhythm, the lizards gather this water and swallow it, thus quenching a thirst that may have been building for months.

How do they reproduce?
Here's what seems to have been an important evolutionary question for horned lizards as they diversified on our continent (their only home): To dig a nest and lay your eggs? or to hold them in your body until development allows them to emerge as live youngsters?

Ten species have stayed with the more widespread adaptation of reptiles, laying white eggs in buried nests, but seven species give live births. The only local species to do so is the Greater Short-horned (usually producing 20-30, but as many as 48, young). Embryo retention in the body is most frequent in species living in high-elevation or high-latitude cool climates. Here females can move within microhabitats, capturing sunrays to adjust to warm temperatures for embryo development throughout the day. Thus a mother can maximize their speed of growth where seasons are short.

How do they repel diverse predators?
Horned lizards see well and pay attention! Their threats are many and diverse, and their brains process information that allows them to use the best defense possible to increase their chances of survival against each type

of predator. Some predators swallow their prey whole (roadrunners, snakes) while others chew it into pieces before ingesting. For the former, prey size, especially if armed with sharp horns around the head, can become a limiting issue especially if the meal is likely to be a throat-choking, life-ending experience.

So when threatened by a Coachwhip Snake (*Masticophis flagellum*), a Texas or Regal horned lizard advertises its size—it spreads its ribs to broaden its back surface surrounded by body-edge extending spiny-scales, tilts its body toward the approaching snake and either rocks forward and backward (Texas) or flips over onto its back exposing a broad, spine-surrounded, white surface (Regal).

The message, "You want to choke on me?"

But if the threat is a Western Diamondback Rattlesnake (*Crotalus atrox*), whose poison kills horned lizards, their response is to just run fast and far. Rattlesnakes, unlike whipsnakes, don't chase prey. They are ambush, venomous, quick-injection biters. Horned lizards know how to ID snakes.

The teeth of foxes, coyotes, and bobcats can easily cut through horned lizard bodies. So, for a horned lizard, it's best to stop this threat before the teeth can do their work. How? Wait until the predator opens its mouth, pick a target—taste receptors—and squirt blood (laced with distasteful chemicals) from the tear ducts of your eye sockets. (See photo page 39.)

The reaction? "I hate this stuff!" And the predator shifts its attention to clearing its mouth—shaking its head, salivating profusely, and wiping its snout on vegetation. Maybe it's a costly defense, but how much is too costly to save your life? Horned lizards don't use a blood-squirting defense with other predators like hawks, ravens, Leopard Lizards, Grasshopper Mice—only with those predators where it's needed.

When predators lurk nearby, horned lizards visually and mentally evaluate the threat and then respond appropriately to enhance their own survival.

Regal Horned Lizard

128

20   **Frogs**

Dawn Wilson

Only two species of frogs are found in the Canyon: the Chiricahua Leopard Frog, which was first described from Herb Martyr Lake, and the Canyon Tree Frog. (Numerous toad species are found in the valleys.)

Chiricahua Leopard Frog (*Lithobates chiricahuensis*)

The Chiricahua Leopard Frog (CLF) is a medium to large, stocky frog with adult lengths from 5.0-13.5 cm (2.0-5.4 in). The ground color of the **dorsum** ranges from green to brown with numerous small dark spots. In southeastern Arizona, frogs are often green, or have green on the head. The species is distinguished from other Arizona leopard frogs by a salt-and-pepper pattern on the rear of the thighs. During the breeding season, male frogs have a dark, swollen area at the base of the thumb that allows the male to obtain a tight grip on the female during reproduction.

This frog is a pool or pond breeding amphibian that uses both terrestrial and aquatic habitats during its complex life cycle. The egg and tadpole stages are entirely aquatic and the juvenile and adult stages are largely aquatic. Ponds provide habitat for reproduction and foraging, and their adjacent wetlands and streams provide areas for **refugia** against the unpredictability of the pond. Historically, the CLF occurred in a wide variety of wetland habitats, including rivers, creeks, springs, and cienegas, but in

Small adult Chiricahua Leopard Frog in a SWRS pond
All photos by Dawn Wilson unless indicated otherwise.

129

recent years in the Chiricahuas, it has been restricted largely to stock tanks and other manmade ponds free of non-natives. CLFs are active during the day or night. Activity patterns increase during the monsoon season, and frogs can move overland along drainages.

Egg mass laid in a pond on SWRS property (large tadpole in the background)

Egg laying (**oviposition**) has been observed in any month of the year but shows noted peaks of reproduction in the spring and summer. The mating call of the male frog can be heard throughout the breeding season and sounds like a low-pitched snore. CLFs can call below or above the water surface. The jelly-coated eggs (as many as 1,485) are laid in masses that are attached to vegetation growing in shallow areas of the ponds. Hatching occurs within a few weeks, and the tadpoles develop in the water.

Compared to other leopard frogs, the tadpoles are relatively dark, mottled, and stocky. They graze on vegetative matter such as algae, as well as other small food items. Depending on the temperature of the water, tadpoles metamorphose into small frogs within three to nine months. However, if egg masses are oviposited in late fall, the tadpoles may overwinter in the pond and not metamorphose until early spring of the next year.

The juvenile frogs and adults eat a wide variety of aquatic and terrestrial invertebrates, small fish, and frogs—including juveniles of their own species.

Predators of the tadpoles include aquatic insects, crayfish, native and non-native fishes, garter snakes, Great Blue Herons, and other birds. Predators of juvenile and adult CLFs include some of the tadpoles' predators—fish, garter snakes, and birds—but also include many mammals: rats, coyotes, foxes, raccoons, ringtail cats, coatis, bears, badgers, skunks, and big cats, as well as the non-native (to Arizona) American Bullfrog.

Historically, the range of the CLF included parts of Arizona, New Mexico, and Mexico. The range of this species is divided into two large areas. One includes northern montane populations along the Mogollon Rim and associated mountains in central and eastern Arizona and west-central New Mexico, and the other includes southern populations located in the mountains and valleys south of the Gila River in southeastern Arizona and southwestern New Mexico, extending into Mexico along the eastern slopes of the Sierra Madre Occidental. This species is patchily distributed within its range is fragmented due to the aridity of this region. The type locality for this species is located at Herb Martyr Lake, 6 miles southwest of Portal. Although the species can still be found in several areas throughout its range, in Arizona it has disappeared from about 85 percent of historical localities.

The CLF was federally listed as threatened by the U.S. Fish and Wildlife Service in June of 2002, and a recovery plan was adopted in 2007. The decline of this species is due to the reduced quality and quantity of its **riparian** and wetland habitats, as well as the spread of an infectious skin fungal disease, chytridiomycosis (*Batrachochytrium dendrobatidis*).

The frog's degraded habitat has been caused by many factors: the introduction of non-native species such as bullfrogs and crayfish; stream channelization and groundwater pumping; agricultural development and grazing by livestock; mining, as well as drought and catastrophic wildfires.

In 2010 the Southwestern Research Station began a partnership with the U.S. Fish and Wildlife Service and the Arizona Game and Fish Department to aid in this frog's recovery. That summer, the Station constructed an enclosed facility to raise ("head-start") tadpoles that were collected at the Leslie Canyon Wildlife Refuge. Head-starting is a reestablishment program where animals are raised or

These small frogs were raised in the outdoor enclosure at the SWRS and then released into one of the ponds on SWRS property.

rehabilitated in zoos, aquariums, and/or private facilities and then released into their natural habitats. In June 2011, the Station observed its first reproduction in the outdoor enclosures.

In October 2011 frogs were released into a pond on Station property. Since that time, over 15,000 eggs have been laid in the Station ponds.

Canyon Tree Frog *(Hyla arenicolor)*

The Canyon Tree Frog is native to rocky plateau areas of the southern U.S., primarily in New Mexico and Arizona. Its range extends to Utah, Texas, and Colorado, and as far south as the Mexican state of Oaxaca. This relatively small frog can be found in habitats near the desert's edge to higher mountain habitats of pinyon-juniper, oak, and mixed conifer.

©R.Wyatt Mendez III 2014

Canyon tree frogs are small, 32-57 mm (to around 2.2 in). The dorsum of the frog ranges in color from rusty-brown, gray-brown to olive green with random green to gray spotting. The ventral surface of the frog is cream to orange-yellow. Adult males can have a dark throat patch and yellow to orange coloration on the inner surface of their hind legs. The color of the frog usually matches the soil or rock coloration of their native habitat, which serves as camouflage. Tadpoles typically have dark spots, and become speckled with golden or bronze coloration as they mature.

The species is mostly nocturnal and can be found in semiarid rocky habitats near permanent water sources. They breed in the spring and during the early part of the summer monsoon season. The sudden, explosive mating call of the male is a loud, rattling series of short trills. Females lay 100 or more eggs that may be floating or attached to vegetation. Eggs hatch in less than two weeks, and tadpoles metamorphose usually between 45-75 days. The adult frog feeds on a variety of small invertebrates and the tadpoles eat organic debris, algae, and plant tissue.

Like other tree frogs, the Canyon Tree Frog has enlarged toe tips with adhesive discs that make them great climbers. This species can be found attached to large boulders in pools at the bottom of mountain drainages. In the spring or summer, you can find them crowded together, lining a shallow rock crevice. They also take refuge in the far reaches of rock crevices during arid times of year and winter months. Their rough, warty skin helps prevent desiccation. So, if you want to see one of these well-camouflaged frogs, go out at night with a headlamp and walk along riparian areas in the rocky canyons—peering into the cracks and crevices of the boulders.

In Arizona, this species has tested positive for chytridiomycosis, but no studies have shown that they are adversely affected by the disease.

21 Ants

Howard Topoff

The Chiricahua Mountains and surrounding high deserts are biodiversity hot spots. More than 125 species of ants have been collected from these areas, which represents about 25 percent of all the ant species in the United States. Not too shabby indeed!

Although ants might not be on the top of your list of important animals, as a visitor to the Chiricahuas we hope you think about ants as more than pests at a picnic. And so you should. Besides being a significant part of our ecosystem, ants share one important trait with humans, other primates, cetaceans, termites, bees, and wasps: They are groups of individuals interacting behaviorally to modify their environment, and they form a society based on complex forms of communication.

Simply put, if we are interested in the evolution of social behavior, ants cannot be ignored!

A worker of *Polyergus topoffi* carries a pupa of *Formica* back to its nest after a slave-raid. When mature, the slave *Formica* workers feed the *Polyergus* workers and queen, clean the nest, and even defend the colony from predation by army ants. *All photos by Howard Topoff*

Ants, of course, are insects and, together with bees and wasps, form the insect order Hymenoptera. Just about all the ants you see are female—whether they are small workers or much larger soldiers. Male ants are typically produced in the nest about once each year. Their sole function is to mate with new queens, after which they drop dead! The life span of male ants is typically measured in days. Female workers can live for a year or two. But the longevity prize goes to the colony queen (or queens in some species), who can easily live for more than 10 years.

The one dominant group of ants in the Chiricahuas is known as harvester ants. These husky red ants of the genus *Pogonomyrmex* seem to be everywhere. Their nests are easily recognized as large circular platters on the ground, devoid of vegetation and covered with small pebbles. They are diurnal seed-eaters and form distinct trails meandering through the scrub in search of food. If you traipse around near their nests, you would do well to tuck the bottom of your pants into your socks. This will prevent the ants from delivering a memorable sting. It is really one time you don't want ants in your pants! They are not like fire ants—they don't swarm all over you. Nevertheless, their sting packs a wallop and burns for hours.

Speaking of fire ants, we have 'em, at least two species. Fortunately, these desert dwellers are not the imported fire ants that cause ecological havoc in the Southeast and California. Our fire ants, in the genus *Solenopsis*, are native. Their populations are kept in check by naturally occurring predatory species.

On a more exotic note, about six species of army ants make

(Top) Workers of the Harvester Ant *Pogonomyrmex barbatus*. (Bottom) Nest of the harvester ant. This is the commonest ant nest you will see in the Cave Creek area. The size of the platter can vary from less than a meter up to two meters, depending on the age of the colony.

Workers of the army ant *Neivamyrmex nigrescens*. The banana-shaped brood are larvae. The ones that look like white adults are pupae.

their home in the Chiricahuas. Army ants are rather infamous ever since Hollywood "glorified" them in the 1954 movie "The Naked Jungle" starring Charlton Heston and Eleanor Parker. In the movie, millions of these six-legged marauders swarm across the jungle, devouring everything in their path. They are of tropical origin, and most species are still found in the wet forests of Central and South America. Nevertheless one genus, *Neivamyrmex*, has evolved to live in more temperate conditions, and is found in the U.S. as far north as Kansas. In arid Arizona, they have adapted by becoming essentially nocturnal. With colony sizes of around 10,000 they are strictly insectivorous wandering ants and use temporary nests (bivouacs) instead of a fixed underground nest. When larvae are present in the nest, the colony is nomadic. During this two-week long phase, nightly raids are conducted against other ants and termites, and the colony emigrates to a new nesting site at the completion of each raid. When the larvae pupate, the colony's food requirements drop substantially. The ants then enter a relatively quiet, **statary** phase. Raiding intensity and duration is reduced (or absent altogether), and the colony remains at the same site for approximately three weeks.

In 1863, The National Women's Loyal League gathered 400,000 signatures on a petition for a constitutional amendment to abolish slavery. And while it took another two years for the Thirteenth Amendment to be ratified, the ant world took little notice. Slavery among ants may be one of the most unusual forms of social behavior, but workers of the genus *Polyergus* live exclusively on slave labor and would die without workers of *Formica* ants to take care of them. Ants that are parasites? That make slaves? You bet!

Strictly speaking, parasitism is a form of **symbiosis,** a broad ecological concept that also includes beneficial associations, such as between humans and the intestinal microorganisms that aid their digestion. **Parasitism,**

135

however, is decidedly one-sided, with the parasite living at the expense of its host, and sometimes even killing it. Among vertebrates, the best known of these symbionts are avian brood parasites, such as cuckoos. In these species, the female parasite lays an egg in the nest of another species, and leaves it for the host to rear, typically at the expense of the host's young.

Polyergus ants are social parasites that have traveled down an unusual evolutionary road. They have lost the ability to care for themselves. The workers do not forage for food, feed their brood or queen, or even clean their own nest. To compensate for these deficits, *Polyergus* has become specialized at obtaining workers from the related ant genus *Formica* to do their chores. This is accomplished by a slave raid, in which several thousand *Polyergus* workers travel up to 150 meters, penetrate a nest of the ant *Formica*, disperse the *Formica* queen and workers, and capture the resident pupal brood. Back at the *Polyergus* nest, some of raided brood is consumed. But a portion of it is reared through development, and the emerging *Formica* workers assume all responsibility for maintaining the permanent, mixed-species nest. They forage for nectar and dead arthropods, and regurgitate food to colony members of both species. They also remove wastes and excavate new chambers as the population increases.

Perhaps the most exciting adaptation evolved by *Polyergus* is the unique method of colony founding used by *Polyergus* queens. Because she too is a parasite, the *Polyergus* queen requires the help of slaves to rear even her first brood. Newly mated *Polyergus* queens accomplish this by invading a nest of *Formica*, killing the host queen, appropriating the pupal brood, and immediately becoming accepted by the slave species' workers. These resident *Formica* slaves then rear the broods of the parasitic queen, until her worker population is sufficiently large to supplement the slave force by staging raids on other host colonies. The process of host-queen killing is crucial, because it allows for the transfer of key chemicals from the *Formica* queen to the *Polyergus* queen.

We hope this small sampling of our ant fauna convinces you that ants are indeed fascinating creatures. When you return home to your gardens, keep in mind that tunneling ants turn over as much soil as earthworms do, aerating the soil and redistributing nutrients. On a grander scale, ants are also part of the world recycling crew: acting as scavengers, collecting dead insects and turning them into fertilizer for your soil.

Any questions? Send them to htopoff@mac.com.

22 Butterflies
Richard G. Zweifel

More than 170 butterfly species are recorded from the Chiricahuas. Within the Cave Creek drainage—Main, North, and South forks—between Portal and an elevation of about 5,500 feet, I have found more than 130 species, or about three-quarters of the known Chiricahua fauna. Many species are highly seasonal, others are rare or at least difficult to find, so the casual seeker should not expect a bonanza, but knowing when, where and how to look can be rewarding. You will need names to keep the species sorted out; check the **Further Reading** section at the end of the book for useful resources.

There is a lot more to identifying butterflies than looking at pictures. What was it doing? Nectaring? On what flowers? Basking in the sun or slipping into shaded vegetation when disturbed? Behavior may often identify a butterfly before you can get a close look. Size is one of the initial criteria for identification. Many of the most interesting and beautiful species are scarcely larger than your fingernail, so serious watchers will require close focusing binoculars to facilitate or confirm identifications. But anyone can profit from just naked-eye viewing.

When to search for Cave Creek butterflies?

Whenever you are here.

Southern Dogface
All photos by Richard G. Zweifel

Weather permitting, some butterflies are active all year, even in the winter months. I view the year in butterfly periods rather than formal calendar seasons. Spring starts, for me at least, with the first sighting of a Sara Orangetip, generally late February to early March. Already by then you may have seen Mourning Cloaks that overwinter as adults and show up on sunny winter days. In March things really start moving. A walk up the South Fork road with close attention to the catkin-laden willows (best at the bridge) usually reveals several species—tiny Spring Azures and Brown Elfins, Satyr Commas hungry after months of hibernation, along with Mourning Cloaks and several others.

As April progresses, look for spiny, roadside shrubs with small white flowers, Fendler Ceanothus. Many species come to it, but Hairstreaks seem especially to be attracted. You are almost certain to see a small gem, the Arizona Hairstreak, and its larger cousin, the Gray Hairstreak, or even the magnificent Great Purple Hairstreak. Hairstreaks have an annoying habit: they keep their wings closed while feeding so their colorful upper surfaces are not in view.

By mid-May the spring butterfly season is in full swing. Dozens of tiny Marine Blues (so called from the wavy lines on the wing's undersides) crowd around muddy spots while Arizona Sisters, conspicuous with their black and white orange-tipped wings, occupy sunny territories along the roads.

You may see some rather large, bright blue butterflies alternately perching and flying in a restricted area or on the move and fluttering while feeding at flowers. The first, the Red-spotted Purple, mimics in colors and pattern the other, the Pipevine Swallowtail. The Pipevine is poisonous to eat, as it inherits and stores in its body noxious chemicals from the plant diet of its caterpillar. A predator might mistake the edible Purple for a Swallowtail, giving the mimic some protection.

Late May and June are good times to move up the canyons. Follow the main road to signs pointing left to the entrance to the Southwestern Research Station. Visitors are welcome on the grounds (but not in the laboratory buildings) where there

Arizona Sister

138

Two-tailed Swallowtail

are flowers planted to attract insects.

Upon returning to the gate, a left turn puts you back on the road that follows the main branch of Cave Creek. Two Forest Service campsites by the creek, John Hands and Herb Martyr, often have a good variety of butterflies. The wet gravel filling Herb Martyr Dam is highly attractive in the June heat. Here the large, yellow Two-tailed Swallowtails that you may have seen floating above you, come down for water and allow a closer look. If you spot one in good condition but with only one tail on each wing, it may be the Western Tiger Swallowtail, more common at higher elevations.

At this season, before the summer rains begin, one can safely walk up the creek from the Dam. Diverse flowering annuals and shrubs in the creek bottom and on the adjacent slopes offer potential nectar feasts.

The summer rainy season may start as early as late June or not until mid-July. Those seeking butterflies may have to do much of their searching by mid-morning before the clouds build up. The sites mentioned earlier, and many more, remain attractive through the summer and can produce additional species that respond to the rains. A bonus is the late summer "southern influx" of species more characteristic of northern Mexico.

As fall approaches, the searcher finds the number and variety of butterflies lessening until mid-October, when Rabbit Brush starts to bloom. This yellow-flowered shrub grows in seasonally moist but well-drained sites (Cave Creek Wash below the Portal Bridge is one) and blooms well into November. Florally, it is the "only game in town" by this time and attracts

Acmon Blue

a host of hungry bees, flies, and butterflies. A large patch of the plants in full flower can offer scores of butterflies and dozens of species.

Skippers

Readers familiar with butterflies may wonder why I have placed this large group of species last. This is because their great individual and species abundance, coupled with subtle differences among species, make most of them difficult to identify on sight. I suggest that you look up the following four species in your field guide: Silver-Spotted, Golden Banded, Common Checkered, and Dull Firetip. These you are likely to see along Cave Creek—but not in the same season.

Then thumb through the several pages of photos of skippers to get some perspective on the problems involved.

'Nuff said.

Silver-spotted Skipper

23 Moths
Michael Van Buskirk

All diamonded with panes of quaint device,
Innumerable of stains, and splendid dyes ...
Gene Stratton-Porter, *Moths of the Limberlost*

lone shadow sails along Cave Creek in the silent moonlight of late evening. It is a female Oculea Silk Moth (Antheraea oculea), a large and beautiful creature in the Chiricahua Mountains night skies during monsoons. She follows the meandering creek as water rushes over rocks and slows into sparkling whirlpools. The round transparent windows on each of her wings glisten in the moonlight, and her feathery antennae "sniff" the trees and shrubs lining the creek. Her favorites are oaks and walnuts.

After emerging from her cocoon three days ago in early morning, the female mated at dusk, and is now examining various oaks on which to lay her ova. Depositing eggs began soon after mating, and this is her third night of activity. She has already placed

Female Oculea Silk Moth (top) has narrow antennae and broad wings. The male Oculea Silk Moth (bottom) has narrower wings and broad pectinate antennae. The "eyes" of both are defensive markings to ward off predators. *All photos by Christopher Conlan*

The streamlined Typhon Sphinx has swept-back wings, allowing fast and agile flying. During daylight, the subtle markings help the moth blend in with a background of bark and leaves, creating safety while at rest.

100 brown-banded, disc-shaped ova on the underside of individual leaves of host plant trees. She has a deadline—she does not feed, her stored fat reserves will run out in a week, and she will die.

Not far below our Oculea, a Typhon Sphinx female flies at ground level along Cave Creek. Looking like a nocturnal hummingbird, she buzzes around and into an immense tangle of Wild Grape vines, depositing spherical transparent green ova. At dusk she extends her 6-inch **proboscis** *to probe deeply for nectar from bright yellow Evening Primrose blossoms.*

Moths (*Macroheterocera*) are a family within the order Lepidoptera, along with Butterflies and Skippers (*Rhopalocera*). More than 30 families of moths are found in Cave Creek Canyon with perhaps 100 species (new ones are discovered often). Found in all sizes and shapes in an endless array of shades and color, these nocturnal beauties are mostly hidden and seldom seen by visitors in the monsoon darkness. Some are minute species with a ¼" wingspread, up to the giant Oculea Silk Moth with a 5-6" wing spread. Nine other species of silk moths (*Saturniidae*) and 20 species of sphinx moths (*Sphingidae*) are found in Cave Creek Canyon. The largest sphinx moth is the beautiful Typhon Sphinx (*Eumorpha typhon*).

So, where can you see moths in Cave Creek Canyon? Wherever lights are bright: outbuildings, visitor centers, car headlights, even the large mercury vapor streetlights at the Portal Store. Butterfly gardens and stands of wild flowers have sphinx moths "nectaring" at dusk. However you might see them, it is an exciting experience. Keep your camera ready!

The female Oculea glides past campgrounds down the Canyon, depositing ova whenever she finds a suitable host plant. A steady breeze gently moves the trees and brings the delightful fragrance of wet creosote from the desert floor.

A thunderstorm pelted Cave Creek with more than an inch of rain earlier in the day. The Oculea female flutters by a large Sycamore at South Fork, passing an Elegant Trogon hidden and sleeping in the branches.

Suddenly, a dark form stealthily moves in behind the female. In an instant the large moth is captured in the jaws of an even larger Mastiff Bat. The bat crunches noisily on his easy meal. The female has reached the end of her short lifespan. For now, the female Typhon Sphinx fares better—she is fast, agile, and a capable escape artist from the large bat.

Adult predators

Many predators threaten Oculea Silk Moths and Typhon Sphinx Moths during their adult lives. Mastiff bats are just one of the lethal dangers to the moths. Other bats and owls feed on these and many other species at night, especially the larger moths. During daylight, birds, rodents, lizards, and even other insects take a large toll of adult moths each monsoon season.

Life history

Both the Oculea Silk Moth and Typhon Sphinx develop through four distinct life history stages, termed complete metamorphosis: egg, caterpillar (larva), pupa, and adult moth. Development of the first three stages within Cave Creek Canyon spans most of the summer monsoon season, from July through September.

Tiny new larvae hatch within 7-10 days. The monsoons create abundant, tender new growth on host plants. Each larva is a leaf-eating machine, increasing body volume many hundreds of times during the larval stages. Each stage of the larva is called an **instar.** Larvae shed their skin at the end of each instar, and there are five instars in total. The larvae of both species face intense survival pressure from their environment—predators such as birds, mammals, lizards, and the worst of all, fly and wasp parasites. Parasitism will kill many larvae, and the variety of those that attack both

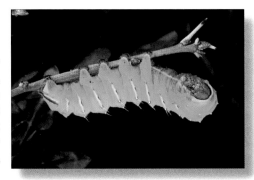

The fully mature Oculea Silk Moth larva is a stout 4" long. Settled deep in oak tree foliage, it nearly disappears. The metallic spots, lateral stripes, oval red breathing apparatus (spiracles), and scattered white hairs combine to mimic dappled sunlight and effectively hide and protect the larva.

moths is significant. Survival rate for both species of larvae is 1-2 percent. Only one Oculea larva, and just two Typhon larvae have survived. All is in perfect balance—larval casualties are nourishment for higher members of the food chain.

Finished feeding, the Oculea Silk Moth larva spins a silken cocoon. Inside the cocoon the next phase of metamorphosis occurs; the larva sheds its skin for the last time into a pupa.

Typhon Sphinx Moth larvae begin pupation using a different process. Each larva leaves the grape vines and races quickly across the sandy soil and rocks, looking for a soft place to burrow. They dig down about 12 inches, push out a hollow space, and pupate in the soil with no cocoon.

The cocoon and underground pupae **diapause** through the fall, winter, and following spring. When the summer monsoon rains begins in July, both emerge in very different ways.

The Oculea Silk Moth hatches from the cocoon, hanging upside down from the bottom of the cocoon, and expands its wings. Once expanded, the wings take several hours to fully dry before the adult moth can fly.

Moisture from the rains penetrates the dry soil around the two Typhon Sphinx pupae, increasing humidity, encouraging emergence. A strong spine **(cremaster)** on its end allows the pupa to corkscrew backwards through the soil to the surface, where the adult moths break out from their pupal shells, finding a twig or rock to climb up and expand their wings.

Each species of moth in the Canyon has a similar cycle. Throughout the year, these moths complete their life cycles and become adults, often hidden during development in a multitude of host plants. The array of beautiful moths in all shapes, sizes and colors is seemingly endless.

These are indeed the hidden jewels of the night!

Mature Typhon Sphinx larvae are masters of camouflage, using either a dark purple (shown here) or bright green color form. The darker color mimics the woody stems of the Wild Grape while green larvae are perfectly hidden within the foliage.

24 Dragonflies

John Alcock

Birdwatchers, and I am a lifelong practitioner, have been discovering that certain insects have much in common with birds when it comes to providing an enjoyable identification challenge.

There are now several good field guides (see **Further Reading**) to help us identify the dragonflies and damselflies, both of which are placed in the insect order Odonata. Dragonflies are generally larger than their more delicate relatives, and the two subgroups differ in how they hold their wings when perched; dragonflies spread their wings out flat when resting while damselflies usually hold their wings together over their backs while sitting on a rock or twig. Both sub-groups have many distinctively colorful members whose species identity can be determined by persons willing to take a look. I recommend doing so, particularly when you happen to be near streams, ponds or rivers. Binoculars can be employed to good effect with **odonates** as well as birds.

A male Red Rock Skimmer perched on a rock in the manner of a territorial individual at a stream. *All photos by Pierre Deviche, www.azdragonfly. net*

The various branches of Cave Creek in the Chiricahuas are populated by many dragonflies and damselflies that provide grist for the identifier's mill. In addition, the behavior of these insects can be readily observed by any reasonably patient individual, a fact that provides a real bonus for the birdwatcher.

In the late spring and early summer, one of the most abundant species in Cave Creek Canyon is the Red Rock Skimmer, also known as *Paltothemis lineatipes*. Its common name reflects the fact that the attractive red-eyed males do seem to skim along over the rocks of Cave Creek as they cruise back and forth along the stream.

If you were to capture a set of males—no easy task as they are extremely agile—and mark their wings with paint spots, you would find, as I did, that males are faithful to a territory, which can be a mere 3 meters in length (when there are many competitors present along the stream) or considerably longer (when rivals are few in number).

Females of Red Rock Skimmers are bluish, not red, as seen in this photograph of a female resting on the ground.

When a patrolling male encounters an intruder at the edge of its territory, the resident engages the other male in a swirling chase that almost invariably sends the intruder on his way.

You may wonder why males of this, and many other species of odonates, are willing to invest time and energy defending a bit of watery real estate. The answer to this question is provided by the females of the species, which only occasionally appear at the stream. When a bluish female does slip down to the water's edge, the local resident territory-holder is quick to spot and catch her using the claspers at the tip of his abdomen. The male grasps her by the thorax just behind her head. He then transports the trailing female to a spot that he has previously identified as a potential egg-laying site.

Females that are taken to small patches of sand or fine gravel in shallow, fast moving water usually twist their abdomen around (while still being held in flight by the male) so that their genital opening covers what passes for a penis in the odonates, a projection from the underside of the male's abdomen where the male has previously deposited sperm for just this moment. The sperm can then migrate into the female to be stored for use in fertilizing her eggs as she lays them.

The Red Rock Skimmer's copulatory behavior is typical of the entire order, with all these insects employing the "wheel position" as the means of transferring sperm from male to female. How odonates evolved this uniquely bizarre method of sperm transfer has puzzled many entomologists.

After a very brief copulation, the male releases his partner. She flies over the egg-laying site while dipping her abdomen into the water there. The eggs that she releases presumably drop to the floor of the stream and infiltrate the sand or fine gravel present in the spot. Meanwhile, initially the male stays very close to the egg-laying female, hovering about and ready to attack should another male even think about approaching the female. "Mate-guarding," in which males try to prevent other males from coming in contact with and copulating with a recent partner, is very common in odonates, many of which (particularly among the damselflies) do not release their females after sperm transfer but retain the tandem position until egg laying is completed.

So now we know why males of the Red Rock Skimmer are territorial. A male defends areas along streams with one or more little egg-laying spots that gravid females are likely to use when steered there by a sexually active territory holder. In this way, the resident male secures the chance to fertilize eggs and leave descendants. Because egg-laying places are often identifiable and because egg-laden females often remain sexually receptive for some time when **ovipositing**, territorial behavior coupled with mate guarding are widespread characteristics of dragonflies and damselflies.

But each species has its own intriguing behaviors. Some males may accompany a female elsewhere if she does not find an oviposition site to her liking in his territory. Other males are non-territorial but instead cruise great stretches of stream looking for a female. The behavior of many species remains undescribed.

You do not have to be a professional entomologist to make novel observations or to appreciate the remarkable diversity of form, color pattern, and behavior in the Odonata.

Give it a try; you'll enjoy what you see.

A copulating pair of the Canyon Rubyspot, *Hetaerina vulnerata*, a common damselfly in Cave Creek. Note the wheel position adopted by the male (in front) and the female, the standard method of copulation in the Odonata. Note also that the rubyspots are holding their wings together in the standard position adopted by most damselflies but not dragonflies.

25 Other Invertebrates
Shane Burchfield

ave Creek Canyon hosts a fascinating and abundant number of invertebrates. The term "invertebrates" includes a multitude of creatures such as spiders, beetles, and many undersized others that fly, jump, and swim. Insects alone account for 75 percent of our planet's animal species and are equally numerous within the Chiricahua Mountains. They play an important role as plant pollinators and fertilizers, and they have other assorted jobs within the ecosystem. Cave Creek Canyon specifically boasts native invertebrates from forests, grasslands, and deserts all within one region.

Most important, the majority of these invertebrate inhabitants are completely harmless to humans and quite captivating.

Spiders, including tarantulas, are easily recognized by their two body sections and eight legs, but they vary in size and shape. The Desert Tarantula (*Aphonopelma* sp.) is more than 2.5 inches in length, and, in

Male Desert Tarantulas are a common sight during monsoons. *All photos ©Ray A. Mendez 2014 unless otherwise indicated*

Female Black Widow spider (top) and Brown Recluse (bottom). Contrary to legend, the female Black Widow only eats the male if they are enclosed in a small container. In the wild several males can be found living on her web.

summer and fall, males are commonly seen searching for mates. In order to escape injury or death, these graceful animals defend themselves by kicking off barbed **urticating** hairs, which are as light as air and very irritating to a predator's airway. Tarantulas also have large fangs than can inflict a painful but harmless bite. You can avoid being bitten by not aggravating them and by giving these animals plenty of personal space.

Two of the most venomous inhabitants of the Canyon are the Arizona Brown Spider, or Desert Recluse (*Loxosceles* sp.), and the Black Widow Spider (*Latrodectus* sp.). Adult female Black Widows are completely black except for a red hourglass-shaped mark on the underside of their abdomen. The web of a Black Widow is a messy-looking tangle that goes in all directions made up of extremely strong strands. The egg sacs are circular, yellowish, and about the size of a dime.

Desert Recluse Spiders can also inflict a venomous bite, but they mostly live up to their name and remain shy and out of sight. Generally, they have a small, white, silky web on the ground, usually in a dark and undisturbed location.

Other commonly encountered spiders include wolf spiders, which are grey, sometimes bigger than a quarter—and a boon for insect control in Cave Creek Canyon.

Cellar Spiders (*Pholcus* sp.) have very long thin legs and are found year-round preying on other spiders and smaller insects. They are often seen in corners of walls and ceilings and are dull yellow with a small gray marking on the upper body. These are often confused with Daddy Long Legs, or Harvestman Spiders, because of their long jointed legs; Cellar Spiders can be quickly differentiated by their two body segments compared to Harvestman Spiders, which appear to have only one. Daddy Long Legs (*Phalangium* sp.) are actually not spiders at all: They lack fangs, don't bite, and aren't venomous. In winter these imitators can be found in large groups with all their legs interlaced as insulation to survive the cold season.

Like spiders, scorpions also have eight legs, in addition to the two front claws and a stinger. Although the highly venomous Bark Scorpion (*Centruroides* sp.) has been recorded here, sightings are quite rare. Far more common is the Stripe-Tail Scorpion, which upon closer look, has several stripes along its tail. The sting of this common scorpion is similar to a bee sting, and the pain usually subsides within minutes.

Interestingly, all scorpions glow at night when illuminated by a special black light bulb or ultraviolet light.

The Vinegaroon (*Mastigoproctis* sp.) is often called a Whipscorpion, but it is distinctly different from common scorpions. These brown, alien-looking creatures resemble a scorpion with their eight legs and pincers, but they lack a stinger. Instead they have a fine, straight, string-like appendage

Striped-tail or Bark Scorpion. Newly hatched scorpions ride on their mother's back for protection. After their first molt, they dismount to fend for themselves.

Vinegaroon, also known as a Whipscorpion, although they lack a stinger. Like scorpions, they also carry their young on their back until the first molt.

that they use for sensing vibrations—but, if the animal is disturbed, it can also spray a concentrated acetic acid. This chemical defense smells like vinegar and often deters predators. Otherwise, these ferocious-looking creatures are harmless and are often seen after rains or during monsoons.

Centipedes and millipedes are often confused. The most common species of centipede is *Scolopendra* sp., which ranges from 1 inch up to 8 inches. Active at night, they eat mostly insects but are also found under rocks or logs in the day. They have one pair of jointed legs per body segment and the front pair of legs are modified fangs to eat prey. Their fast pace is another distinction from the slow speed of a millipede whose adult size averages around 5 inches. Cylindrical in shape, millipedes have two pairs of jointed legs per body segment and are usually brown or grey in appearance. They are largely vegetarian, consuming foliage and plant matter. Desert millipedes, *Orthoporus* sp., are harmless but will secrete a cyanide solution as defense if agitated.

A wide variety of insects populate the Chiricahua Mountains, in particular the riparian zone of Cave Creek Canyon. You can recognize them by their

Female centipede with eggs. She holds, protects, and licks her eggs until they hatch. The licking keeps them clean and free of fungus and other infectious agents.

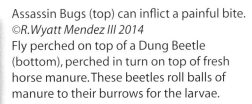

Assassin Bugs (top) can inflict a painful bite.
©R.Wyatt Mendez III 2014
Fly perched on top of a Dung Beetle
(bottom), perched in turn on top of fresh
horse manure. These beetles roll balls of
manure to their burrows for the larvae.

segmented body over six legs. Among the most notorious locals are Cone Nose or Assassin bugs (*Triatoma* sp.) These small dark-colored bugs take flight to find a mate and locate their next blood meal. They have been known to carry Chagas disease, but it's undocumented in our area and very uncommon in the U.S. The most frequented spots are pack rat nests and lights at night that often result in a new and unwelcome house guest. If you're bitten, sanitize the area, and check your sheets and mattress carefully.

Similiarly shaped but far larger are Leaf-footed Bugs, and the most commonly encountered is the Mesquite Bug (*Thasus gigas*). These are bigger yellow and brown bugs with red and black banding. They have odd-looking long antennae with disc shapes near the ends that are used to detect sensations. They eat plant and tree juices primarily of mesquites.

Beetle species worldwide outnumber plant species on our planet, and within Cave Creek Canyon, there are dozens of these critters to be found. The small Bombadier beetles (*Brachinus* sp.) gather underneath rocks and are easy to identify by their orange head and dark wing covers. They're well named: When provoked, they defend themselves by sending a blast of hot chemicals at 100 degrees C. towards the predator.

Dung beetles (*Canthon* sp.) are the size and shape of a pea, and they are mostly all black but sometimes green. These specialists partake in the dirty job of rolling a ball of dung to a burrow where the adults and larvae grow.

Among the most colorful and impressive are the Scarab beetles. One of these, the Fig Beetle (*Cotinis* sp.), a regular inhabitant of the Canyon, feeds on nectar and fruit, flying from one sweet spot to another. The sound of their wings buzzing in flight can grab your attention, and their bright green appearance with a yellow marking around the body gives away its identity. Equally impressive in color are the neon-green *Plusiotes* sp., or Jeweled Scarab beetles, that often fly to lights at night. They feed mostly on oaks

Tarantula Hawk Wasp. The females can be found on mountaintops where they find groups of males waiting to mate.

and junipers and are typically encountered in summer and fall. One type of Jeweled Scarab beetle (*Chrysina* sp.), in particular induces amazement and wonderment with symmetrical gold stripes covering its body.

But it's the massive Rhinocerus, or Hercules, beetle (*Dynastes* sp.) that has the most extensive flying ability. These majestic beetles are capable of reaching several inches in length and vary in color from grey, dull green, to almost completely black. Adults are often seen (and heard) flying into lights at night. Males sport two large horns, but these gentle giants are harmless.

By far the largest and most overlooked insect is the Walking Stick (*Diapheromera arizonensis*). The creatures resemble brown, green, or gray twigs, and their defense tactic is to remain completely motionless. They commonly reside on creekside plants and are abundant during summer and fall.

Wasps come in many sizes and colors, but the large Tarantula Hawk Wasp (*Pepsis* sp.) boasts an immense body and wings exceeding 2 inches. These insects inflict a temporarily excruciating sting, but they aren't hostile—unless you're a tarantula. To feed its young, the Hawk Wasp finds an adult tarantula, paralyzes it, then drags it to a burrow as food for its larvae. The sight of a wasp dragging a tarantula is startling to many but a normal feat of strength and determination in the invertebrate world.

The invertebrate residents of the Chiricahuas far outnumber the human inhabitants, so you are bound to cross their path in your Canyon ramblings. Remember that most are peaceable and not aggressive unless provoked. You can respect and honor their beauty and service in our fragile environment by photographing and then releasing them during your stay.

26 A Highway for Wildlife
Kim Vacariu

Long before people arrived in the Chiricahua Mountains, the range was a key segment in a heavily traveled system of continental "highways." Of course, that ancient route had no traffic signs and was not traversed by any vehicles. Instead, it was used intuitively by wide-ranging native wildlife species as a multi-lane throughway connecting them with distant relatives, seasonal food sources, and preferred weather.

Back then, Jaguars quietly prowled along the stream-filled Chiricahua canyon bottoms on their way from hunting near the Grand Canyon to their breeding grounds in northern Mexico. Gray Wolves loped north and south through Chiricahua hill country grasslands in search of new mates. Ocelots and Jaguarundi ventured northward through these mountains from Mexico seeking new food sources. Black and Brown Bears moved back and forth through the Chiricahua "Sky Island" wilds as part of their daily activities. Above, a crowded north-south flyway served as a key corridor for many bird species, including colorful flocks of Thick-billed Parrots.

Today, some of the native species that formerly traversed these Chiricahua pathways (wolves, grizzlies, Jaguars, and Thick-billed Parrots) are gone due to excessive hunting and eradication efforts in the early 20th century. But the historic wildlife corridors through which these magnificent creatures maneuvered still exist, ironically now also relied upon by thousands of people who use the corridor trails every year for recreation and scientific purposes. Those trails continue to be shared, of course, by the wildlife that

Species that use the Chiricahua Flyway include the White-crowned Sparrow. *Narca Moore-Craig*

155

remains relatively abundant: Black Bear, Mountain Lion, Coyote, Mule and White-tailed Deer, Javelina, Coati, and hundreds of species of birds, to name a few.

The strategic geographic location and relatively excellent biological condition of the Chiricahua Mountains continue to make this range the focus of many science-based studies and conservation mapping projects that identify this area as a critical link in a "western wildway" stretching along the mountainous "spine of the continent" from Alaska to Mexico. These studies show that the Chiricahua and Peloncillo Mountain complex is the irreplaceable southern link in a chain of critical wildlife corridor connections that must be protected in various ways in order to ensure that existing (and potentially newly recolonizing) species requiring room to roam can remain healthy into the distant future.

As part of Coronado National Forest, including the strictly protected 85,900-acre Chiricahua Wilderness Area, this mountain range has recieved many helpful federal protections over the years. However, conservation biologists note that protection of the range solely as an isolated Sky Island that is disconnected from other protected wildlife habitats will not be enough to allow the return of the now missing—and ecologically necessary—native species that once roamed through the Chiricahuas on their ways to other destinations. That trip now requires crossing seas of grassland and desert carved by freeways and housing developments.

Conservation efforts are now underway to identify, restore, and make safe the pathways most used by wide-ranging species moving between (a) Mexico's Sierra Madre Occidental and the southern Peloncillo and Chiricahua mountains, and (b) the northern Chiricahua, Dos Cabeza, and northern Peloncillo mountains toward ranges further north—eventually connecting to the Rocky Mountains. Private land conservation and wildlife bridges over highways that allow passage of these large and important animals will, one can hope, someday restore the full habitat corridors connecting the Chiricahuas with these other mountain ranges along the spine of the continent.

Science-based mapping projects have identified the Chiricahuas as a critical link in the "Western Wildway," which stretches along the mountainous "spine of the continent" from Alaska to Mexico. These studies show that the Chiricahua and Peloncillo Mountain complex makes up an irreplaceable southern link connecting the temperate Rocky Mountains and associated ranges in the U.S. to the subtropical Sierra Madre Occidental in northern Mexico.

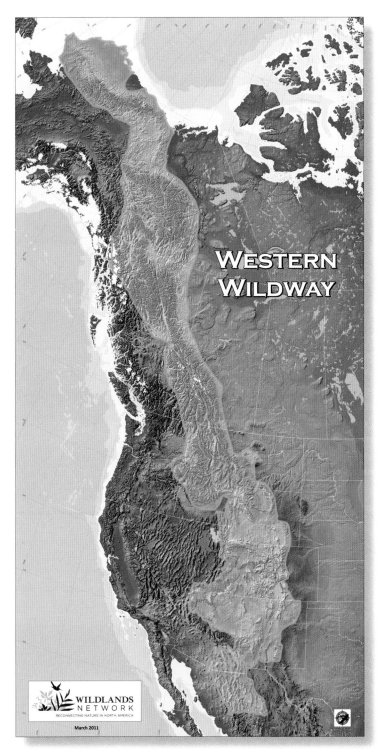

WESTERN
WILDWAY

WILDLANDS
NETWORK
RECONNECTING NATURE IN NORTH AMERICA

March 2011

157

The need for connected wildlife pathways linking the Chiricahuas with other surrounding and protected habitats is made more essential and timely by the onset of climate change, which is forcing wildlife of all types to change the location of their normal habitats as well as the duration of their stays. As weather warms beyond normal in northern Mexico, for example, many species may move north toward the Chiricahuas where the climate might more closely resemble what they require.

Without safe wildlife corridors allowing them to make that move, species could ultimately be greatly reduced in numbers—or die out entirely.

By the same token, as climate change increases, species that already live in the Chiricahuas may also need to migrate to maintain appropriate living conditions, making protection of habitat pathways that radiate farther north from the range just as important. Over the long term, climate change may be the single greatest reason to identify and protect wildlife corridors both within and outside the Chiricahua Mountains.

Recent catastrophic and habitat-altering forest fires, the frequency of which may also be associated with climate change, are another reason for wildlife corridor protection, both within and surrounding the Chiricahuas. As unnaturally severe fire drives some animals to make habitat changes, or to simply avoid immediate fire threats, they must be able to move quickly and safely along protected routes to surrounding landscapes, unhampered by large-scale impediments that can essentially "trap" species.

When strolling along the Chiricahuas' spectacular Crest Trail, hikers, bird watchers and scientists alike can revel in the knowledge they are walking along the 40-mile spine of one of Arizona's longest and tallest contiguous mountain ranges—and wildlife corridors. While passing through the range's cluster of promontories, including 10 mountain peaks in excess of 9,000 feet, it is easy to envision oneself as a legitimate part of the historic parade of wildlife that has passed along the trail over the eons.

We can hope that, in the future, the variety of species that will continue to use the "Chiricahua Connection" will increase to its nature-intended level. But for that to happen, those who appreciate this great mountain range and its ageless, ecologically critical wildlife corridors, must take responsibility for ensuring that safe passage for animals—and people—will continue for ages to come.

Human History

Although humans have been in the Canyon vicinity for around 12,000 years, they have left little impact. *Painting by Sherry Nelson*

Pottery sherds   *Mel Moe*

27 Early Peoples
Mel Moe

uman habitation in the Chiricahuas is not new. The first people known to have seen the Chiricahua Mountains arrived between 11,000 and 12,000 years ago. This was at the end of the last ice age, and the climate was much cooler and moister than it is now. The region was inhabited by many kinds of large mammals. These included mammoths, giant bison, horses, camels, and ground sloths.

The Clovis Culture

The first humans to arrive are called the Clovis Culture by archeologists. They were big game hunters, killing animals as large as mammoths with hand spears. The spears were tipped with large and distinctive, finely flaked spear points. These distinctive points with a characteristic groove on each side are called Clovis points. Mammoth kill sites have been found in adjacent valleys, including one with eight spear points found with its bones.

The Cochise Culture

By about 8,000 B.C. the climate was much hotter and drier, and the mammoths and many other species of large mammals were

Atlatl spear point from the Cochise Culture
All photos by Mel Moe

extinct. This may have been due to the habitat loss associated with climate change or a combination of this and overhunting by the Clovis People.

With the loss of big game, the people inhabiting this region had to change their lifestyle. They became much more dependent on plant foods which they gathered from the landscape, as well as hunting smaller game such as deer and rabbits.

Archeologists call them hunter-gatherers, and they labeled the culture they developed the Archaic Culture. In this region the local subset of the Archaic culture is called the Cochise Culture. These people gathered small seeds and roots and ground them in shallow stone basins, called metates, with small handheld stones, called manos. They also ground deep mortar holes into the bedrock of the foothills and canyons for grinding food. Instead of long handheld spears, they used shorter spears that they launched with an atlatl, or spear thrower. This is a stick about 18 inches long that in effect lengthened the thrower's arm. The spears were tipped with triangular points, either side-notched or corner-notched, that were much smaller and more crudely made than the Clovis Points.

These people lived in small groups, probably families, and roamed over large areas to find enough food to survive. They moved back and forth between mountains and valleys as the seasons changed and different foods became available. They lived in temporary shelters or rock shelters or caves. Population densities were low, but the culture was very successful and survived in this area for about 8,000 years. A few signs of these people still remain. Metates, manos, and spear points are still found, and there are numerous grinding holes in the bedrock.

Another sign of their residency is rock art. It is hard to date, but undoubtedly some of the pictographs (paintings on rock) and petroglyphs (figures pecked into rock) found in this region came from this culture.

The Mogollon Culture
The local cultures started to change in the last millennium B.C. At some time during this period, corn agriculture arrived from Mexico, and some of

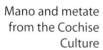

Mano and metate from the Cochise Culture

Rock Art of either the Cochise or Mogollon Culture. This style is called Mogollon Red.

the Archaic peoples started cultivating corn in small plots although they still relied largely on hunting and gathering wild foods. Then, between 100 and 200 A.D., squash and beans were added as crops, corn varieties improved, and two new innovations arrived, also from Mexico: pottery and the bow and arrow. Pottery provided for better food storage and preparation, and the bow and arrow improved the efficiency of hunters. With these changes, the land could support higher population densities, and people could settle more permanently in villages where they could care for their crops although hunting and gathering were still important.

The culture that evolved with the advent of pottery in this region is called the Mogollon culture by archeologists. By about 1200 A.D., sizable pueblos, now mostly identified by low mounds and pottery sherds, had developed at the mouth of every canyon in the Chiricahuas, and along water sources in the adjacent valleys.

A severe drought ravaged this area in the late 1300s, and by 1400 it appears that all of the settlements had been vacated. The Mogollons had moved on to more hospitable regions, perhaps to join the Zunis in the north or the Pueblos along the Rio Grande—no one is quite sure where. Pottery sherds and rock art are the most noticeable remains of the time when they inhabited this area. Small, mostly abstract, red pictographs found in rock shelters and on cliff faces in this area are called Mogollon Red by archeologists and are attributed to the Mogollon people.

Coronado called this region a *despalado,* or uninhabited land, when he came through in 1540, and there is little evidence of people living in the Chiricahuas until the mid-1600s. At that time, Spanish settlement to the south reported problems of raids from nomadic tribes they called the Janos and Jocomes who used the Chiricahua Mountains as a stronghold. It is possible that these people could have been living here the whole time, unknown to the Spanish.

The Apaches

The Apaches are believed to have arrived in the Chiricahua region in the early to mid-1600s, about the same time as the Spanish settlement of nearby Northern Mexico. Apaches were identified as joining the Janos and Jocomes on attacks of the Spanish for the first time in 1685. Anthropologists believe that the Apaches moved into this region from Northwestern Canada. They speak nearly the same language as the Athabascan Peoples of the Yukon and Northwest territories and are believed to have split from these people sometime in the last 2,000 years. Apache tradition, however, maintains that they have been in this region since the time of creation. The Apache have a rich religious tradition centered on Mountain Spirits.

One group of Apaches settled in the Chiricahua Mountain region, and became known as the Chiricahua Apaches. These people lived a hunter-gatherer life style, with the hunting expanding to raiding agricultural settlements for livestock.

The Apaches left few signs of their time here except for distinctive rock art, which included the depiction of horses and Mountain Spirits. (More about the Apaches is in Chapter 29.)

Places to visit

To learn more about the Mogollon Culture, you can visit Gila Cliff Dwellings National Monument, located north of Silver City, N.M.

Fort Bowie National Historic Site, located south of Bowie, is an excellent place to learn about the conflicts between the Apaches and the American Army.

Those interested in Apache Culture in this region can visit the San Carlos Apache Cultural Center at Peridot, Ariz., the White Mountain Apache Cultural Center at Fort Apache, Ariz., and the Mescalaro Apache Cultural Museum at Mescalaro, N.M.

Apache rock art depicting a Mountain God on a horse.

28   Archaeology
BAlvarius

It is always interesting and exciting to find remnants of former inhabitants when hiking in the Chiricahua Mountains. Whether it is evidence of historic use or something earlier, finding traces of others who lived on and used the landscape creates a sense of context and provides insight into how others viewed and lived in the Chiricahuas and surrounding valleys throughout time.

Evidence of historic usage

Historic visitation to this area began during the Spanish colonial period when expeditions from New Spain (modern-day Mexico) began looking for Cibola and the rumored riches of the New World.

The most well-known of these early Spanish explorations was the Coronado Expedition of 1540. The nearby Coronado National Memorial marks the location believed to be close to where Coronado entered the modern United States. Although other routes have been proposed, including entry at San Bernardino, and up the San Simon Valley, little physical evidence exists to mark the route taken by the early Spanish. But a series of presidios was eventually established across southern Arizona/northern New Mexico by the Spanish to mark the northern boundary of their protected holdings while they continued their northern expansion.

The closest presidio was located on the modern San Bernardino Wildlife Refuge. With the arrival of the Spanish and subsequent westward expansion of European settlers from the east in the early to mid-1800s, the Chiricahuas began receiving more visitation and settlement. The formal incorporation of the region into the United States through the Gadsden Purchase continued to open up the area. The ongoing conflict with indigenous peoples, which resulted in the loss of life on both sides, was eventually resolved, making more areas open to settlement.

Evidence of prehistoric usage

While evidence of early historic usage is more easily found in the Chiricahua Mountains, evidence of prehistoric usage abounds throughout the area. As noted in Chapter 27, "Early Peoples" the earliest humans documented on the landscape were the Clovis culture. The majority of physical evidence for Clovis culture comes from a number of sites west of the Chiricahua Mountains along the San Pedro River, but a documented fragmentary Clovis point was recovered east of the Chiricahuas in the Playas Valley, and local residents report finding evidence of these earliest inhabitants.

Perhaps the most abundant evidence of past landscape usage in and around Cave Creek Canyon is associated with the Mogollon culture.

Members of the Mogollon culture inhabited a large area of southwestern New Mexico and southeastern Arizona. A specific cultural subset, the Mimbres, are perhaps best known for their classic black on white picture bowls. The San Simon valley and eastern flanks of the Chiricahuas appear to be the most westward extension of this group, and their unique

A turn of the century grave from Jhus Canyon in the Chiricahua mountains. Note pottery fragments left on the sandstone grave marker.   *All photos by BAlvarius.*

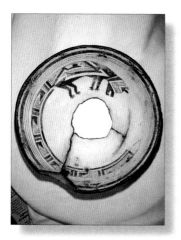

(Top) A classic Mimbres black on white bowl from a private collection.

(Bottom) Mimbres masonry field house foundation from the San Simon valley.

pottery fades from history after the Mimbres reorganization between 1150 and 1200.

The Mogollon were primarily agriculturalists living in villages but farming the landscape where they maintained field houses for easy access to farmed plots. As a result, evidence of their presence is frequently found near former water courses across the valley and into the mountains.

While the Mimbres built with stone creating masonry rooms and pueblos, others living in the area built with adobe. Adobe construction is typified by Hohokam villages found to the west of the Chiricahuas, as well as later Animas phase sites in the San Simon valley on the east side of the mountain range.

The Apaches were the last indigenous cultural group to utilize the Chiricahua mountains. Evidence of their presence on the landscape is known from both historic references and a number of sites in some of the more remote areas of the mountain range.

Relationship to the geography

The Basin and Range topography of southern Arizona and New Mexico funneled animals, early hunter/gathers, and settlers along north south paths, which were eventually settled, especially those sites with or close to permanent water sources. In combination with a day's travel on foot, larger concentrations of human activity (villages) are found about every 10 miles up the valleys surrounding the Chiricahuas, while on smaller drainages individual homesteads of one or several rooms are often encountered.

Important considerations

The Archaeological Resources Protection Act prohibits the disturbance of archaeological sites or collecting of artifacts on Federal lands. As such, the best approach is to photographically document a find and pass the information along to a local U.S. Forest Service official. If this is not possible, it falls to the discoverer to continue the story of the artifact or site by careful recording of information and redistribution.

Through careful observation and recording, it is possible to glean more information about those who came before us and how they used the landscape, thereby enhancing the experience of a trip to the Chiricahua Mountains.

Granary with mud-plastered rocks and sticks from the Chiricahua Mountains is evidence of the Apache presence.

29   Apaches and the U.S. Cavalry
Bill Cavaliere

To understand the history of the Chiricahua–U.S. military conflict, one must begin by knowing the area that comprised the homelands of the Chiricahua Apaches, commonly known as "Apacheria." This area was composed of southwest New Mexico, southeast Arizona, and, in Mexico, northeast Sonora and northwest Chihuahua.

The Chiricahua Apaches were divided into four bands: the Chokonen (Red Cliff People), who ranged west toward the San Pedro River and east to the Peloncillos. This is the band that was found in the Chiricahua Mountains, including Cave Creek Canyon. Cochise and Naiche were prominent Chokonen chiefs. The second band was the Chihennes (Red Paint People), also known as the Warm Springs or Mimbreno Apaches, who ranged roughly from the Burro Mountains east to the Rio Grande. Victorio, Nana and Loco were all Chihenne chiefs. The third band was the Nednhi (Enemy People), who ranged primarily in the Sierra Madre in Sonora and Chihuahua of northern Mexico, north into the Bootheel of New Mexico and east to the Florida Mountains. Juh and Nolgee were well-known Nednhis. The fourth and final band of the Chiricahua Apaches was the Bedonkohe (no known translation), who ranged north of the Gila River. Mangas Coloradas and Geronimo were Bedonkohes. The ranges of the four bands were not set by any kind of negotiated boundaries, and there was much overlap and even intermarrying among bands.

The Chiricahua Apaches derived from Athapascan-speaking peoples who migrated from the north. For many years, anthropologists had set the date of their arrival in Apacheria at around the year 1500. Recent research, however, has now moved that date back to 1200-1300.

The Chiricahua Apaches had been traditional enemies with Mexicans since the first arrival of the Spaniards in the early 1500s. When the first white

Americans, traders and trappers, began arriving in the 1820s, an uneasy peace was maintained. Some early pioneers claimed that Cochise and his Chokonens even supplied firewood to the Butterfield stage station near Apache Pass. This relationship was shattered on January 27, 1861, when Coyotero Apaches raided a ranch near Sonoita Creek, kidnapping a boy and taking some cattle. The kidnapping was reported at Fort Buchanan, and 2nd Lieutenant George Bascom was ordered to recover the child. Bascom had no prior experience dealing with Indians and had been an officer less than three years. What followed severely damaged the relationship between the Apaches and whites.

Probably due to the fact that the Chokenen chief's name was well-known to many in the area, Bascom assumed that Cochise was responsible. In early February, he and his soldiers arrived at Apache Pass and sent word that he wanted to speak with Cochise. After Cochise and some family members entered his tent, Bascom accused him of kidnapping the boy. Cochise rightfully proclaimed his innocence and even offered to try and locate the boy. Bascom accused Cochise of lying and had the tent surrounded by soldiers. At this point, Cochise withdrew a knife, slashed the side of the tent open and ran out, surprising the soldiers, who fired at him as he ran. The Indians remaining inside were taken prisoner. Cochise later captured four Americans, who he had killed when Bascom still refused to negotiate. Bascom retaliated by having some of the Apache prisoners hung. Thus began a decade of warfare between the Chiricahua Apaches and the Americans.

One of the first raids by Apaches after the Bascom Affair occurred just two months later, in April, when Cochise and his warriors attacked a stage and two wagons passing through the east mouth of Doubtful Canyon in the Peloncillo Mountains, killing a total of nine Americans.

On July 14, 1862, Captain Thomas Roberts arrived at Apache Pass with about 70 soldiers, several wagons and two small cannons. The Apaches fired at the soldiers, trying to prevent them from watering at the spring. Roberts positioned the cannons and fired them on the Apaches, killing several and scattering the others. Realizing that future attempts to obtain water there would produce similar confrontations, Roberts recommended a fort be built there to guard the spring as well as protect citizens. Therefore, in 1862, Fort Bowie was established. It would become the command center for military action against the Chiricahua Apaches.

July 1864 saw an Apache/U.S. military incident occur in Cave Creek Canyon. An expedition of soldiers led by Captain Thomas Tidball

Naiche, the last hereditary chief of the Chiricahua Apaches, and son of Cochise. *Photo taken by A. Frank Randall in 1882. Courtesy Arizona Historical Society*

encountered Indians travelling along the south side of the canyon. Their chief, called Plume, began shooting arrows and throwing rocks at the soldiers, delaying their advance while the women and children escaped. His bravery resulted in his being shot and killed by soldiers, who later found the Apaches' camp near Portal Peak.

Despite this one victory for the military, Apache depredations increased between 1864 and 1869 until Captain Reuben Bernard, commander at Fort Bowie, called Cochise "one of the most intelligent hostile Indians on this continent" and described the Chokonen warriors as "recklessly brave."

Major James Gorman clashed with Cochise's band on November 5th, 1865, near Sentinel Peak, killing seven warriors and wounding several others. Gorman also destroyed 14 Apache wikiups, along with all the belongings.

On October 8th, 1869, a clash took place between troops led by Lieutenant William Winters and Cochise and his warriors, who were caught leading a large herd of stolen cattle near the south end of the Chiricahuas. The battle resulted in about twelve Apaches killed and the cattle recovered. This incident proved to be the beginning of several engagements between the military and the Apaches in the Chiricahua Mountains that didn't conclude until November 2nd, with much of the action taking place in the Rucker Canyon area. However, clashes between the military and the Apaches soon resumed and continued unabated over the next several years.

Ten days after Lieutenant Winters' battle, Captain Reuben Bernard and his troops clashed with Cochise and his warriors in Tex Canyon on October 18, 1869, which resulted in one soldier wounded and several Apaches killed.

On October 21, 1871, Captain Gerald Russell and 25 men followed the trail of Apaches into Horseshoe Canyon, where the soldiers were attacked while watering their horses at a spring, resulting in one American and an undetermined number of Apaches killed.

Desiring an end to the ongoing hostilities, on August 1872, General Oliver O. Howard asked Tom Jeffords, the only white man Cochise considered his friend, to take him to Cochise in the hopes of negotiating a peace treaty.

After meeting with Cochise in his stronghold in the Dragoon Mountains, Cochise told Howard that he too wanted peace, but rejected Howard's request that the Apaches move to a reservation in New Mexico. In the end, Howard agreed to a location for a reservation suggested by Cochise himself: the tribe's ancestral homelands. The new reservation would be bound on the west side by the western base of the Dragoon Mountains, on the north by a surveyed line stretching from Dragoon Pass east to Stein's Peak, on the east by the New Mexico line, and on the south by the Mexican border for 55 miles west, where it then turned north to meet the point of origin. The reservation centered around the Chiricahua Mountains and, at Cochise's suggestion, its first agent was Jeffords.

Cochise died two years after the establishment of the Chiricahua reservation, and in 1876, just two years after his death, the U.S. Government disbanded the reservation. Most of the Apaches were taken to the hated San Carlos reservation, with the exception of a large group who escaped, to live a life of raiding and murder. Among those who slipped away was Goyathlay, also known as "Geronimo." And along with him went another decade of Apache/U.S. military warfare.

One incident that took place during this period occurred in Cave Creek Canyon on September 29, 1885, when Chokonen chief Chihuahua and his warriors, with the army hot on their heels, killed a lone prospector before turning north the following day and killing a rancher near Galeyville, and then another man in Morse Canyon on October 1.

There were other engagements in the Chiricahua Mountains between the Apaches and the U.S. military; this chapter covers only the more well-known and better-documented incidents. The killings and kidnappings of civilians by Apaches that did not immediately involve the military are not recorded here.

Furthermore, only battles that occurred in the Chiricahua Mountain region are covered here; there were many more conflicts that occurred throughout Apacheria's hundreds of square miles, clashes that didn't end until a small group of Apache hold-outs surrendered for the final time on September 4, 1886, at a place called Skeleton Canyon.

30 Two Early Settlers—
Stephen Reed and John Hands
An Old Settler

By spring of 1879, Stephen Reed and son Wesley had hacked through 4 miles of cypress, oak, sycamore, and pine along the banks of Cave Creek Canyon as it twisted between towering reddish cliffs. Stephen's father, Leonard, used oxen to uproot stumps and haul trees to the side. Thirty years before, headed to the Gold Rush with his father and 200 other Forty-Niners, 19-year-old Stephen had noticed this verdant cleft in the distance-purpled mountains.

Half a lifetime later, he was back to stay.

After a year on California's Merced River, the Reeds had abandoned sluice boxes for ax and whipsaw. They supplied logs to burgeoning towns till Stephen married Nancy Nestor, settled to farming and had a son, Wesley. Nancy died after the Civil War, and he married a widow with a baby daughter named Lucinda Isabella.

In 1875, the family stowed their possessions into a wagon and reached the year-old farming community of Safford, Arizona Territory, in the spring of 1876, in time to clear land to plant a crop. The Reeds got acquainted with Brannick Riggs, a Confederate veteran, his brother James, and their families. During the winter, Stephen's wife died. He determined to make one final move, to that haunting entrance in the Chiricahuas. The Riggses liked the prospect and joined the Reeds in traveling south that fall of 1877.

At Camp Bowie, they learned they had been unbelievably lucky not to meet any of the Apache bands raiding through nearby parts of the Arizona and New Mexico territories. The families decided to spend the winter near the camp. They earned money by cutting and hauling firewood and prairie hay to supply the soldiers, work the Indians had done till marched off to the detested San Carlos reservation.

By autumn of 1878 the Reeds had journeyed from Camp Bowie to Cave Creek Canyon while Brannick's family went by Apache Pass to settle on Bonita Creek at what is now the Chiricahua National Monument.

For his final home site, Stephen chose an oak-studded expanse where Cave Creek's North Fork joined the main creek. There was an excellent warm spring, good grazing and silt-enriched soil for plowing. Stephen may have also thought Apaches would avoid a place only a mile from where an encampment of 30 women, children, and old men had been recently massacred by soldiers.

That fall, the men raised a cabin of logs squared with a broadax brought from California, along with the whipsaw they used to make a floor and door and window frames. The roof's pine shakes were hammered in place with nails brought from Silver City. Twelve-year-old Isabella probably did the cooking, scrubbed out laundry at the warm spring, and tended the corn and garden they had almost certainly planted as well as an orchard. As soon as they could, the Reeds acquired hogs, poultry, and more cattle and horses.

In 1880 when the Southern Pacific, building from west to east, reached what had been the San Simon Station of the Butterfield Overland Mail, Stephen was only 35 miles from a market for his farm products and a point from which he could ship cattle. A much closer market opened with Galeyville and its Texas Mine that same year, about 5 miles away. In 1882, Stephen

The old Reed place   *Collection of Zola Stolz*

174

and his 15-year-old stepdaughter, Isabella were married by Gus Chenowth, a freighter and self-ordained parson. Leonard, now over 80, may have considered this improper. He and Stephen had a quarrel that sent Leonard raging out of the cabin he'd helped to build and in which he had surely expected to die.

Through the canyon and across the cruel scrubland, Leonard made his way to the San Simon Cienega where the Chenowths took him in. He suffered a heart attack, followed by a fatal stroke. Gus Chenowth, knowing Leonard loved the vista from the mouth of Cave Creek Canyon, took him back in a wagon and buried him there.

Isabella bore six children before she was killed in 1898, still a young woman of 31. She was riding through a corral gate that 10-year-old Glover (who would die in the influenza epidemic of 1918) had opened for her. He let go of the gate too soon. It struck the filly. She jumped out from under Isabella whose foot caught in a stirrup. She was dragged to death.

That winter Stephen boarded his children in San Simon. Lula, the eldest at 17, and Claudie, a year younger, looked after their siblings down to 7-year-old William Jennings Bryan.

Stephen missed his family, so he built a little wood schoolhouse and made a lean-to on the side of his cabin for the teacher, Miss Ida Hively from Arkansas. She got a cowboy's wage, $30 a month with meals and lodging.

In February 1912, Arizona became a state. Next month brought warm rains that melted mountain snow and sent Cave Creek roaring through the canyon. Stephen's meadow flooded.

Water surged against both doors although it never flowed under them. After the waters calmed, Stephen died. In his 83 years, he covered a lot of country, buried three wives, sired seven children, and left a cabin that stands to this day. His youngest son, William Jennings Bryan, "Bill," cooked for the Southwestern Research Station, according to Carol Cazier, whose all-embracing job, while her husband, Mont, served as the first director, was to keep everything running smoothly. The Station occupies the Reed homestead, and Stephen's cabin, where William had grown up, is still the director's home.

§ § §

John Hands, 18, had toiled at low wages for five years in a large Scottish plant nursery when he read a Southern Pacific Railway booklet urging settlers to take up land in the western United States. John set out in 1884. He worked his way from New York to San Antonio, where, in 1887 he met the Walker brothers from Arkansas, Joseph W. and George W. (The latter is not to be confused with the George Walker who married Stephen Reed's eldest daughter, Lula.)

The three young men pooled their money to buy a wagon and team, and see what they could find in the Arizona Territory. It was a long journey. Arid West Texas and southern New Mexico Territory must have made them wonder, but at Granite Gap they were rewarded, seeing the great cottonwoods and sycamores shading the marshes of the San Simon Cienega below, and the valley's grasslands stretching between the Peloncillos and the Chiricahuas offering enticing green canyons. After rumbling across the valley, the young men camped among the wreckage of Galeyville.

After talking over the prospects, the Walkers decided to try to hire on at the San Simon Cattle & Canal Co., commonly known as the H's because of their brand. Hands chose to make his way to Stephen Reed's cabin and stayed on working for room and roof. That was the summer of the great earthquake that was felt hundreds of miles from the epicenter in Bavispe, Mexico.

Isabella Reed had two young children and another coming, and the house was full. When John's older brother, Frank, turned up on a hot June day the next year, having walked all the way from San Simon with his suitcase, Stephen Reed suggested they start a place of their own. They found a perfect spot at the Cave Creek Cienega just outside the canyon, a refuge and resting stop for man and beast time out of mind.

An existing rock-walled dugout probably built by Albert George after he sold out to the San Simon Cattle and Canal Co., gave shelter to the Hands brothers, now three when young Alfred joined them. They built a cabin of squared cypress logs with four glass windows and a loft. Even the dog house was well made. They may have kept chickens and they certainly kept goats, building a fence with a low rock wall around the lower part.

Alfred took care of the goats while Frank and John worked in mines and prospected. In March, 1896, John was working in the Sulphur Springs Valley, and Frank was at the Dunn Mine in Pinery Canyon. He decided to ride over and spend a few days with his younger brother. He found the cabin door open and feathers all over from ripped pillows. Frank called for Alfred and rode warily around the cabin. Alfred lay halfway to the dugout, shot in the head, and battered by stones. Frank knew that Stephen Reed, on his way home from Solomonville near Silver City with supplies, might spend that night at Red Top Ranch six miles north on Turkey Creek. Reed was just unhitching when Frank rode up. Afraid for Isabella and his children, Reed hooked up the team again. Frank tied his worn out horse to the tailgate and climbed up beside Stephen. Next morning, while Frank pursued vengeance, Stephen and a helper made Alfred's coffin from boards of the Hands' cabin's ceiling. They took the boy from Scotland up the canyon and buried him near Wesley Reed, who had recently died.

Frank returned to his Pinery camp. Fort Bowie had shut down two years earlier, so he sent word to Fort Grant on Aravaipa Creek north of Willcox. A lieutenant came to Pinery with a few Apache scouts. Frank took them to the Hands cabin and they followed the trail south. John Slaughter and his foreman rode with them from the San Bernardino Ranch.

A few days after crossing the Mexican border, the party found an Apache camp with fires still burning. A 2-year-old baby girl had been forgotten. She wore a skirt made from a cloth election poster taken from the Hands cabin. She also wore a shirt that had belonged to Eliza Merrill, killed along with her father three months before as they hauled grain to sell in Clifton.

Stephen Reed (center) with Alice, Claudie, Walter, and Bill with John Hands, circa 1907   *Collection of Alden Hayes*

Slaughter took the baby home, called her May, and developed such love for her that, after her death from scalding soap when she was 8, he sat on his veranda in the evenings, gazing off into Mexico.

Alfred's murder is often blamed on the Apache Kid, a former army scout, or on Masai, who had escaped from the Florida bound prisoner train, but it could have been any small band out to raid in their old homeland.

John and Frank kept digging and chipping away at the limestone near their homesteads on the North Fork of Pinery, hiring out when they were short of dynamite or beans. In 1909, John helped Neil Erickson, the Chiricahua Forest Reserve's first ranger, string telephone wire from Barfoot Park around the shoulder of Ida Peak to Erickson's headquarters on Bonita Creek.

Arthur Zachau, the forest supervisor, had his office in a tent at first, but he had a telephone that reached Paradise and on up to Barfoot. He allowed local people to buy their own telephones and connect to the forest line, a practice that continued for many years.

Zachau also helped Stephen Reed file documents entitling him to the land he had lived on for almost 30 years. The title came through after Stephen's death. All the Reed children except Bill, the youngest, had married or moved away, so to give them some cash, John Hands paid down on the place with his little stash accrued from the sale of small shipments of silver, lead, zinc, and copper from the Dunn Mine area.

Alfred Hands' twin, Percy, had come from Scotland to work with his older brothers. They called their outfit the Hilltop Silver/Lead Mining Company, but that didn't give them the money to develop their discoveries. In 1913, they worked their way over the ridge into upper White Tail Canyon. In 1915, John Fife and Chicago investors paid the brothers $120,000, which, according to Alden Hayes, was the most money anyone, before or since, ever made out of a California District Mine (the local mining district centered on Paradise). They earned it.

Frank Hands married and settled on his Pinery homestead where he and his wife, Grace, are buried.

John paid off the Reed children and lived at the old cabin where he had found welcome and a lifelong friend in Stephen Reed, whose kids still called him Uncle John. In 1919, he built four little cabins and named the place Bide-A-Wee Ranch. A visitor of that year wrote that he ate the fresh butter while everyone else got the old. Whatever the reason, John later tired of the venture and sold to men who planned to make the homestead a resort.

John held a mortgage on the Oasis Orchard outside the canyon and moved there when the farmer, Jim Reay, gave up his 25-year struggle to succeed. Jim took his family to California, as did other farmers and homesteaders who welcomed a chance to sell to John and seek better prospects. John, living in the adobe on what he renamed the Desperation Ranch, owned a producing orchard and a huge expanse of San Simon Valley range. He wasn't much interested in either fruit or cattle. Most of the trees Jim Reay had fought to water dried up, and such cattle as John accidentally acquired with the land, survived as best they could or were adopted by neighbors.

Though he was well-to-do for those times, John lived frugally. If company came, he might shoot a rabbit, skin and clean it, and toss it in the pot of beans simmering at the back of the stove. No longer compelled to earn a living, he traveled to Mexico with Dr. Byron Cummings of the University of Arizona to help with excavating ruins. Fascinated by what they uncovered, John volunteered his time and growing ability as an amateur archaeologist to various expeditions. He built the small white museum still to be seen near the Portal Rescue building and filled it with artifacts, which earned accolades from professionals. His monument and grave are close by.

The Cave Creek Cienega place where the Hands brothers raised their first cabin was occupied by other families until it was sold back to John in 1929. When, in the last few of his 72 years, he began to need some help, Stephen Reed's grandson, Reed Walker, and his wife Una, moved their house down from the foothills and set it close to John's.

John died in 1939 and left the Walkers the Cienega place. Not long afterward, they moved Reed's mother, Lula (Stephen's daughter), into John's former quarters. His life had been interwoven with the Reeds since he first walked up the canyon in 1887; it was fitting he passed away among them.

Sycamores in Snow   *Watercolor by Marge Fagan*

31 **Pioneer Graves**
Bill Cavaliere

efore the establishment of organized cemeteries, early Cave Creek Canyon pioneers buried the deceased in family plots or, oftentimes, in single graves just a short distance from where the person died. Some of these graves are adorned with tombstones made from expensive granite, while others have the deceased's name crudely chiseled onto a rough rock. Some were topped with wooden crosses that have deteriorated over time, causing the location to be lost forever, and others were simply piled over with rocks minus a headstone, leaving an obvious location but without a name of the occupant.

There are two examples of family plots in or near Cave Creek Canyon. The first is known as the Reed family plot, located within the canyon.

The first person to be buried here was Wesley R. Reed, the son of Stephen. Wesley's gravestone, a rectangular-shaped rock, simply has "W. R. Reed" on it, and nothing else. Although his exact date of death is not recorded, it is known that no one else was in the plot at the time of his burial.

Leonard R. Reed wanted to be buried at the mouth of the canyon near the view he had always admired.
Photos by Bill Cavaliere unless otherwise indicated

The second burial in the Reed plot was Alfred Hands, the youngest of the Hands brothers and a family friend of the Reeds. Carved on his simple stone marker is "Alfred Hands 1875–1896."

Recently in Arizona from England, Alfred was tending goats at the Hands' cabin near the mouth of Cave Creek Canyon when he was killed by Apaches on March 28, 1896. Since the Chiricahua Apaches had formally surrendered 10 years earlier, the Apaches who killed Alfred were known as "Bronco Apaches." This was the name applied to those few who had escaped immediately after the final surrender as well as those who never surrendered at all. This small group lived a perilous existence, mainly raiding vacant homesteads or killing lone individuals, while constantly being hunted themselves by both Americans and Mexicans. The last documented raid by Bronco Apaches in the United States occurred in 1924, and well into the late 1930s in Mexico.

When pioneer Stephen Reed homesteaded here, he was a widower. Since women were scarce in the Chiricahua Mountains in that era, Reed married his stepdaughter Isabella, who eventually bore him six children. In 1898, Isabella was killed when her horse bolted (see Chapter 30). Her tombstone, another plain slab of stone, reads "Isabelle Reed–Died 1898."

A fourth burial in the Reed plot is marked by a small headstone that simply has the two words "Wolfe Baby" chiseled on a small rock, with no other information. If examined closely, one can observe that for some unknown reason, both the word "Wolfe" and "Baby" are in parentheses. There is scant information regarding this grave, but it was more than likely the newborn infant of Ed Wolfe and his wife, who were the only family known with that name in the Chiricahuas. Ed Wolfe ranched in Tex Canyon in partnership with Jesse Benton in the late 1890s. The child was probably stillborn, due to the fact that it hadn't been named at the time of burial. The Wolfes were more than likely visiting the Reeds when the child died, or possibly they were there because Isabelle Reed may have offered services as a midwife.

The Reed plot was slowly growing. Stephen Reed, patriarch of the large family, was the first white settler in Cave Creek Canyon. Born in Missouri in 1829, he arrived in the Chiricahua Mountains in 1877, not long after the Chiricahua Indian Reservation was abolished. He eventually built a cabin, which is still in use today on the grounds of the Southwestern Research Station. Reed died in 1912 of natural causes at the age of 83, outliving both his younger wife Isabelle and his son Wesley. His plain rock marker is made of stone similar to the other four already there, and bears the inscription: "Stephen Reed 1829–1912."

The winter following Stephen Reed's arrival in Cave Creek Canyon, his father, Leonard R. Reed, arrived. He was the only family member not buried in the family plot. He had expressed his desire to be buried at the mouth of the canyon, a view he much admired. His tombstone, supplied by the CCC and located near the Portal Ranger Station, lists 1880 as his date of death.

The next burials in the Reed family plot took place 68 years after Stephen Reed's. Matthew Pugsley was a doctor who came to Cave Creek Canyon to work as a physician at the CCC camp during the 1930s. After he left the CCC, Pugsley, or

The plaque on John Hands' grave. *Cecil Williams*

"Doc" as he was called, joined the army and achieved the rank of colonel in World War II, where he lost an eye after the vehicle he was in drove over a land mine. Returning to the Canyon, he met and married Anna Roush.

As was their tradition, Doc Pugsley and Anna (known as "Aunt Duck") made weekly trips into Douglas. In his later years, the sight in Pugsley's remaining eye began to fail. To compensate for this handicap, he often drove in the very center of the road, using the centerline as a guide, but straddling both lanes. This would cause oncoming vehicles to be forced off the road. Oftentimes he'd drift off the road and onto the shoulder, then suddenly swerve back onto the road again. Locals who were fortunate enough to recognize his car would pull off onto the shoulder when they saw him approaching, giving him enough room to pass by.

However, on December 5, 1980, while on one of their trips to Douglas, Pugsley drifted off the road and struck a bridge railing. Anna was killed instantly, but Pugsley lingered on in the hospital for two more days, occasionally regaining consciousness and asking for Anna. He died two days later, on Pearl Harbor Day. When he and Anna were buried together, his funeral featured a full military honor guard.

Anna Pugsley was born Anna M. Pence in Kentucky in 1886. In 1907, the diminutive woman married Raymond Roush. Seven years later they moved into a homestead in Horseshoe Canyon. While her husband was away working for the railroad, Anna ran a trap line. One day she found a wolf in a trap, which she shot in the head. She began dragging it home with its front legs pulled over her shoulders. After a while it began to feel lighter. Apparently she had only grazed it, and the wolf had regained consciousness and was walking along with her on its hind feet. Anna eventually divorced Roush and opened a general store in Portal, where she met Pugsley.

Probably the most impressive grave in the Cave Creek Canyon area is that of John Hands, Alfred's older brother. Born in 1866 in Great Britain, Hands died of natural causes in 1939. During his time in the Chiricahuas, Hands was variously employed as a miner, rancher, and archaeologist. The 7-foot high monument at his grave, constructed of stones and Indian metates, bears a brass plaque that denotes the dates of his birth and death, his place of birth, his various occupations, and a likeness of his face as well. (See Chapter 11.)

Another family plot, this one located in Round Valley, belongs to the three members of the May family. Clarence May Jr. was shot and killed in 1910 by neighbor Earl Sands over a dispute involving Sands' goats watering at the Mays' spring. Clarence Sr. was buried there in 1924, and his wife Isabel was the last to join them, in 1945. The graves in this plot, located near the site of the May homestead, are covered with a cement slab and surrounded by a metal rail.

Many other interesting pioneer graves are located throughout the Chiricahua Mountains, but this chapter is limited to just those in Cave Creek Canyon and vicinity. If planning on visiting graves, please be respectful of property ownership. Do not trespass.

Chiricahua Place Names Quiz

With the Chiricahuas being the largest Sky Island, one could imagine some confusion over the origin and meaning of many of the names given to all the canyons, springs, peaks, and creeks in the area. For example, the region has more than one Brushy Canyon; even "Chiricahua" could be an Opata word for "turkey," or it could be an Apache title (in either case slightly altered by Spanish and English).

Here is a light-hearted test to help the visitor or long-time resident learn how this small sampling of local landmarks acquired their current labels.

1. Barfoot Park and Peak are named for

A) a former resident in the late 1800's, Malcolm Barfoot, B) the pioneer term for the prevalent "bear tracks" seen in the vicinity, C) the common summer practice of taking off shoes and walking "barfoot" in the cool pine-shaded black soil, D) none of the above.

2. The first large hikeable drainage, on the northern side of Horseshoe Canyon is Pothole Canyon. It derives its name from

A) a synonym for "cave," used in geology, B) the rough depressions formed in the now-obsolete roadbed near the mouth of the canyon, C) the priceless early-Spanish kettle found on the side of Pothole Peak that had been used for target practice sometime in the mid-to-late 1800's, D) none of the above.

3. The tallest mountain located more than a mile to the southeast of Portal, at about 8573 feet is

A) Rodeo Ridge, B) San Simon Summit, C) Portal Peak, D) Topoff the Mountain, E) none of the above.

4. Herb Martyr is the name of a dam and campground located along Cave Creek, upstream of the Southwestern Research Station. Herb Martyr refers to

A) the body found riddled with arrows among the ferns belonging to newly-arrived Baltic-immigrant preacher, Dats Schmartz, in 1883, B) Herbert Martyr, a U. S. Forest Service (USFS) ranger who died too soon with tuberculosis, C) all the rare flora that perished in the subsequent flooding required to make the trout lake of the mid-20th Century, D) none of the above.

5. Sage Peak, south of Price Canyon and north of Tex Canyon, is named for

A) the Apache shaman, Tse-daza or "Juanito" who lived in a nearby cave until his death at about age 102, in 1941 B) the abundant shrubby vegetation growing along the mountain's slopes C) Harley Sage, a USFS ranger who died in 1918, D) none of the above.

6. A mountain near Silver Peak, "Sceloporus," is named after

A) a genus of small lizards, of which a number of species live in the area, B) a titan of Theban lore that guarded the mountain pass to a lush magical paradise , C) "Sunny" Sceloporus, who quarried low-grade marble in the flats below the peak until he went bust in 1931, D) none of the above.

7. Fly Peak, at 9,666 feet, is named after

A) the hang-gliding craze that proliferated along its eastern face and is now prohibited, B) the Tombstone, AZ photographer C. S. Fly, who captured images of enemy Apaches and had a ranch below the peak, C) the many winged insects that torment visitors amid the moist summer slopes, with the most persistent biting pest being Chrysops cochisii *D) all of the above.*

8. How did Silver Peak, west of the Cave Creek Ranger Station, acquire its name?

A) There was a modest vein of silver struck by Galeyville prospectors in the basin to the west of the peak in 1884. B) Over the generations countless senior citizens individually made the difficult walk to the summit to prove they still, in hiking terms, "had what it takes." C) The name was changed from "White Rock" to "Silver" to encourage settlement and investment in the area by Paradise promoter, George Walker. D) all of the above.

9. The impressive hike that ascends in elevation west of Herb Martyr Campground, known as the Greenhouse Trail (in Greenhouse Canyon), is named that because

A) there once was a house located along the trail that was painted green, B) the USFS staffed a plant nursery near the base of the trail for reforestation efforts beginning in 1934, C) the canyon in which the trail meanders is so verdant with plants and trees that it reminds one of a giant greenhouse, D) none of the above.

10. Which canyon was named for a known outlaw of the Old West?

A) Ketchum Canyon, B) Tex Canyon, C) Leslie Canyon, D) Ringo Canyon, E) none of the above.

— Craig McEwan

(Answers are at the end of the Authors section.)

32   Mining

Al Bammann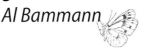

Mining played virtually no role in the earliest Anglo history of the Chiricahuas, due to the mountains' location in a core portion of the Apaches' homeland, and later their reservation. Some prospecting went on just south of Apache Pass in the late 1860s due to protection by soldiers at nearby Fort Bowie. Soldiers and others located gold prospects, but there was little development until the reservation was closed in 1876. Miners swarmed into the Chiricahuas soon after the Apache people were removed to the San Carlos Reservation.

Central to the business of mining is the Mining Law of 1872. Signed by President Grant, this law made it the policy of federal agencies to encourage exploration, development, and extraction of minerals from federal lands. It supports the sale of federal land (at rock-bottom prices) to miners if it is beneficial to their operation. Most of the privately owned (patented) parcels within the Forest boundary were acquired under provision of the Mining Law of 1872. In a few cases the land with the mine itself wasn't patented, but the access route and a nearby town site was.

The Mining Law is still in effect. Many new requirements have been added to protect the land, natural resources, and the public. Mining operators on federal lands are now required to clean up and re-vegetate the area when they close. Currently there is a moratorium on new applications for mineral patents.

Finding a spot with potentially valuable minerals was just the first obstacle for a miner. Filing a claim with the County provided a legal right to mine that location and blocked others from "jumping the claim." Miners then needed physical access to their mine. Maybe it began as just a foot and horse trail, but eventually a road would be needed. The cost of developing a mine was often more than a lone prospector could afford. Many mining claims were quickly sold to developers who had the money to hire workers, build roads, and purchase equipment.

Copper, lead, zinc, and silver were found on the east slope of the Chiricahua Mountains in 1879. This find resulted in the most famous mines in the area and gave rise to the towns of Chiricahua City, Galeyville, and Paradise. Miners found food, lodging, equipment, and entertainment in these new communities.

Roads were built to connect the railroad stations (at Rodeo, Willcox, Bowie, and San Simon) with these first small towns and the major mining operations. Men and supplies came in, and the ore was shipped out. Many of the local roads driven today were constructed in the late 1800s and early 1900s for the mining industry.

The mining boom created a huge demand for wood. Boards were needed to build the towns, and large timbers were used to support mine shafts and tunnels. In addition, most machinery used in the early mining era was powered by burning wood. Much of the logging in our local forest was done to supply the mining industry.

Abandoned mines

The interior of the Kasper Tunnel, which is part of the old Hilltop Mine complex.
All photos by Jonathan Patt

are mostly located along the eastern side of the Chiricahua Mountains from Apache Pass (near Bowie) south past the mouth of Cave Creek. Miners found mineralized rocks in complex quartzite veins within limestone formations.

The majority of mines are in the California Mining District, which is centered in Jhus Canyon. Mines that supported Galeyville and Paradise are over a ridge, to the south. Numerous mines are in Round Valley and on Davis Mountain, to the east. Several miles to the northwest are the Hilltop group of mines. Some exploration and small diggings occurred on Limestone Ridge just north of Portal. Gray patches of waste rock are visible on private lands above the Portal to Paradise Road.

Stay out—and stay alive!

Before anyone considers visiting old mines, they need to remember several things:
- Most mines have been closed for 50 to 100 years.
- They were dug before any safely regulations were in effect.
- None is maintained.
- Timbers that once supported roofs or walls are rotten or were removed.

No mines are safe to enter!

Additionally, most are on private property, and owners seldom allow visitors due to liability risks.

The most abundant metal found in the local mines was lead. It was extensively used in paint, plumbing, and gasoline. It is now known to be extremely dangerous to humans, animals, and the environment. Lead ores are often yellowish or dull yellow-green. Bright blue and green coatings on rocks are copper ores. Silver and gold were found in some mines but always as an alloy with lead.

A mine was profitable only as long as the price of metal was high, labor was plentiful, and the ore was easy and cheap to extract and ship to a smelter. The valuable metals were separated from rock by heating to very high temperatures. Metals could be separated from each other because they each melted at different temperatures. Most smelting was done at Douglas or El Paso. Small smelters were briefly operated at Galeyville and west Hilltop in the early 1880s.

Most mines operated only a few years. Galeyville boomed in the 1880s when rich ore was discovered at a time of high copper prices. The town died when copper prices fell. Paradise followed the same pattern in the period between 1900 and 1920. The mines at Hilltop produced some lead and zinc from the 1890s through the 1920s. Several Chiricahua mines reopened in the 1950s when high metal prices returned. The last local mine was closed in 1972.

In the 1990s Newmont Mining Corporation, a large international company, located a promising deposit of gold-bearing rock a mile south of Portal. Local opposition convinced Newmont that the natural resources were more valuable than gold. The corporation worked with the U.S. Congress to exempt the Portal and Cave Creek area from the Mining Law.

Shale formations deep under the Chiricahua Mountains were recently identified as having the potential to contain oil and natural gas. The hydraulic fracturing (fracking) technique has been successfully used elsewhere to produce hydrocarbons from similar rock formations.

However, some geologists believe the volcanic activity millions of years ago vaporized any oil or gas that may have once been present.

An example of the condition of many vertical shafts that can still be found in the Chiricahuas, illustrating the need for caution when walking near where mining may have occurred.

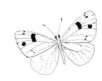

33 Paradise Reminiscences
Winston Lewis

$\mathcal{J}$ ust the word "Paradise" evokes visions of a place of complete happiness.

Paradise, Arizona, in the Chiricahua Mountains, located about 6 miles up-mountain from Portal is such a place. Quiet, remote, surrounded by National Forest lands, one would hardly suspect or know that it was a mining boom town that started up in 1902 and went bust after the Money Panic of 1907.

The town came into being after the Chiricahua Development Company located a vein of ore nearby. A post office was established in the same year, and, at one time, 300 people drew their mail in Paradise.

Estimates are that during peak boom time, the area was home to 2,500 souls hoping the nearby mine held good ore and Paradise would be their final bonanza.

Arriving in the peaceful hamlet of Paradise, it's hard to believe it was once a rollicking town bursting with 2,500 hopeful miners.
Jackie Lewis

The town boasted a German restaurant, 13 bars by one count, 14 by another, two general merchandise stores, one combination hardware store/lumber yard, one dry goods and ready-made clothes store, one variety shop, and one notions store. The red light district and a jail were located across the creek. As we enter 2014, Paradise boasts three full-time residents, several weekenders, and a snowbird or two.

There are several stories as to how Paradise was named. One is that early travelers to the area came across a flowing stream, East Turkey Creek, and named the area Paradise after slogging through the short grasslands and finding a source of cool, clear mountain water. Another story is that the idea of building a town next to nascent mining operations came to George Walker and George Myers under a Silver Oak, or Madrone tree.

The story we like best is that George Walker named the area Paradise to honor his honeymoon with Lulu Walker.

When booming, the town also sported a school, a weekly newspaper titled *The Paradise Record*, a butcher shop, at least one tonsorial parlor, and a boarding house/hotel for the miners. When the miners were not working at the mine, they were often employed building the road from Portal to Paradise.

Back then, there was no radio, Wi-Fi, or television. People entertained themselves with singing and fiddle playing. Small groups of folk would gather during the day and sing popular songs while someone might eke an accompanying tune out of a fiddle. Evenings and weekends there were "socials"—many of them. Stories are told of all-night soirees, which ended when the hard-rock men headed back to work. Driving a double or single jack with a hangover most likely caused the sale of cough syrup in quantity. Back then, cough syrup was laced with opiates. Perhaps they provided a little relief to head and body aches!

When the mine closed, people began to head to the next boom town. As they left, houses were knocked down, the lumber tossed into wagons and structures rebuilt wherever the wagon stopped. Very few original Paradise buildings exist today, and there are only 29 structures by Forest Service count. We do still find a nail or two in the road, especially after a heavy rain.

Enough people stayed in the area to keep the post office open until 1937 or 1943, depending on which source is referenced. Even after the closing, a few hardy souls continued to stay in the area, and a few newcomers came into town to make homes in Paradise. Bill Sanders owned and operated the Leadville mine above the town and was able to haul out several tons of good lead ore. The vein was not large, and soon the Leadville mine was also played out. In the late 1970s a band of hippies established a commune at the Paradise Ranch and tried their hand at living and loving off the land. The Chiricahuas are a hard place to survive in. One year will bring 20 inches of rain, another many inches of snow, and the next? Drought.

The Madrean Sky Islands provide species richness and biodiversity that bring bio-researchers and birdwatchers from around the world. The George Walker House birdwatching "yard list" boasts 158 or so species of birds that can be seen in the yard during the year. Northern and southern migrations bring a riot of bird colors. Orioles and tanagers nest nearby, as do Magnificent, Black-chinned, and Blue-throated Hummingbirds. According to Pam Hulme's mother, Betta Lou Wakefield, who spent her honeymoon in the Chiricahuas, the first recorded account of a bird watcher in Paradise was around 1918 when one stopped by and asked if a Barred-tailed Trogon had been seen in the area. No one remembers the answer given, but an occasional trogon has been seen in Paradise. Turkeys have been re-introduced to the area and seem to be thriving.

Wildife is plentiful. It is not uncommon to see Coues Deer, also known as Desert White-tailed Deer, and Javelina. Other mammals in the area include: Mountain Lions, Bobcats, Gray Foxes, Black Bears, Coatimundis, Ringtails, all four species of skunk, Apache Fox and Rock squirrels, various species and subspecies of pack or wood rats, kangaroo rats, and mice. Bats also abound. Nineteen separate species have been identified in and around Paradise. The closest breeding population of Jaguars is in Mexico, about 130 miles southeast of the Chiricahua range. While not seen in the range recently, it is possible a Jaguar or its little cousins, the Jaguarundi and Ocelot, might also be observed.

The kitchen was next on this bear's list.
Jackie Lewis

A natural progression from bird watching is butterflying. More than 100 species of butterflies can be found within a mile of Paradise. But, for a real challenge, take on the moths. There are possibly 2,000 species of moth in the Chiricahuas, and every year or two several new species or subspecies are discovered and named.

Paradise also boasts the Paradise Cemetery, where early settlers and a few modern folk are interred. Only hard-rock miners would place a cemetery on bedrock! Indeed, Bill Sanders was on the Cemetery Committee because he was the last person in town licensed to handle dynamite. It took three to seven days to dig a grave back then. Blast and shovel, blast and shovel.

If you stop by to do a little headstone reading, pick up a copy of *Resting in Paradise* to guide you through the graveyard and back into time.

Also, be sure to bird the Cemetery, the junipers, and the nearby fields. Montezuma Quail may be found anywhere in the area!

Male Montezuma Quail
Narca Moore-Craig

34   Sawmills
Jonathan Patt

Logging operations in the Chiricahuas began in mid-1879 when Philip Morse and Jacob Gruendike arrived from San Diego and established a steam-powered sawmill in what is now Ward Canyon, off West Turkey Creek.

A government contract to supply lumber to Fort Bowie and Fort Rucker soon followed, and by early fall, they were producing 20,000 feet of lumber per day and had added a shingle mill to their operation. Orders came in from Tombstone, Tucson, and elsewhere, and early on they were frequently unable to meet demand.

Later that same year, Major William M. Downing established his own sawmill in Pinery Canyon, near the site of the old Apache reservation agency buildings. By the next January this mill was running as well, with "an abundance of orders already on hand." Around this time there were reports of a third operation beginning, possibly in the Rucker Canyon area.

By early 1880, Morse had added a planing mill, and Tucson papers reported receiving a shipment containing "tongued and grooved surfaced flooring and ceiling," which was "the first surfaced lumber manufactured in Pima County that has come to this town." Frequent advertisements in newspapers could be seen during this time seeking teamsters to haul lumber from sawmills, and the mills appear to have had constant difficulty obtaining enough transport to meet demands, with large quantities of wood frequently sitting at the mills.

In 1881, Downing moved his operation south into Pine Canyon. Not long after, both he and Morse filed with the county to establish toll roads up the respective canyons to their mills, maybe as part of an attempt to recoup costs for maintenance of what were often reported to be terrible roads.

Daniel Ross, initially in partnership with Jacob Scheerer, a teamster who had been working to haul logs from the Chiricahua mills to Tombstone, purchased a mill of his own in 1883 in either John Long or Mormon Canyon, later moving it into Rock Canyon. Morse left the Chiricahuas in the same year, and it is unclear what happened to his mill after he left, although there is some evidence it may have been taken over by Ross. Scheerer sold his share of the business after three years and returned to freighting.

By this time, the Copper Queen Mining Company in Bisbee had become one of the largest buyers of lumber from the Chiricahuas, primarily using the wood for mine timbers. Both Downing and Ross were sending a majority of their output there, and some reports even referred to the mills as if they belonged to (or were fully contracted by) Copper Queen. Whatever the situation was, the mills appear to have become so tightly linked with the mines that when Copper Queen temporarily ceased operations in the summer of 1889, both sawmills shut down as well.

Riggs sawmill on west side of Barfoot Park
Photograph by A. F. Potter, 1902. Courtesy Coronado National Forest

Foundation of sawmill in Mormon Canyon.
Jonathan Patt

Operations resumed soon enough, however, and demand was sufficient that Ross had to move his mill farther up canyon, having apparently logged all the trees in the vicinity of the previous location. He appears to have repeated this several times over the years until reaching nearly the head of Rock Canyon on the west side of Fly Peak. Downing similarly moved his mill in Pine Canyon several times.

Around this time, the federal government began investigating the extensive cutting of timber in the Chiricahuas, and in 1890 arrested Daniel Ross for "cutting and disposing of timber from government land." Shortly after, both he and the Copper Queen Mining Company were sued for a sum of $90,000 over 3 million feet of lumber allegedly harvested illegally,

Ross was acquitted two months later, but appeals by the U.S. went on during the next 12 years until reaching the U.S. Supreme Court where the case was ultimately thrown out.

Despite the eventual win, the cost of fighting in court proved too much, and, four years after his arrest, Ross shut down his sawmill for good. Downing followed shortly after, selling to the Riggs brothers in 1895. In 1898, both Ross and Downing died, just six days apart: Ross of pneumonia and Downing of unknown causes at the age of 74.

For several years the Riggs brothers, running Downing's old mill, appear to have been the primary lumbermen operating in the Chiricahuas. In 1902, Albert F. Potter was sent to survey the range following the establishment of the Chiricahua Forest Reserve. (See Chapter 35.) The map he created documented extensive cutting across the west side of the Chiricahuas, as well as 12 sawmill sites—with only the Riggs mill, now moved all the way up Pine Canyon to Barfoot Park, still running. The Riggs brothers stayed in operation for nine years before selling to Edward F. Sweeney of the Duluth & Chiricahua Development Company for $8,000 in 1904.

Sweeney improved the short, steep road between Barfoot Park and Paradise, which was used to transport lumber into town, where it was sold and used to build many of the early buildings. The steepness of the road required the use of six-horse teams, with the majority of the horses at the rear of the fully loaded wagons during their descent.

Within two years, the mill at Barfoot Park was sold again, to the operators of the Commonwealth Mine in Pearce, but stayed in operation only a short time before the Chiricahua National Forest was established, and it was removed in the spring of 1907.

Over the following decades, several other sawmills were established—including the Webb sawmill in West Turkey Creek, which burned down in 1921, and the Davies-Mason mill, which cut wood out of Pine and Rattlesnake Canyons in 1941—but the mining boom had ended, and with it so had the need for local timber on the scale that had been provided by the early mills.

Today, it's still possible to come across the remnants of logging roads and the clearings where the mills once stood, but with the forest now regrown and not much in the way of debris to definitively identify the sites, it can be hard to imagine the bustling activity that once took place throughout the Chiricahuas.

Abandoned logging road lined with rocks at confluence of Saulsbury and Ward Canyons.   *Jonathan Patt*

35   U.S. Forest Service History
William B. Gillespie

On April 20, 1902, two new employees of the Bureau of Forestry named Albert Potter and Royal Kellogg began a two-week inspection tour of the Chiricahua Mountains. Potter and Kellogg had been assigned by Bureau Chief Gifford Pinchot to visit the major mountain ranges of southern Arizona and evaluate their suitability for designation as Forest Reserves. Theodore Roosevelt, who had ascended to the presidency in September 1901, was very interested in creating new Forests under the authority given him by the Forest Reserve Act of 1891, the law that allowed presidents to set aside areas for the protection of timber resources and watersheds.

Kellogg and Potter were particularly interested in whether the timber resources of the mountains were still worth protecting. They found that the western side of the Chiricahuas had been heavily logged, particularly in Rock Creek and Turkey Creek, where the Copper Queen Mine Company of Bisbee had done extensive cutting. The U.S. Department of the Interior had been battling with the Copper Queen Company for years, starting in 1890 when the government presented the company with a bill for $187,000 for

The original Portal Ranger Station, built about 1910, was located on the mesa above the present-day Cave Creek Visitor Information Center. *All photos courtesy of Coronado National Forest*

the unlawful removal of an estimated 5.9 million board-feet of timber from government lands and arrested Daniel D. Ross, the operator of the sawmill. But after 12 years of litigation, the government was unsuccessful in making its charges stick, and the company prevailed in court. Ironically, it was while they were inspecting the Chiricahuas that Potter and Kellogg learned of the final judgment of the U.S. Supreme Court in favor of the company, affirming the decision the Arizona Territorial Supreme Court had made.

Kellogg remarked that much of the pine forest on the range's western flank had been "completely skinned" although the higher mixed conifer forest was little touched. Despite the extensive cutting they observed, Kellogg and Potter recommended that the Chiricahuas were indeed appropriate for designation as a Forest Reserve. On July 30, 1902, President Roosevelt issued a Proclamation stating "… the public good would be promoted by setting apart and reserving said lands as a public reservation," thereby establishing the 169,600-acre Chiricahua Forest Reserve.

The original Forest included the central portion of the mountains, from what later became Chiricahua National Monument on the north to Tex Canyon on the south. Boundary adjustments in 1906 and 1911 added major areas to the north, south, and east nearly doubling the size of the Forest. In 1907, the Chiricahua Forest Reserve was renamed the Chiricahua National

Forest Service trail crew working in the Chiricahua Mountains, about 1920.

Forest, as all Forest Reserves were renamed National Forests to emphasize Gifford Pinchot's philosophy that Forests should be open to multiple uses of Forests, and not simply "Reserves." In 1908 the Chiricahua National Forest was enlarged again to include the former Peloncillo National Forest to the southeast. But the Chiricahua National Forest lost its autonomy in 1917 when it was merged with the Coronado National Forest, with its Supervisor's Office in distant Tucson; the Chiricahuas have been part of the Coronado National Forest since that time.

Charles T. McGlone, first Forest Supervisor for the Chiricahuas, started with no employees, but over his five-year tenure built up a small staff of Rangers and Forest Guards. McGlone first located his office at Willcox, then Barfoot Park where Brannick Riggs operated a sawmill under permit, then Paradise, and finally Douglas, a considerable distance from the Forest at a time when travel was mainly by horseback.

Supervisor McGlone was replaced in 1908 by Arthur Zachau who a year later moved the Chiricahua National Forest headquarters back to the mountains, to Cave Creek just upstream from the tiny settlement of Portal. The first Forest Supervisor's Office at Portal was a small brick building on the mesa north of the present Visitor Information Center. The Portal facility served as the Forest Supervisor's office until the 1917 merger with the Coronado, and for many years after that time continued to be the primary Ranger Station for the Chiricahuas. In 1924 Ranger Carl Scholefield was allocated $1,000 to build a new residence for himself and his family. Scholefield had the old office dismantled and the bricks reused in the new building. This, one of the oldest surviving administrative buildings on the Coronado National Forest, now serves as the Forest's Cave Creek Visitor Information Center.

Other early Ranger Stations were established at Rucker Canyon, at the railroad town of Apache, in Tex Canyon, and in West Turkey Creek. In the mid-1930s Douglas again became the main Ranger Station for the Chiricahuas, a role that continues today.

In the early days, Forest personnel were mainly concerned with regulating timber sales and with the detection and prevention of wildfires that were perceived as a threat to timber reserves. Early Forest personnel built trails to access remote areas, erected wooden, and later metal, fire lookout towers, and strung telephone wire to connect the lookouts, administrative sites, and local ranches. Rangers also evaluated and inspected Forest Homesteads, issued permits for grazing in the Forest, and, beginning in 1906, collected fees for grazing, something that local ranchers initially found objectionable.

Catering to the desires of the public for recreational opportunities was not a priority for the early Forest Service. Camping became popular in places such as Cave Creek and Rustler Park, but few developed facilities were available before the 1930s when Civilian Conservation Corps crews developed a large number of campgrounds. The "Wonderland of Rocks" became an attraction in the 1920s, and, with the support of Governor George W.P. Hunt, was designated as Chiricahua National Monument by President Coolidge. The Forest Service administered Chiricahua National Monument until 1933 when all national monuments were transferred to the National Park Service. One of the first recognized wildernesses in Arizona was the 18,000-acre Chiricahua Primitive Area, established in 1933. This area was renamed the Chiricahua Wilderness Area when the Wilderness Act was passed in 1964, and was enlarged to 87,700 acres in 1984.

Today the bulk of the Chiricahuas are managed by the Douglas Ranger District of the Coronado National Forest. The Forest Service strives to meet the challenges of balancing multiple uses of the Forest, providing a variety of recreational opportunities, working with ranchers who hold permits to graze on the Forest, and protecting historic structures, archaeological sites, and a variety of threatened and endangered plants and animals. Current objectives focus on the restoration of watersheds, springs, and forest ecosystems to healthier conditions, including efforts to reduce the risk of catastrophic fires that have impacted the mountains in recent decades.

In 1924, the Forest Service found funds to build a residence for Ranger Carl Scholefield and his family. Walls were built using bricks from the old office on the mesa behind the structure. This building now serves as the Cave Creek Visitor Information Center.

36   Ranching
Diana Hadley

Both to the east and west of the Chiricahua Mountains, vast north-south trending valleys have served for millennia as corridors for movement of plants, wildlife, and humans. During the 19th century these rich semi-arid grasslands gained fame as classic examples of the Open Range Cattle Boom. Today they are still home to cattle ranchers, many of whom have been here since the days of the Wild West.

West of the Chiricahuas, the Sulphur Springs Valley (some 1,600 square miles) drains southward into Mexico, part of the Río Yaqui watershed. East of the Chiricahuas, a barely perceptible watershed divide near the town of Apache separates the San Simon and San Bernardino valleys. The northern portion of this vast grassland, the 1,200-square-mile San Simon Valley drains northward through the ephemeral San Simon River into the Gila River. South of the divide, the smaller San Bernardino Valley, with more than 400 square miles in Arizona, drains into Mexico through the San Bernardino River, which flows in turn into the Cajon Bonita, the Río Bavispe, the Río Yaqui, and the Sea of Cortes.

During most of the 17th and 18th centuries, Apaches prevented Spanish or Mexican ranchers from raising livestock on these prime grasslands. Although raiding parties likely held stolen livestock for slaughter in the box canyons at the valleys' edges, there is no evidence that Apaches practiced stockraising in or near the Chiricahuas. The earliest ranching took place at the end of the 18th century, when an unknown Sonoran rancher, who likely owned a ranch headquarters farther south in Sonora, began pasturing his cattle near the headwaters of the San Bernardino River at the abundant springs and cienega. From 1775 to 1780 a Spanish military post operated at the site and constructed a defensive adobe fort and outbuildings. The 55 soldiers at Presidio San Bernardino maintained a herd of beef cattle and a *remuda* of up to eight horses per soldier. In 1820, Lieutenant Ignacio Pérez, acquired a land grant at the abandoned "rancho San Bernardino." Pérez and his wife, both members of the powerful frontier elite that dominated mining, stockraising, politics, and the military in Sonora, promptly stocked the grant with 4,000 head of cattle, but soon abandoned the ranch because of Apache raiding.

In the decades following the Gadsden Purchase (1854), the end of the Civil War (1865), and the termination of the Chiricahua Apache Reservation (1876), cowboys working for organized cattle companies drove thousands of head of cattle into the valleys. In the Sulphur Springs Valley two companies established by Pennsylvania entrepreneurs dominated the grazing ranges. The Chiricahua Cattle Company (the Three Cs), whose largest stockholders included pioneer surveyor Theodore White and the Vickers brothers, controlled the northern end of the valley, their holdings comprising over 1,500,000 acres. To the south, the Erie Cattle Company, incorporated by members of the Shattuck family and friends from western Pennsylvania, held title to only 2,200 well-watered acres near the international border, but controlled almost 1,000 square miles of Cochise County rangeland, in addition to leases in Mexico nearly the size of Rhode Island. Both companies began by marketing scrawny Mexican *corriente* steers to mining camps, military posts, Indian reservations, and Southern Pacific Railroad crews. By the end of the 1880s, both companies had evolved into large well-capitalized enterprises, active in establishing livestock associations, operating slaughterhouses, lobbying legislatures, and importing higher quality cattle to the area.

Huge round-ups were held each year in spring and fall to brand and move the cattle. *Arizona Historical Society*

In the San Simon Valley, two established Texas cattlemen, James H. Parramore and Claiborne W. Merchant, began acquiring claims at water sources. In the early 1880s, they bought a preemption claim from one of the Chiricahuas' earliest and best-known residents, Judge John C. Hancock of the Galeyville

> **Acts used to Acquire Land**
>
> • Preemption Act (1841)
> • Homestead Act (1862)
> • Timber Culture Act (1873)
> • Desert Land Act (1877)
> • Forest Homestead Act (1906)
> • Enlarged Homestead Act (1909)
> • Stock Raising Homestead Act (1916)
> • Taylor Grazing Act (1934)

mining camp. Not interested in owning large parcels of land, the partners focused on controlling water sources as a means to control the surrounding rangeland. When they acquired title to the San Simon Cienega, they changed the name of their company to the San Simon Cattle and Canal Company, acknowledging the importance of water. Although the partners reportedly drove their first herds of longhorns by foot from Texas, after the completion of the Southern Pacific Railroad they began shipping entire trainloads of cattle to the valley. In 1883 they unloaded an estimated 12,000 head at the San Simon station. After 1902, the El Paso and Southwestern Railroad provided an even closer means to export cattle, inducing the partners to move their headquarters from the cienega to Rodeo, N.M., near the station's huge shipping pens. The company remained in operation into the 1920s and was instrumental in developing the townsite of Rodeo.

In the San Bernardino Valley, former Cochise County Sheriff John Slaughter purchased the former Spanish land grant, after a lengthy process of validating the title with the Court of Private Land Claims. Long before receiving title in 1900, Slaughter grazed thousands of cattle on the grant. His 73,000-acre ranch extended 30 miles southward into Sonora from its headquarters on the international boundary. One of his ranch buildings had rooms on both sides of the border, and the dozens of wells he drilled— many with artesian water—captured the cienega's underground water in both Arizona and Sonora.

Although legal homesteading peaked between 1910 and 1920, land-hungry "nesters" with a few head of cattle moved into the valleys and the Chiricahua Mountains at the time of the arrival of the cattle companies. They filed preemption claims or simply "squatted" on a piece of land, erecting tiny shacks and digging hand-dug wells sometimes as deep as

70 feet. The homesteaders joined the corporate ranchers in overstocking the grazing ranges, the resulting competition for water sources and forage sometimes erupting into violent conflicts. No regulations were in place for control of the unfenced "open ranges," allowing cattle to move freely to the best forage. Huge communal round-ups, or "works," were held in the spring for branding and in the fall for shipping cattle to market. Each ranch sent one or more "reps" to participate. They sometimes followed the chuck wagons for months. One round-up in the San Simon/San Bernardino Valley contained an estimated 50,000 head of cattle, some of which had been driven from miles beyond the unfenced Mexican border. In the 1880s, cattle rustling was rampant and was a cross-border enterprise.

Periodic droughts occurred in 1885, 1892-93, 1902-04, and 1932-34, increasing grassland degradation and leading to intense suffering on the part of ranchers and livestock. Ranchers themselves began the outcry for a system of regulation of the open range. In 1902, an estimated 75 percent of the cattle in Cochise County died of starvation, having consumed all the grass down to roots and accelerating desertification. In 1902, Dr. Robert Forbes, director of the University of Arizona's Department of Agriculture, singled out the San Simon Valley as one of the most severely eroded and denuded grasslands in the country, calling it a "striking example of this process of ruin."

Recognition of rangeland degradation led to the creation of a system of reserves intended to protect watersheds and restore grasslands throughout the West, giving birth to the National Forest system. Prior to the creation of the Chiricahua Forest Reserve in 1902, cattle from the valleys roamed freely into the mountain range. After the reserve became the Chiricahua National Forest in 1908, permits to graze cattle were required, and stocking rates were limited to the estimated "carrying capacity" of the land. The Forest Homestead Act of 1906, intended to increase farming, removed arable land along creek beds from the national forests and provided for homesteading on up to 40 acres if the land were put into cultivation. Many would-be ranchers used the act to acquire title to property within the Chiricahua National Forest, which gave them the right to apply for a Class A grazing permit. After 1934, the Taylor Grazing Act limited and rationalized grazing on the rest of the country's public lands.

Within a few years, controlled legal livestock grazing was allowed throughout the Chiricahuas, and the land along Cave Creek was among the best-watered and most desirable ranch locations.

37 Farming

Craig McEwan

The nurturing of plants and animals for human purposes has gone on in these mountains and valleys for thousands of years. Before the mass migrations in the 1800s, the inhabitants were, at the very least, growing maize, squash, and beans on a small scale to supplement foods hunted and gathered.

Archaeological evidence suggests that irrigation or dry-farming methods were used in the Paradise area circa 1200 A.D. Rock shelters and cavities used as caches or storage rooms for maize still exist at several locations in the area. The last residents of the "pre-American Period," the nomadic Chiricahua Apache, did not grow food; although they mastered riding the non-indigenous horse, they were not raising the equines in a conception-to-death manner as required in animal husbandry. Except for the limited possibility of some minor farming by brief Spanish residents (such as those who built the adobe corral at what would become the Gus Chenowth homestead in the San Simon Cienega), European agricultural methods were not established until United States settlers arrived following the 1876 removal of the Chiricahua Apaches from their reservation. Since that time area residents have attempted, and sometimes succeeded in, growing a number of different crops and livestock.

In about 1880, people began arriving in the Chiricahuas to work in the mining and timber industries. They required a steady supply of provisions that was sometimes hard to obtain. Furthermore, soldiers stationed at nearby Fort Bowie and the temporary Camp Crawford (1886), near Paradise, also desired fresh food. Grains, canned goods, and some meats could be imported by wagon or train. Hunting wild game was usually reliable, but an economy including locally grown produce helped reduce any potential food shortages.

Stephen Reed, son Wesley, and step-daughter—soon-to-be wife—Isabelle were the first permanent "Easterners" to reside along Cave Creek, homesteading here in the fall of 1878 (see Chapter 30). The Reeds grew vegetables, fruit, and beef that they marketed in the mining boom-and-bust towns of first Galeyville and then Paradise. Stephen transported his goods by wagon over a rough road he had cleared to those two communities that were 5 miles distant to the northwest. Many of the small-acreage landowners in the region were supplementing the diets of the region's inhabitants with garden vegetables, molasses, meat, and milk from dairy cows or goats. Besides cattle, the farmers were raising chickens, pigs, goats, sheep, and horses. Two farmers growing staples, such as potatoes, along the crest of the Chiricahuas, were Malcolm Barfoot and C. S. Fly.

After the arrival of the Spanish to the Southwest, local grasslands and, to a lesser extent, mountain terrain supported large numbers of non-native herbivores. Feral horses ranged in the San Simon Valley and were captured by the Apache for use as transportation and food. Later, ranchers utilized remnants of these horse herds, along with large numbers of feral (Spanish origin) and released (English-breed) cattle for export at a profit until a devastating livestock famine began in 1891. The two-year drought harmed small and large ranchers, as well as subsistence farmers who grew grain crops, harvested the native grasses for hay, and established orchards as well as vineyards. Into the early 20th century, a series of rainy years would trigger an increase in the number of farms; the inevitable dry years that followed would shrink that same statistic.

Horticulture was the preferred branch of farming in Cave Creek Canyon. Several old apple trees still survive at the Southwestern Research Station, where the Reeds once lived. Jack and Emma (Sanders) Maloney, who lived downstream from the Reeds, planted about 8 acres in fruit trees in the early 1900s.

The Maloneys also gardened and sold vegetables in the area. In the vicinity of Portal, the Gurnett family owned about 400 acres that included a hay field, a chicken- and turkey-raising shed, and nearly 20 acres planted as an irrigated orchard of mostly apple trees (Stark's Red Delicious and Winesap cultivars) and a vineyard.

After 20 years in the canyon, the Gurnetts sold their holdings to Arthur and Jane Greenamyer in 1941. The Greenamyers added a fruit-packing shed near the road that divides today's Portal. Since the water supply was not dependable, the orchard was phased out by 1946.

Adjacent to that now-vanished orchard, Bill Stuart and his new bride Eula (Chenowth) signed a mortgage on 80 acres in 1913 to the Stark Brothers' Nursery in Missouri; the couple bought 1,647 fruit trees for $580. They could water their trees from an irrigation ditch they had constructed with Jim Reay and others in 1911. The "Portal Ditch" diverted water from Cave Creek first to the Forest Service, then to the Stuarts, and eventually on the east to the short-lived Oasis Orchard (established before the "Ditch") of Reay. The intermittent flow of water in the ditch did not provide enough moisture for Reay to maintain his orchard.

The Portal community experienced a water shortage around 1913-1917. Irrigating all those trees exacerbated the issue of who had the natural vs. legal rights to the creek water. A feud between the Chenowth clan and the water-deprived farmers climaxed with Eula's brother killing a neighbor who was not directly involved in the water controversy.

The following year, 1918, was an extremely wet one, and everyone had plenty of water again. In the 1920s the area water rights were adjudicated; thereafter, the irrigation side-streams legally belonged to the prior users of several ditches. These farmers retained the water rights as long as they continued to yearly harvest the diverted Cave Creek water when it was flowing. The Stuart Orchard survived through several purchases.

In 1932, "Doc" Adamson, a Douglas physician, and wife Anna bought and improved the fruit-growing business, drilling an agricultural well in 1935. Dr. Theodor Troller, an Austrian immigrant, bought the property in 1952. Besides buying and processing local growers' apples for sale—such as Maloney's harvest—and making cider, Troller expanded the business with a peach orchard of about 10,000 trees (bought from Stark Brothers), making it one of the largest peach orchards in Arizona at the time. With summer temperature fluctuations that could reach 50 degrees F. in just a few hours, the peach trees' fruit production rates fell substantially by the late 1960s.

Falling production, increased labor costs, and other unfavorable market conditions pushed son Ted Troller to remove the trees by the mid-1970s.

Gretchen (Greenamyer) Hayes admiring her family's blooming apple trees at the Sierra Linda Ranch in 1942. *Courtesy of the Chiricahua/Peloncillo Historical Society*

By the 1930s, lack of ground cover caused the U.S. Department of Agriculture to seed the area's former grasslands to Lehmann Lovegrass, an African import that thrived in extremely dry conditions. It quickly became established and considerably helped bind the earth to prevent soil erosion by wind and water.

Originally, only land near springs and drainages, as within the marshy San Simon Cienega, could support farming. However, after World War II, returning veterans could start or improve farms with Veterans Administration loans. Large numbers of wells were drilled, and the agriculture industry began utilizing synthetic fertilizers and pesticides, which enabled farms to expand into the vast arid plains. This well-pump irrigation was used to grow a few species of crops in any given time period.

With government subsidies and the Korean War driving up prices, grain sorghum and cotton became profitable. For a time, chili peppers were a commodity. While alfalfa is still grown locally, the agricultural enterprise that has increased the most in recent years is nut production. In the central San Simon Valley, pecan trees have been the dominant tree planted, along with pistachios, and English walnuts. More land has also been tilled for grape production.

Most farming within the Chiricahuas has dwindled to garden, home orchard, and small livestock operations, along with open grazing by some of the larger cattle ranches. Honey harvesting from domestic bee hives has been successful during wet seasons that allow for mass-flower-blooming. Locally grown produce—with a substantial amount raised organically, or all-naturally—can still be purchased through farmer's markets or from producers, and Portal has a Seed Savers Club that exchanges garden seeds and plants from members' time-tested varieties. High-tech irrigation practices, such as drip irrigation, have allowed the landscape to grow more crops using less water.

Only time will decide if humans can overcome the region's wind, heat, and scant precipitation in order to make the desert and mountains "bloom" with food.

38 Early Visitors
Reed Peters

ntil the arrival of the motor car, visitors to Cave Creek Canyon were few. Determined friends and relatives of early settlers might make a visit, but the effort of getting to Portal and Paradise was daunting.

The railroad came to Rodeo in 1902, but there was still the arduous stage trip—five hours uphill to Portal, where there was liquid refreshment for man (liquor) and beast (water) under the big sycamore to the east of today's post office, and then a further five-hour stage to the mines, saloons, and boarding houses of Paradise, where most passengers were bound.

By the early 1920s, motoring made Portal more accessible, and visitors began arriving who had heard about its beauty and abundance of wildlife to hunt. The Southern Pacific Railroad promoted Arizona guest ranches via its Sunset Route. Service extended to Rodeo and Douglas. The railroad called Cave Creek Canyon "the Yosemite of Arizona." The moderate climate, the allure of its very recent frontier status, coupled with the fame of Geronimo and Cochise, made the area attractive to visitors from the East. Many of these were looking for a "Western" experience, as ranching fascinated Americans of the time. During this period many ranches in southeast Arizona began accepting guests, as cattle ranching no longer paid the bills.

Some Portal area residents had been accepting paying guests, and a few went a step further. The first homestead in the canyon had been Stephen Reed's, who coexisted peacefully with the Apaches in the 1880s. The property was purchased upon his death in 1912 by John Hands, who in 1919 named it the Bide-a-Wee Ranch to attract visitors (see Chapter 30). By all accounts it was fairly primitive, although in a spectacular setting. John found that he didn't enjoy the role of host and soon sold the ranch to two Douglas promoters who added more cottages and the swimming pool.

Around the same time Emmett Powers, the owner of what later was called

Cave Creek Ranch, began accepting hunting and fishing guests. By the end of the 1920s, families were coming to stay, and a few upgrades were needed. Gordon Newman purchased the property in 1930, built guest cabins, and a swimming pool was constructed using ruined iron bedsteads from the recently burned Gadsden Hotel in Douglas for the rebar.

Mrs. Anna Roush in Portal ran the La Siesta del Monte Ranch in the late 1930s, offering a rest home with horseback riding, dancing, hiking, and pack trips, and accepted up to eight guests. An active entrepreneur, she had built and opened the first grocery in Portal, and became first postmistress in 1927. She later married Col. ("Doc") Pugsley, and lived to be 94, known as "Lady Ann" Pugsley or Aunt Duck (see Chapter 31).

The Toles sisters, Elsie and Myriam, also accepted guests in the summertime at their El Portal Ranch. In 1922 Elsie was the first woman elected as State Superintendent of Public Instruction. In the 1950s Vladimir Nabokov was their guest when he visited to search for butterflies and work on his novel Lolita.

But the best place to stay in the 1930s was undoubtedly the Sierra Linda Ranch. Elizabeth Gurnett of California bought much of the unsold Portal town site from Emmett Powers and his son-in-law Fitch McCord (for whom the McCord trail above their property was named). She established a working farm with a large U-shaped adobe house. She later added separate cottages

Small dams were constructed in Cave Creek and Rucker Canyon by the CCC to create ponds that were stocked with fish. This 1941 photo is in Cave Creek. *Courtesy of Coronado National Forest*

that accommodated visitors for $30 and up per week. A saddle and a horse were included.

With an apple orchard, vineyard, turkey house, dairy herd, and vegetable garden, the ranch needed a number of hands. Mrs. Gurnett's ranch manager was a well-educated Englishman, Neil Carr, who had come west for his health having been a hungry prisoner in Germany for all of World War I.

That was a wet period in the canyon, when fruit and vines did well. Subsequent drier times have made the orchards of those days a distant memory.

By the early 1940s the Sierra Linda and Bide-a-Wee returned to being private homes; what became known by the late 1940s as Cave Creek Ranch continued to operate as Rancho Risco.

In 1950 Hollywood briefly found Portal. "Branded," starring Alan Ladd and Mona Freeman, was filmed on the AVA Ranch at the entrance to the canyon. Residents of Portal were surprised when watching the movie as riders left the canyon in one scene and reappeared around the bend somewhere hundreds of miles away!

In 1956, in a happy turn of events, the former Bide-a-Wee became the American Museum of Natural History's Southwestern Research Station, and again began accepting guests, as it does to this day.

Brochure from 1939-40 season,
Arizona Highway Department Travel Bureau.
Arizona State Library and Archives

213

Coatimundis are a common sight in the Canyon.

Maya Decker

39   Game Wardens

Craig McEwan and Kim Murphy

When Arizona became a state in 1912, a framework for protecting against the over-harvest of hunted animals had been in place for 30 years. Originally this thinly staffed agency, called the Arizona Fish Commission, monitored the state's limited numbers of fish and regulated the hunting of deer and turkey.

Within the first decade of the new state, all sheriffs' deputies and livestock inspectors were appointed as deputy game wardens in addition to their other duties. The Chiricahuas were also being patrolled during deer season by a part-time game ranger from Rucker Canyon, E.O.B. Mann.

In 1929, the newly renamed Arizona Game and Fish Department hired Chiricahua Mountains resident Ralph Morrow to patrol the southeast corner of the state. At the age of 5, Morrow had moved to Paradise with his family in 1903. (He could remember, from those early years, Thick-billed Parrots in the area.) With wife Juanita (Kuykendall) and daughter Audrey, he moved to Hilltop in Whitetail Canyon after accepting the deputy game warden position. Some of the many tasks he was assigned included:

• Inspecting game meat in cold storage
• Reducing predator numbers of Coyote, Mountain Lion, bear, wolf (in 1960, he saw his last Mexican Gray Wolf in the area) and eagle

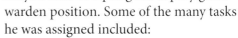

Ralph Morrow was one of the first Chiricahua game wardens for the Arizona Game and Fish Department. *Collection of Michael Morrow*

215

• Controlling "pest" populations, by such methods as the "rabbit drives" of the 1940s
• Conducting animal research projects, and
• Enforcing game codes and aiding standard law enforcement agencies.

During his tenure, the agency unsuccessfully tried to reintroduce several animal species, such as turkey. The least researched idea appears to have been releasing beaver in South Fork, where torrential rains made the creek's speed and volume too volatile for beaver habitat.

As a dedicated ranger, Morrow frequently logged in 85 hours per week, and he moved his family, which now included son, Wayne, over the years to Douglas, Fort Huachuca, and back to Hilltop. He worked as a Cochise County deputy sheriff for two years after being laid off as a game ranger because of funding shortfalls during the hard times of the Great Depression.

Morrow maintained an exemplary record throughout his career in which he was known for his courage, fairness, and staunch honesty. His citation-writing days ended with a forced retirement in 1962 (he had reached age 65), but that resulted in a promotion to Arizona Game and Fish Commissioner two years later. In 1976, Ralph Morrow completed a most fulfilling life and was buried in the Paradise Cemetery in the heart of his beloved Chiricahuas.

David Roe was game warden for six months in 1963. He was replaced by Buddy Bristow, who had the job for a year and a half.

In January 1965, Kim Murphy, raised in Colorado, took the warden's position. Murphy inherited a district that bordered Mexico,

Kim Murphy holding a rescued bear cub whose mother had been shot by a javelina hunter in 1988. *Collection of Kim Murphy*

New Mexico (where he could legally stay in pursuit of suspects fleeing his authority), the future I-10 to the north, and the old Route 666, which became Highway 191, in the Sulphur Springs Valley to the west.

Although Ralph Morrow lived in these mountains longer than any other game warden, Kim Murphy holds the distinction of having patrolled the Chiricahuas the longest, retiring at the end of 1998. He was trained by Morrow, and the two remained friends.

In 1979 the Douglas district was divided, and Murphy took the northern end. He has resided along Cave Creek, just east of Portal, ever since.

Murphy has watched game populations rise and fall, as with the White-tailed Deer, which have slowly rebounded from the over-hunting of does during the 1950s. Most of the wettest years he has witnessed have long since passed, so recent animal numbers have declined in relation to lack of vegetation caused by drought.

One aspect of his former job that has nearly disappeared is writing citations for over-fishing. During the 1970s, the Chiricahua district boasted several trout lakes. There were the small reservoirs of John Hands and Herb Martyr, both along Cave Creek. The larger Rucker Canyon Lake could net 30 violations on crowded days, such as those over Easter weekend. All the stocked fishing holes have disappeared, filled in by post-fire mountain floods that sent boulders, gravel, and soil into the man-made ponds.

Some of the most defiant lawbreakers Murphy ever encountered were fishermen. He humorously states that he would rather face a hunting-violator with a gun or a knife than one armed with a fishing pole. In one story, he explains how the driver of the trout-stocking truck, after releasing his precious aquatic cargo in the Cave Creek reservoirs, would stop at the Portal Store for refueling and a bite to eat. The store's owner would call his friends with the news of the latest fish population boom. Soon a convoy of anglers' vehicles were headed toward the mountains. Murphy would show up later and write over-limit tickets to nearly everyone on the scene. He became *persona non grata* in the community after a few of these incidents.

Like those officers before and after him, Murphy had to always be judging the mind-set of his poacher opponents. That strategy has helped keep game wardens, who mostly work alone and isolated in Arizona, alive. Possibly his best method of defusing the unpredictability of an angry and bewildered violator was having a large dog or two in the vicinity. A person looking to escape an embarrassing citation would think twice about acting on impulse with a patient Rottweiler waiting in the background. Yet, Murphy could not avoid being verbally threatened on several occasions, such as when he was bluntly told by a life-long local hunter that one of these days "we're gonna be shootin' at one another."

Some of his most dangerous encounters were with wildlife, however. Besides brushes with rattlesnakes, bears, and Mountain Lions, he has watched Javelina run underneath his horse—while he was on the horse! Coatis fighting his dogs have given Murphy a few scares too.

Protecting people from aggressive animals, and vice versa, has been integral to the duties of conservation officers. Murphy recalls how June was always the month for live-trapping bears. The hottest, driest, and most food-deprived time of the year hovers near the summer solstice. Rains could come pouring down by late June, but previous precipitation may not have reached the Earth since January, or earlier. The Black Bears' hunger would bring them too close to area orchards, chicken pens, bee hives, and kitchen refrigerators. Once captured, a remote release did not ensure that a bear would not return, as evidenced when Murphy helped in the relocation of a bear to the White Mountains. Eventually the bear journeyed the roughly 80 miles back to the Chiricahuas.

The Department of Game and Fish now monitors the northern Chiricahuas from Willcox. Gilbert Gonzalez has been the regular agent patrolling this area since the district's most recent division in 2000. He has helped in the successful reintroduction to the area of the rarest of the United States' turkey subspecies, Gould's Wild Turkey. The unique nature of these mountains in relation to the geographical convergence of many different climate and terrain zones means there are many rare creatures living here. So Gonzalez is vigilant against poachers removing legally protected animals from eastern Cochise County. He has ticketed a number of individuals stealing snakes from the Cave Creek area.

The subtleties of the game warden's job may change from inspecting a hunter's freezer for venison to looking in a poacher's car trunk for captured snakes, but the mission of protecting the area's wildlife for future generations has remained constant.

40   Civilian Conservation Corps (CCC)
William B. Gillespie

In 1933, the country was nearly four years into the throes of the Great Depression with no firm prospects for improvement of the struggling economy. Unemployment was extremely high, the stock market was extremely low, many banks were closed, and businesses were struggling. When Franklin Roosevelt took the oath of office as president on March 4, 1933, he initiated his "New Deal," a suite of programs aimed at reducing unemployment and righting the economy. The first of Roosevelt's programs was the Emergency Conservation Works Act, which was passed by Congress within weeks of his taking office. This legislation created what soon became known as the Civilian Conservation Corps.

Roosevelt conceived of the program as having two goals: reducing the level of unemployment by putting young men to work, and improving the condition of the nation's natural resources, especially its forests and eroding watersheds, exemplified graphically by the Dust Bowl of the Great Plains.

The Cave Creek CCC Camp was one of the first to open in Arizona in 1933 and last to close in 1942.

All photos courtesy of Coronado National Forest

As the President put it: "Our program is two-fold: conservation of our natural resources and conservation of our human resources. Both are sound investments for the future."

The program's goals at the beginning were very ambitious: The President wanted 250,000 young men enrolled by summer, assigned to new camps throughout the country, and working on conservation projects. Initially, enrollees were to be unmarried and unemployed men, ages 18 to 25, and from families living on relief. They would be paid $30 each month ($25 was to be sent home to their families), and would also receive food, clothing, medical care, and educational opportunities. Soon after the program began, out of work World War I veterans protested that they should not be excluded. As a result, Roosevelt had the enrollment qualifications changed to include veterans, though they were placed in companies separate from the "junior" companies. One of the few veterans companies that worked in Arizona started out at the Rucker Canyon CCC Camp.

The initiation of the program required remarkable mobilization by a number of federal agencies. The Labor Department was responsible for finding and enrolling members. The War Department's responsibilites were to build and staff camps and provide enrollees with a physical exam and basic training at a US Army post, assigning them to a company, and transporting them to a camp. Land-managing agencies such as the U.S. Forest Service and National Park Service were responsible for assigning and overseeing work projects.

The camps were typically designed to house a company of 200 men plus a military leadership staff, cook crew, and medical, technical, and educational staff. As many as 30 buildings were erected, typically including four barracks for 50 people each, a mess hall/kitchen, officer/technical staff quarters, recreation hall, and smaller buildings such as medical dispensary, lavatory and showers, tool room, blacksmith shop, and garages.

The Chiricahua Mountains hosted four of these major CCC camps; F-10-A at Cave Creek, F-12-A in Rucker Canyon, F-47-A in West Turkey Creek, and NM-2-A in Bonito Canyon. The "F" in the identifier stood for "Forest Service," "NM" for "National Monument," and "A" for "Arizona."

In 1935, Congress established another federal agency, the Soil Conservation Service (SCS), and it soon began to use CCC labor for soil-conservation work projects. Both the Cave Creek and Rucker CCC camps were turned over to the SCS for periods in the late 1930s and were renumbered Camps SCS-22 and SCS-24 respectively. Not all these camps were used during the entire 1933-1942 existence of the CCC, and not all four were in use at the same time, but they still indicate how important the CCC was in the Chiricahuas.

Two camps in the Chiricahuas, in Cave Creek and Rucker Canyon, were ready to go during the first enrollment period in the summer of 1933. The Cave Creek camp (F-10-A) was one of the first to open in Arizona, on June 1, 1933. The camp, located between the town of Portal and the Portal Ranger Station, was occupied by Company 865, and included many enrollees from Texas. One of the first projects the company undertook was improvement of the nearby Portal Ranger Station, adding landscaping walls and fences around the Ranger's dwelling and a new distinctive cobble-walled office building. Crews also worked on the roads in Cave Creek and over Onion Saddle to Pinery Canyon. Roadwork was hazardous, and tragedy came early as one of the enrollees from Texas was killed in a blasting accident in July 1933. The camp was named in his honor—Camp Harold C. Riley—although it continued to be widely known as the Cave Creek CCC Camp. Three more enrollees—Arnold Garrett, Nalty Lee, and Ralph Case—were killed in 1940 by a cave-in as they cleaned a debris-filled culvert.

Another early project Cave Creek CCC crews took on was the installation of over 6,000 rock and log check dams in the drainage basin of the North Fork of Cave Creek. In 1934 Cave Creek camp enrollees built a 60-foot fire lookout tower on Fly Peak. They also built the campgrounds in Cave Creek Canyon, constructed four bridges on the Cave Creek Road, and put in bridges and culverts along the Portal to Paradise Road.

A single structure remains at the site of the CCC Camp: a stone-masonry house built as a garage

CCC laborers constructed many miles of trail in Chiricahua National Monument.

for motor-vehicle maintenance and repair and later used as a telephone exchange. Both this building and the 1933 cobblestone Ranger Station Office have recently been rehabilitated and been made available to the public as part of the Forest Service's cabin rental program.

In summary, the CCC program had a huge impact on the infrastructure of government-managed lands in the Chiricahuas. Practically every campground here was either built or substantially improved by CCC crews. The list includes multiple campgrounds in Cave Creek and Rucker Canyon, plus facilities in Bonito Canyon, Turkey Creek, Pinery Canyon, and Rustler Park. The majority of these campgrounds are still in use, many of them with little modification other than improved sanitation.

All the major roads in the mountains were improved with the addition of culverts, bridges, and cattleguards. New buildings were constructed at administrative sites at Chiricahua National Monument, Portal Ranger Station, and at Cima Park and Rustler Park. New fire lookouts were built at Sugarloaf Mountain and Fly Peak. CCC crewmembers staffed these and other lookouts and served as the main fire-suppression force when wildfires broke out. Telephone lines and fences were repaired or replaced, trees were planted, and thousands of erosion-control structures were installed.

Perhaps the greatest change was in the development of recreation facilities. Prior to the 1930s, the Forest Service rarely received funding for developing and managing recreation facilities. Suddenly having access to hundreds of laborers allowed all the land-managing agencies to take on far more projects than ever before.

The program often had life-changing impacts on the enrollees as well. Becoming gainfully employed and learning new job skills prepared them for their future careers.

Company 2870 was stationed at the Portal CCC Camp from 1938 to 1942 after previously working out of the Turkey Creek and Rucker camps.

41 Portal Reminiscences
Zola Stoltz

It was December 1955. George Pat Stoltz had been discharged from the Air Force and we, with our 8-month-old daughter, stopped in Portal on our way to Los Angeles where he would return to his old job with the Southern Pacific Railroad. He was raised to the age of 6 by his grandparents, Emma and Jack Maloney, on the Maloney ranch roughly 4 miles from Portal. The land was homesteaded in 1886 by Joseph Sanders, Pat's great grandfather, and, has remained in the family since.

My husband, Pat, raved about the beauty and excitement he experienced as a youngster living on the Ranch, and all the summers he spent with the Maloneys. The entire trip from Michigan, Portal was all he talked about. It was nothing like Oscoda, Michigan nor was it like anything in the coastal areas of southern California where we both grew up. I was curious and anxious to get out of the car for a couple days, even though I had no idea what to expect. I had never seen my husband so happy.

From Lake Huron across many states, I spent my time alternately entertaining our daughter and napping. We carried a Porta-crib in the mini rear seat of our black Ford coupe and towed a tiny trailer with our possessions, including a diaper pail—no paper diapers then. We had a few stops at

The old Maloney place
Collection of Zola Stolz

motels where I did a hand wash, as we didn't want to get to California with moldy baby clothes.

From Road Forks, Pat's excitement bordered on extreme. I looked around me constantly wondering what beauty he saw in brown hills, cactus, and rocks. How I longed for all the evergreens that had surrounded us in our little log cabin by the Ausable River. Once off the interstate, I thought the view would change. The only thing that changed was Pat's tone, as he described what I would see when we got to our temporary destination. I actually thought my husband had gone a tad crazy. I felt alien in these surroundings and could not see a shred of the beauty he raved about.

We crossed the state line, and I watched the majestic towers of rocks come into view and loom over us. He put the window down, saying he wanted to smell home. We stopped at Newman's Store with a single gas pump in front. I carried Lyn and followed Pat inside. My first impression was that I'd stepped into a movie: A few older men sat around a wood stove, all in long-sleeved flannel shirts and jeans, appearing as from one family rather than individuals. Western hats adorned a few knees and the floor. There was a pickle barrel beside the counter, and the mixture of wood smoke and tobacco made my eyes burn. I tried to take in my surroundings, while listening to my husband asking questions—generally about men he had grown up with. I don't remember being introduced to anyone.

I do remember being told how the gas pump worked and being allowed to put gas in the car. Strange how some things resonate in the memory and others do not. That pump was a curiosity, and seeing it today on a porch brought back how I pumped the handle until the glass "bowl" at the top of the pump was full, and then allowed the gas to flow into the car.

Driving the crooked road up to the property, I thought we had entered a fairy tale as we got deeper into the canyon. Pat gave me crazy names of different formations—like "Donkey's Ears" (I think the locals now call it "Mule's Ears")—but I was mesmerized by the coloring and the sheer beauty.

As we drove past what Pat called the "white rock," he told me that the road was moved in the '30s. That enormous rock had to be blasted and in doing so a young man had lost his life. I remember crossing the creek, with some trepidation, and being greeted by the grandparents. Grandmother Emma was an outspoken wonder of a woman in a dress and stockings—on a ranch! If she ever wore trousers, I never saw her in them. We put Lyn on the board seat of her makeshift potty chair that had been also used as a car seat where Pat and Granddad could watch her in the warm sunshine.

Grandmother and I went into the kitchen so she could show me her pride and joy. It was a grand wood stove the likes of which I had only seen in books. It had a water reservoir on one side that provided hot water as long as there was wood burning in the stove, which was most of the time. The rich aroma emanating from a pot bubbling on that big black marvel made my stomach growl. My eyes were drawn to the pump on a metal drain board in the center of the kitchen. She explained that the well was right there. I really was intrigued by that little pump standing where faucets should have been.

The living area was centered around a small wood stove that kept the house warm along with the heat from the kitchen. She said that the night would be freezing and hoped that I had sufficient nightwear that would keep our baby comfortable. I could hear Lyn's excited squealing; a cat and two small dogs had come up close to investigate. Lyn had never seen pet animals—only the ones in the books I read to her all the time. She was so beside herself—arms and legs pumping. I had never seen her like that. Grandmother picked up the cat and held it down in front of Lyn who simply leaned over and put her face down on the cat's fur. Then she lifted her head and took to making so much noise that the poor cat clawed to be released. (In the 58 years since that day, Lyn has always had cats and a couple of dogs. She loves them as much as she loves her child!)

I inquired about a bathroom or outhouse. As I recall there was neither. There was plenty of vegetation to hide in when the need arose. I was familiar with outhouses, as my Grandmother had one. However I was not accustomed to using Mother Nature as a bathroom.

That night I wrapped Lyn in pajamas, then into a snug sacque, and I even put a hat on her and snugged her blanket around her. I placed a wool Army blanket over the entire crib to help insulate it. She slept through the night, which is more than I can say for myself. Pat and I were sunken in his old feather bed with such heavy blankets over us, I felt choked, confined, and uncomfortable.

In the early morning I was amazed at how warm the rest of the place was as I helped set the table for the breakfast. Granddad's job before any other chores was to stoke the embers at night and stir them up in the morning as he added wood. I watched Grandmother pour a mound of flour on a board, add a few other ingredients, knead them all together and, in less than five minutes, a large pan of biscuits was ready for the oven. I do not recall the exact menu of that morning, but there was red-eye gravy, bacon that Granddad had cured himself, (along with cattle, they also had hogs and chickens), and the best biscuits I had ever eaten. That is saying something, as my own grandmother made great ones. Part of the taste had to be her Damson Plum jam. Anyone who was privileged to have some knows what I say here is true. It was Pat's favorite.

During the day I explored the old place, which had been a visitor center down where the Ranger Station is today, possibly on the site of the rock house. The building had been dismantled, loaded on a flatbed, and hauled up canyon across the creek, and reassembled where the remains now stand. Granddad had added a kitchen and another bedroom and built a washhouse out back, shaded by a weeping willow. Their old house had burned down in a fire. It had been located over a root cellar, the remains of which are still across the meadow from the existing place. The house insulation was newspapers, covered by burlap. Curtains were made from printed feed sacks. It all worked and was quite homey.

They did have electricity and the old washer was electric. It worked fine, and her own lye soap made diapers sparkling white. We got to California with clean clothes and a happy baby.

The creek bed, where the concrete platform is, has dropped a good 5 feet at the spot where we once drove across—most recently in the '60s—in a VW camper van. That platform was poured in the late 1920s or early '30s and was used for community gatherings. Granddad Maloney was known for his barbeques. He had strung carbide lights in the trees surrounding the pad and had ditches on either side as cooking pits for pork, lamb, or beef. Ranchers and their families came and danced, listened to music played by talented locals, and the women brought food to share. The closeness of those days among Portalites and those from Rodeo has continued to this day.

Familial camaraderie is part of what makes this area so unusual and wonderfully so.

Motorists had to pump enough gas to fill the glass bowl on top before the fuel could go into the car.
Cecil Williams

The Portal School

I am Sheila Clark, then Sheila Rivers.

The Portal School started about 1910, back when the teachers got paid about $75 per month. The adobe building was built about 1930. Paradise consolidated with Portal also in 1930. Hilltop school closed in 1937 and went with Portal as well.

I started school in Rodeo for 1st and 2nd grade. Then I went to Portal School in 1965 in 3rd grade. I continued there for the next six years. My first teacher at Portal was John Pirtle. There were 35 kids. Nine were from the Rivers family— six from my family and three of my Dad's brother's family.

The summer of 1966 the parents and neighbors got together and painted the school red and did a lot of cleaning inside and out. The building used to be painted a yellow tan with white trim.

The year I went to the 9th grade in Animas, they said all the Arizona kids had to go to San Simon. So I went to 10th grade in San Simon. They just had Grades 1–3 at Portal School a couple more years, then closed it altogether in 1974.

My dad bought the farm outside Rodeo, so I finished 11th and 12th grades back in Animas school.

Here are a few more details of my school days at Portal School:

In 1965 or 66 we went on a field trip to Tucson to the Desert Museum, Old Tucson, the dairy, and the Rainbow Bakery. We had a small 4-H group for two years. We made aprons and knitted pot holders that we entered in the Douglas fair. I think I got a red ribbon.

The stage had a huge curtain that could be pulled by a drawstring for the main curtains, and it also had two side curtains so we could have plays.

There was also a big Halloween party at the school. The older kids made a haunted house out of sheets in one corner of the room. When we crawled into it, the big kids would have us stick our fingers in a slimy mess. They said it was someone's brains. It was only a bowl of boiled spaghetti.

The next year the Halloween party was at the Research Station. A couple of sheets that looked like ghosts were hung on some of the trees. We sat around a big campfire while Vince Roth told ghost stories. Someone held a sheet on a cross pole, and this floated into view at the right time in Vince's story.

For Christmas we would have a name exchange and buy gifts for the people whose names we drew. We had a party in the afternoon and a night-time program for the community where we sang songs or put on some kind of play. Sally Richards always played the piano for us at these events.

We celebrated Easter with an egg hunt on the school grounds.

Several times we went on field trips to the Research Station, or sometimes Vince Roth would bring some critter down to the school. I remember him bringing a big tarantula and another time a big python that he had us line up and hold in our hands.

One year the teacher wanted to teach us about our solar system and the different planets. So he covered a basketball for the sun and other sizes of balls for the other planets and hung them with string from the ceiling in the right order.

I believe this is the same year the astronauts went to the moon. The teacher let us go over to the teacherage and watch the blast-off on the television.

The county health nurse would come out once a year to give us shots and check our eyes, ears, and teeth. I remember them showing us how to brush our teeth properly on a giant set of dentures. Plus they would give us a new toothbrush and a small toothpaste.

Sometimes at lunch break we walked to the store (which John Jensen had at the time) to buy little cartons of milk, candy, and gum. We had to bring our own lunches from home. We had tin lunch boxes that we always put in the back left corner.

One year the ants discovered our lunch boxes and were crawling all over them. The teacher got on my sister Sally for calling the ants "piss ants" and told her they were sugar ants.

Sometimes the teacher would let us eat our lunches down by the creek, which in those days always had running water in it. To end the school year we would have a picnic at Sunny Flat and a big baseball game.

I really enjoyed my Portal school days.

— *Sheila Clark*

The Portal School circa 1970
Cochise County Historical Society

42   The Southwestern Research Station
Dawn Wilson and Carol A. Simon

The Southwestern Research Station (SWRS or the Station) is a year-round biological field station owned and operated by the American Museum of Natural History (AMNH) in New York City. The SWRS is located in Cave Creek Canyon, 5 miles west of Portal, Arizona. Since 1955, the Station has served biologists and geologists interested in studying the diverse environments as well as the wide range of plants, animals, and fungi of the Chiricahua Mountains and surrounding areas. Researchers and students come from all parts of the U.S. and from abroad to work on their own projects or to assist others. Much of the research conducted here has contributed information for other chapters in this book.

The Station is also rich in history. In 1849 the Leonard R. Reed family passed by Cave Creek Canyon on their way from Missouri to find gold in California. A son, Stephen B. Reed, and his family came back to the Chiricahuas to live. In 1879, they built a log cabin of felled juniper and pine on the property the SWRS owns today. The original cabin still stands as part of a larger home next to the laboratory buildings. The Reeds were the first white family to settle in the area, and rumors persist that Stephen Reed and Geronimo were on friendly terms.

After several owners, the property was named Painted Canyon Ranch, and was purchased in 1950 by

The log cabin built by Stephen Reed is still used today as the residence for the Station's Director.
All photos collection of SWRS

authors Weldon F. and Phyllis W. Heald, whose experiences in the canyon are chronicled in Weldon's 1975 book *Sky Island*, republished in 1995 as *The Chiricahuas, Sky Island*.

By 1953 Dr. Mont Cazier, chairman of the Department of Insects and Spiders at the American Museum of Natural History, had become aware of the property and wished to acquire it as a biological field research station for the museum. This was accomplished in 1955 with funding from David Rockefeller, who shared Dr. Cazier's passion for beetles. Dr. Cazier then became the first director of the station and set the standard of research excellence the SWRS maintains to this day.

Subsequent directors were Vincent Roth, Dr. Wade Sherbrooke, and Dr. Dawn Wilson. All have made significant contributions to the Station in their own ways.

The AMNH chose Cave Creek Canyon in particular because of the rich biodiversity found here. The Station is at an elevation of 5,400 feet within the Madrean Pine-Oak Woodland habitat. Within 10 miles, elevations range from 4,000 to almost 10,000 feet. Because of their insular nature, sky islands such as the Chiricahua Mountains, serve as **refugia** for many species stranded by warming climates since the last ice age. Both the sky islands and the surrounding deserts and grasslands are globally important because of their highly diverse species and habitats. This biodiversity is one of the great attractions for scientists to Cave Creek Canyon.

Scientists are also drawn to the SWRS because of the uniqueness of the fauna and flora in the surrounding habitats. Many of the plants and animals

studied by researchers here are of conservation interest because they are either at their distributional limit or **endemic** to the area.

Scientists who use the Station's facilities are affiliated with a variety

The Station is nestled among sycamores, junipers, and oaks at an elevation of 5,400 feet.

Students of all ages benefit from the Station's volunteer, intern, and outreach programs.

of institutions including universities, museums, and government agencies.

The National Science Foundation has been a long-time supporter of facilities development, which has helped the expansion of plant and animal collections, laboratories, supplies, and equipment. Additionally, an outdoor aviary complex, an animal behavior observatory, and a multi-room live-animal holding facility are used for behavioral ecology studies. Scientists work in areas of entomology, herpetology, ornithology, mammalogy, botany, geology, arachnology, and animal behavior, as well as population, behavioral, physiological, and conservation ecology.

Many long-term studies are in progress, including communal breeding in Mexican Jays, spadefoot toad reproduction, behavior and sexual selection in Striped Plateau Lizards, and the evolution of social behaviors in ants. As of 2014, the Mexican Jay study has been ongoing for more than 40 years! Scientists working at the Station have produced more than 1,200 scientific publications. Much of the research has helped guide land management decisions for the surrounding national forest areas.

The SWRS welcomes educational groups, and training workshops have become an integral part of life here. Topics include specific training on the conservation of organisms such as bats, bees, butterflies, ants, and lizards, as well as training on broader topics such as animal behavior, native plants, and wetland design and function. Participants leave the courses better equipped to pursue their research, teaching, and/or conservation efforts because of knowledge gained concerning the taxonomy, ecology, and behavior of the organisms studied. Some courses are open to the public.

The SWRS is a leader in mentoring students from the U.S. and abroad by supporting 20-30 interns annually. This program provides an opportunity for many promising young scientists to explore their options in several areas of field ecology. Students receive room and board in exchange for working 24 hours per week doing general housekeeping, landscaping, etc. Most importantly, they have the opportunity to receive training in field ecology and to assist in an ongoing research project or conduct an independent project of their own. The Station began a grant program in 1989 to support student research, and, since then, more than 160 students have received support from this fund.

The SWRS also opens its doors to day visitors and nature enthusiasts to enjoy beautiful scenery, diverse birds and other animals, and numerous hiking trails. A gift shop provides mementos, snacks, and drinks, and an interpretive area includes informative exhibits on native grasses, oaks, and more. A public viewing area with a boardwalk allows visitors to enjoy hummingbirds and other bird species.

In addition, the SWRS participates in outreach programs for the local community. Each year, many scientific seminars are given and are advertised locally to the general public. These events serve to increase the ecological knowledge within the local community and highlight the science conducted at the Station.

Many Station scientists volunteer to give a seminar or lead a field trip when their stay overlaps with that of a science workshop or class. Historically, workshops offered at the Station were geared towards upper-level university students and/or agency personnel. More recently, the Station has reached out to middle- and high school students. Students from several Tucson schools come each year to attend a short summer course that requires them to work in teams to collect and analyze data. At the end, each team presents their results to Station users in a series of short seminars.

From 1955 on, the SWRS has been a premier field station for researchers, an incomparable learning environment for students, and a focal point for the surrounding community.

Cave Creek Canyon would not be the same without it.

Station scientists don't work ALL the time!

Mt. Sceloporus — A New Name in Cave Creek Canyon

People name many things—mountains, streams, locations of significant events, children, ranches—these are names that become part of the landscape. Time and history contribute names, like Cochise County, Arizona. The Chiricahua Mountains (from *tsil* "mountain" and *kawa* "great") were home to a people we have called Apache since the time of their leader, Cochise. The cultural significance of names often runs deep.

So it was in that land when on August 16, 1989, a small expedition from the Research Station set out to name the undesignated peak to the southeast of Silver Peak, notable for its U.S. Forest Service fire lookout tower.

Departing SWRS at 6 a.m. to climb the unnamed landscape of lime-green lichens covering rosy-rhyolite cliffs were Kevin Dixon, Laura Hardy, Bryan Jennings, Ariovaldo Neto, Wade Sherbrooke, and Christina Swartz. The 24" x 28" flag they carried to name Mt. Sceloporus sported an iridescent-blue silhouette of a spiny lizard. The numerous species of *Sceloporus sp.*, spiny or fence lizards, live only in North and Central America. Cave Creek Canyon is home to several.

The significance of the scientific genus name lies in commemorating the multiple scientific research efforts carried out with many organisms by many people over decades at the Station, which has been at the base of the mountain since 1955.

As Station Director, I consulted with visiting USGS geologists John Pallister and Edward du Bray when petitioning the U.S. Board of Geographic Names in Reston, Virginia, to name Mt. Sceloporus. Much to John and Ed's surprise ("The Board never takes any of our suggestions"), the name now officially appears on USGS topographic maps. It may well be the only "mountain" officially named for a genus of lizards on our or any other planet. Locally known Reed Mountain, to the east of SWRS and named for Stephen Reed, was also requested for an official USGS name, but it was not so designated.

— Wade C. Sherbrooke
Director Emeritus, Southwestern Research Station

Mount Sceloporus above the Southwestern Research Station is named for a genus of spiny lizard common in Cave Creek Canyon.

Noel Snyder

43   Trails
Jonathan Patt

The Chiricahua Mountains have long been known by birders, biologists, and other naturalists as an area of high biodiversity.

Perhaps less known to many is the extent of the range's hiking trail system. Spanning nearly the entire range, it totals about 300 miles across approximately 100 trails. From the bottoms of many canyons to the tops of the highest peaks, the trails provide access to a variety of remote, scenic, and otherwise impossible-to-reach areas, with a wide variety of options for both out-and-back and loop hikes.

Linked by the Y-shaped Crest Trail running along the uppermost ridges of the range, many of the trails climb several thousand feet from points along the base of the mountains and canyon bottoms, traversing nearly every life zone along the way, from Upper Sonoran to Hudsonian. Elsewhere, other trails travel for miles along relatively flat riparian areas, staying close to the creek and providing an easy and enjoyable walking experience while also providing access to some of the more popular birding areas.

The trails have a varied origin: some began as early pioneer travel routes while others were constructed for resource management, firefighting and recreational purposes by the Civilian Conservation Corps in the 1930s and later by Forest Service trail crews. (See Chapters 40 and 35.) Occasionally a trail abruptly widens and reveals itself to be a remnant of an old road. These often provided access to sawmills and stands of timber that were cut in the 1800s, or occasionally were part of a former wagon road between settlements.

A wide range of difficulty and conditions can be found across the trail system, with options that appeal to people of all skill levels. For those who prefer easy walking and navigation, consider the Cave Creek Nature Trail,

Running along the spine of the Chiricahuas, the Crest connects numerous other trails into the greater network. *All photos by Jonathan Patt*

the Crest Trail, or the first several miles of the South Fork Trail as it travels along one of the most popular riparian areas in the Chiricahuas.

For intermediate hikers, the Greenhouse Trail, Herb Martyr Trail, Rucker Canyon Trail, Silver Peak Trail, and many others provide access to higher regions and amazing views of old growth forest, volcanic formations, epic canyons, and the surrounding valleys and mountain ranges—at the price of a lot of climbing.

If you enjoy visiting areas seen by few other people and are up for a navigational challenge, there are many primitive trails that receive minimal maintenance and require the use of a good map and compass or GPS: The greater Witch Ridge region, including the Hoovey Canyon, Green Canyon and Fife Canyon Trails, is just one example of this type of area.

For decades, the Chiricahuas have been a backpacking destination for those who seek a solitary wilderness experience with a low chance of encountering other people. Developed springs can be found all over the Chiricahuas, many of which are quite reliable. Combined with backcountry campsites scattered across the range, a large number of multi-day loop options are

The first mile of the South Fork Trail is one of the most well known in the Chiricahuas due to its popularity with birders. Beyond that, it continues along the South Fork of Cave Creek for 3 miles before leaving the creek and climbing over several additional miles to the Crest Trail high above, near Sentinel and Finnicum Peaks.

possible, exposing a backpacker to a wide variety of locations and views that can be difficult to reach in a single day.

With so many trails, it can be difficult to keep them all maintained, especially after a series of major fires—the 1994 Rattlesnake fire and the 2011 Horseshoe 2 fire in particular—which have caused significant erosion damage and frequent deadfall in the most heavily burned areas. Forest Service crews and volunteer groups work in the Chiricahuas several times per year, focusing on some of the most popular and problematic areas.

Volunteers enjoy working in the Chiricahuas so much that they will travel from all over the country at their own expense to help keep trails here open for hikers to use.

Every Thursday, rain or shine, local residents as well as visitors to the area meet up to hike—usually in the Chiricahuas, and occasionally elsewhere. If you're interested in learning more about the trail system but aren't ready to venture into it entirely on your own, the hiking group can be an excellent way to start learning the mountains.

Visit http://www.portalrodeo.com/hiking/ for details about the upcoming hike, as well as its meeting time and location.

Forking off the Rucker Trail near Rucker Forest Camp, the Raspberry Ridge Trail continues up Bear Canyon before beginning one of the steepest climbs in the Chiricahuas to the eponymous Raspberry Ridge and the Crest Trail beyond.

44   Everyday Life in the Canyon

Nearly everyone who visits Cave Creek Canyon gets around to asking: "So, what's it like to actually LIVE here?"

Here's the answer to at least a few parts of that question.

Education in Portal
— Peter Grill and JoAnn Julian

Education in rural areas is always problematic. Small populations spread over large areas tax limited resources. One of the first schools in the Portal vicinity was the Hilltop Mine School. Although originally built to serve residents and workers at the Hilltop Mine in Upper Whitetail, it also served many of the local ranch children. Some took a shortcut through the mine tunnel at the eastern portal of the Kasper Trail. They were accompanied by one of the miners as they passed through the tunnel, and then dropped down the mountain trail to Whitetail Creek.

After the mines played out and the mining population declined, the school closed its doors in 1937. Students from the area transferred to Portal to attend school. The original Portal school was housed in what is now the Myrtle Kraft Library, known then as the "Big Room" and the Portal Post Office known as the "Little Room." The Little Room was for Grades 1-5 and the Big Room for Grades 6, 7, and 8.

In 1973, due to decreasing enrollment, the Portal School merged with the San Simon School District. Now students living in the Portal area have a choice between two elementary schools; the Apache School (K-6), a "one-room" school with two teachers located south of Rodeo, or the San Simon School District (K-12) located in San Simon off Interstate-10 at Exit 378.

Despite facing the problems common to most rural areas—a shrinking population and extended bus trips to school—the San Simon School

District has managed to improve the quality of education and increase enrollment. In the past seven years the enrollment at San Simon, home of the Longhorns, has risen dramatically from 84 students to over 150, with a staff of 28. The school has attained a rating of A+, the highest given in the State of Arizona. The long distances between Portal and the school are covered by bus from the "downtown" area of Portal.

The San Simon District has adopted an open enrollment policy for students who reside outside the district from as far away as Animas, New Mexico, or Willcox. Parents also have a choice of enrolling their children in the Animas School District.

The San Simon School is like many rural areas with a small influx of people, but the area benefits from regional loyalty, both from old-time residents and new residents seeking a more bucolic setting. San Simon has a number of fourth-generation students attending school. Although the relative remoteness of the district would seem to inhibit attracting good teachers, the teachers who do come to the area are excellent and tend to stay and become rooted in the community.

San Simon offers a full academic program. Over the last seven years it has had a graduation rate of 100 percent. Following the state mandate for career and college readiness, 100 percent of the high school students are enrolled in precollege or technical education programs. Fifty-nine percent of the graduates enroll in college or university, and 64 percent have been placed in a career that is related to their college and technical education.

In spite of the sparse population, many local people and businesses sponsor college or technical school scholarships. Eighty-six percent of San Simon graduates have received some form of scholarship. Due to increasing enrollment, extra-curricular activities are numerous. Athletic programs such as archery, football, volleyball, track, baseball, softball and basketball are offered. Character education is addressed through FFA, National Honor Society, student government, and yearbook. The district offers additional classes and accelerated study through a teacher-moderated remote learning system, Odyssey Ware online education.

The education realities of rural living have moved beyond the historic one-room classroom. Although there may appear to be limiting factors in choosing to move a family to the environmentally blessed area of Portal, lack of educational possibilities need not be one of them. This concern is being met by the San Simon School District. The Portal area is now and always has been concerned about the educational needs of its residents.

Meeting Medical Needs
— Frances Grill

In any discussion of medical or health services available, it is important to define terms. In the United States, what is commonly referred to as the Health Care Delivery System (HCDS) is actually designed to deal with sick care. Although preventive health care is nominally addressed and paid for, much of the HCDS, which comprises more than 15 percent of our GNP, is focused on disease after it happens, not on prevention. That is a topic beyond the scope of this chapter, which will focus on what is available in the Portal area to address medical needs, not prevention or health.

In this country, as is true in most of the world, many health or preventive practices are actually provided for in the home or community. For example, eating certain foods to prevent illness, exercise, adequate rest, and handling stress are health practices provided for by the family or community. The Portal/Paradise/Rodeo community has many health and prevention advocates with skills to facilitate these practices: massage therapists, alternative healers, people skilled in the use of essential oils and herbs, and at least one yoga teacher.

Since most health/medical care is being provided in the home or community, the HCDS is available for those times when home remedies and preventative practices fail.

Historically, people who migrated to the west were adventuresome, independent individuals who tended to provide for themselves and their families without much assistance or dependence on outside institutions. They took care of themselves. The Portal/Paradise/Rodeo community was no exception. Several medical care providers have lived here over the years but very few who intentionally set up practice. Doc Pugsley seems to be the most commonly acknowledged provider (see Chapters 30 and 31). Basically, people took care of themselves in the same way they did their animals. Herbal poultices, salves, and purgatives were used for both humans and horses. Since there were so few "professionals" in the area, residents relied on themselves and anecdotal cures.

That mentality has prevailed to current times with some minor changes. With improved transportation, people are more likely to rely on what the "city" has to offer, including medical care. And now, smaller towns also offer medical care choices that did not exist 50 years ago. With increased technology and cure rates, we have also come to expect that our medical needs will be met, unlike years ago, when a more fatalistic mentality prevailed, which allowed people to live out in the rural areas and not expect the latest and best technology possible.

The health issues that face people who live in the Portal/Paradise/Rodeo area are similar to those of the general U.S. population. Diabetes, hypertension, heart disease, cancer, and arthritis occur at the same rate as any other place.

Our area does have some unique health challenges, including various plant allergies, such as juniper and mesquite, as well as animal and bug bites and stings, such as snakes, cone nose beetles, and scorpions. In addition, chemically sensitive folks are drawn here searching for an environment that's less toxic to them.

When people need emergent medical care, expert advice, or simply routine medical care, many choices are available relatively nearby. Some people have established care in the larger cities of Tucson and Phoenix and prefer to periodically make that trek. The smaller towns of Sierra Vista, Safford, Douglas, Willcox and Silver City offer excellent hospitals and clinics. Most of these locations have specialists either practicing there, or bring ones in from larger cities weekly or monthly.

Closer to home, Lordsburg has the Hidalgo community health clinic, complete with dental care, which is open five days per week and operates on a sliding fee scale. A branch of this clinic is in Animas and is open on Tuesday, Thursday, and Friday.

Portal has a privately owned clinic, Walker Family Medicine (based in Willcox), which has a provider available on Mondays and Thursdays. The clinic accepts most insurance plans and accepts walk-ins.

In addition, Portal Rescue, a volunteer emergency service, is available 24 hours a day by calling 911. Three flight companies serve the area for emergencies as well.

There is no hospice and no home care facility available to Portal or Paradise at this time. Assisted living and nursing homes are in most of the small nearby towns mentioned previously. However, many caregivers and nurses are available to meet the needs of folks who prefer to stay home or who are discharged from hospital. One advantage of supporting local services is early detection of disease so that hospitalization may be avoided. Hospital-acquired disease is becoming a huge problem in this country and should be avoided if possible.

This notion of supporting local services, or "locavore," can be expanded to more than just food. If we all want a better quality of life in this community, we need to support services provided locally as much as possible. With the two clinics in Animas and Portal, this is quite possible.

People who move to this area need to familiarize themselves with what is available and decide if they can tolerate a little more uncertainty than might be true near a larger city with more choices. The Portal-Rodeo community has many independent residents who have health-related skills. There are healers, therapists, physicians, nurses, and nutritionists, some retired and some not.

The resources are there to make living in this community safe and comfortable. One can have basic needs provided for quite well with some networking, careful planning, and communicating so that the community can help meet those needs.

Living in a remote area such as the Chiricahuas obviously requires more attention and participation in one's own health care, but, as in most small communities, the more you immerse yourself in the community, the more fully you will be cared for and your needs will be met.

Walker Family Medicine, based in Willcox, has a clinic in Portal that is open
Mondays and Thursdays. *Cecil Williams*

Life in the Boonies
— Gerry Hernbrode

"Portal? Why there? There's nobody out there and nothing to do!"

This was the response of Tucson friends on hearing that I planned to retire in this mountain hamlet.

Wrong on both counts.

There are more than 600 folks in the Portal/Paradise/Rodeo area. Love of the natural world, whether birds, stars, or the great outdoors, is the common thread that weaves them together. These folks are an interesting lot, be they writers, bird watchers, ranchers, astronomers, or retired teachers or biologists. Lots of biologists!

Biologists, who for many summers have conducted research with the Southwestern Research Station 9 miles into the canyon, retire here. Not-so-urban legend has it that they give Portal the highest percentage of PhDs per capita in Arizona. We don't hold it against them. They act like normal folks.

The dark skies attract astronomers, who take advantage of the absence of outdoor lighting to build their observatories in areas such as the Sky Village a couple of miles northeast of Portal.

Four companies that specialize in international nature travel have their headquarters in Portal.

One business here furnishes insects for medical research and museums. Another raises captive-bred reptiles. A third company designs and builds interactive museum displays that they install all around the world.

The Chiricahua Desert Museum on Highway 80, two miles north of Rodeo, not only provides a gift shop that would be right at home on Park Avenue in the Big Apple, but also features a world-class display of live rattlesnakes safely tucked away behind glass. The owners have a thriving publishing company and generously sponsor speakers and parties for the community.

This eclectic mix makes for interesting neighbors.

"But there's nothing to do!"

Quite the opposite. There is much that MUST be done. Fundraisers bring people together and strengthen our sense of community. Keeping these little burgs going requires community involvement—local volunteers staff all the following services:

• The yearly "Octoberfest" helps the Sew What? Club, the ladies' service group, raise funds for local scholarships, Portal Rescue, and a Douglas nursing home.

• An annual "Soup Kitchen" occurs each February to support Portal Rescue, the local Fire Department and EMS service. It draws diners from all over Cochise County who enjoy homemade soups, breads, and desserts as they test their luck in the raffle.

• Holiday events include the July Fourth parade, the "Mixed Nuts" Craft Bazaar, and Christmas Dinner, all in Rodeo, and the St. Patrick's Day parade in Portal.

• Friends of Cave Creek Canyon hosts a spring garden party, a fall event with silent auction, and many work days for worthwhile outdoor projects.

• Heritage Days brings in speakers and hosts field trips each September.

• The Chiricahua Gallery on Highway 80 in Rodeo features works of local artists and authors. It sponsors a yearly concert as well as Spring and Christmas shows and "Art for Kids" each summer.

"But don't you get bored? Without a cinema? A mall? Heavens!"

Portal Library has the largest per capita circulation in Arizona. Through inter-library loans we can obtain just about any book in print. Great for reading pleasure, necessary for ongoing research.

The Sew What? Club sponsors monthly forums on topics ranging from the natural world, travels, history, and comedy to astronomy.

Every election, Portal's "Candidate's Night" draws most of the local politicians because 45 to 50 voters will attend, assuring candidates of a larger and more engaged audience than they get in the cities.

Scientists working at the Research Station during the summer give presentations featuring their specialized fields.

The Circuit Writers, for local writers, and the Sewing Group (irreverently called the "Stitch and Bitch Group" by their spouses) meet weekly in members' homes.

The Book Group, Portal Rescue Board, and Sew What? meet once a month.

The Portal Store hosts music events, including a Celtic Festival.

Local volunteers staff The Chiricahua Gallery and the library.

"But, you've got to eat!"

It's true, folks have to go 60 miles south to Douglas or north to Lordsburg for groceries. The Portal and Rodeo stores carry some groceries and, with the Rodeo Tavern, serve meals. Residents have large freezers. For water, Rodeo has a Water Company while Portal residents have wells.

"What about health and emergency services?

A person has to make an appointment to have a traffic accident in Portal proper, but accidents do occur on Highway 80. A 911 call dispatches Portal and Rodeo firefighters and EMTs. Portal Rescue is a volunteer outfit with regular training and free service to all. The EMTs are certified and qualified to work on any ambulance service in Arizona. These volunteers generously help locals and visitors alike. If the patient is critically ill or injured, helicopters arrive quickly to transport them to Tucson hospitals. See previous section for more about healthcare here.

"What if I want to visit this interesting spot in the boonies?"

Portal and Rodeo have beautiful cabins, a couple of motels, and many bed-and-breakfast accommodations. These hamlets are about three hours east of Tucson and three hours west of Las Cruces. They can be reached by driving on 1-10 and turning south on Highway 80 for 30 miles. Rodeo is on Highway 80. For Portal, turn on a well-marked paved road 2 miles north of Rodeo and head 9 miles east toward the Chiricahuas.

Come visit. You'll be glad you did. That's a promise.

Cave Creek Canyon in clouds
Orchid Davis

45 Local Conservation and Preservation Efforts

O ver the past few decades, various groups and individuals have been active in helping protect and preserve the resources of Cave Creek Canyon. Here are profiles of some of them.

Archaeology Southwest

Archaeology Southwest is a private 501(c)(3) nonprofit organization headquartered in Tucson, Arizona.

For three decades, Archaeology Southwest has practiced a holistic, conservation-based approach to exploring the places of the past. We call this "Preservation Archaeology." By exploring what makes a place special, sharing this knowledge in innovative ways, and enacting flexible site protection strategies, we foster meaningful connections to the past and respectfully safeguard its irreplaceable resources.

www.archaeologysouthwest.org

Arizona Archaeological and Historical Society

AAHS was founded in 1916. It is a nonprofit, educational organization affiliated with the Arizona State Museum. AAHS provides a forum for professionals in archaeology and related fields as well as the general public to share their common interests and enthusiasm for the Southwest's rich cultural history. Activities, announced monthly in the newsletter, *Glyphs*, provide educational and social opportunities to explore these interests. The Society's quarterly journal, *Kiva*, publishes original research in southwestern anthropology and history, and is an internationally recognized professional journal.

www.az-arch-and-hist.org

Chiricahua Regional Council

The Chiricahua Regional Council is a citizens' watchdog group that monitors public agency actions and other issues affecting the Chiricahua, Peloncillo, and Dragoon mountains and nearby areas. We focus on maintaining healthy, intact habitats and protecting the world-famous biological resources of the region. We disseminate information about potential threats to these resources, as those threats arise. We advocate careful land stewardship and seek to educate the public, as needed, on any aspect of natural history, conservation, and land use, including sound grazing and forestry practices. We support policies that encourage and allow quiet public enjoyment of significant portions of the Coronado National Forest.

Diverse interests of the community, from biologists to ranchers, are represented on our Board of Directors. This nonprofit group evolved from a large coalition of people opposed to a proposed gold mine in the Chiricahuas in the early 1990s (see sidebar). That effort culminated in the voluntary withdrawal of the mining company and in national legislation protecting the Cave Creek Canyon area from further threats from mining.

A major strength of the organization lies in its broad constituency. Our membership includes biologists, ranchers, birders, residents, visitors, and other segments of the general public with a strong interest in the region's well-being.

http://chiricahuaregionalcouncil.blogspot.com

Friends of Cave Creek Canyon

Our mission is to inspire appreciation and understanding of the beauty, biodiversity, and legacy of Cave Creek Canyon. We work closely with Coronado National Forest to support their work and mission in Southeast Arizona.

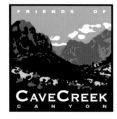

We seek to provide educational opportunities for area residents, visitors, school groups, scientific researchers, and others who cherish the special qualities of our region.

Recent projects include establishing and maintaining a wildflower garden at the Visitor Information

The Gold Mine Battle of Cave Creek Canyon

Residents of Portal were taken by surprise in mid-1990 by a proposal that was projected to lead to a huge open-pit gold mine overlooking the mouth of Cave Creek Canyon. This proposal posed worrisome threats of dust pollution from mine tailings and contamination of ground water supplies with cyanide—not to mention social disruption of the Portal community and a host of negative effects on scenic and biodiversity values of the canyon. The lands involved were all administered by the Coronado National Forest, an agency constrained by the 1872 Mining Law to permit mining activities on lands not officially withdrawn from "mineral entry."

As the lands in question were not already protected from mineral development, residents immediately asked the Forest Service to withdraw these lands from such threats. The Forest Service responded that it was not its policy to initiate protection of any lands as a response to a mineral development proposal. Similar responses were heard from members of the Arizona Congressional delegation.

Despite the refusal of government officials to act, residents began an intensive effort to study the mining law and formed a grass-roots organization to mount a major national effort to stop the development. This organization was the Portal Mining Action Coalition (PMAC) and later evolved into the Chiricahua Regional Council (CRC). With help from concerned parties around the world, members conducted a major campaign of letter writing and interactions with the media, combined with an effort to negotiate matters directly with the mining organization involved—Newmont Mining Corporation.

These activities resulted in numerous articles in national newspapers and magazines, tens of thousands of protesting letters to the Forest Service, members of Congress, and Newmont, but most importantly to a productive meeting with Newmont officials to discuss a potential reconsideration of the proposal. Newmont responded with its own intensive study of alternative values of the canyon and ultimately agreed with the assessment of PMAC. Newmont itself became a supporter of withdrawing the lands from mining development, and this eventually led to a bill called the Cave Creek Canyon Protection Act, which was supported by the entire Arizona Congressional delegation. It was signed into law by President Clinton on August 2, 1993.

None of this would have happened without the concerted and nearly unanimous participation of an aroused community.

— Noel Snyder

Center, publishing a book on Cave Creek Canyon, being a co-sponsor of Heritage Days, hosting multiple guest speakers on topics of interest to the community, organizing and staffing school field trips, initiating a 10-year invasive plant removal project—and more.

www.friendsofcavecreekcanyon.org

Malpai Borderlands Group

The Malpai Borderlands Group is organized and led by ranchers who live and work primarily in southeast Arizona and southwest New Mexico. It is a collaborative effort that is built around goals shared by neighbors within our community. Our group originated as a series of informal discussions among ranching neighbors who recognized that a way of life, and a wild landscape, that they all loved was being threatened by the spread of development and subdivision from nearby towns.

The Malpai Group works in an 800,000-acre region that extends from the foot of the Chiricahua Mountains in Arizona, east to the Playas Valley in southwest New Mexico

www.malpaiborderlandsgroup.org

Northern Jaguar Project

NJP strives to preserve essential jaguar habitat through the establishment, care, and expansion of a safe-haven sanctuary in northern Mexico. We aspire to restore habitat suitable for jaguars and other threatened and endangered species, to support wildlife research and educational programs,

and to reduce conflicts between carnivores and humans. Our goal is to instill pride and respect for regional biodiversity among those dwelling in jaguar country, and to dispel any myths and misconceptions about the species. We recognize that curtailing hunting and trapping of jaguars is the most time-sensitive need for species recovery throughout the region.

www.northernjaguarproject.org

Sky Island Alliance

Sky Island Alliance is a bi-national conservation organization dedicated to the protection and restoration of the rich natural heritage of native species and habitats in the Sky Island region of the southwestern United States and northwestern

Mexico. We work with volunteers, scientists, land owners, public officials, and government agencies to establish protected areas, restore healthy landscapes, and promote public appreciation of the region's unique biological diversity.

www.skyislandalliance.org

Wildlands Network

Wildlands Network, a non-profit international conservation organization with its western field office in Portal, focuses on restoring and connecting the West's most critical wildlife habitat corridors. Through science-based field research and mapping, Wildlands Network has identified the Chiricahua and Peloncillo mountains and the intervening San Simon and San Bernardino valleys as the top priority wildlife linkage connecting Sky Island ranges on both sides of the U.S.-Mexico borderlands.

To raise awareness of the importance of protecting our mountain landscapes, Wildlands Network has also been instrumental in founding and organizing annual "Heritage Days" events every September that bring together a wide range of community residents to celebrate the region's cultural history, archaeology, natural history, and conservation of the landscapes and wildlife that mean so much to the economic and natural health of the Chiricahua and Peloncillo Mountain communities.

For information, call 520-558-0165 or email kim@wildlandsnetwork.org

www.wildlandsnetwork.org

Cochise County Historical Society

The Cochise County Historical Society was founded in 1966 as the Cochise County Historical and Archaeological Society in Douglas. At that time, noted archaeologist Charles DiPeso and others, including those affiliated with Cochise College, were active in exploring archaeological finds in Cochise County. Our main mission is to work to preserve the history of Cochise County by publishing our journal twice a year. We encourage the study of history in Cochise County. The journal is intended to have articles of scholarly interest without being strictly academic. Local writers are encouraged.

www.cochisecountyhistory.org

Chiricahua-Peloncillo Historical Society

A gathering of local history enthusiasts to collect and organize, preserve, and share natural and human history of our area.

The Chiricahua-Peloncillo Historical Society's primary function is to share our history through historical programs and field trips.

For current officers and contact information, please go to the Portal Rodeo website, select Chiricahua-Peloncillo Historical Society, and scroll down.

www.portalrodeo.com

Alden Hayes: Chronicler of the Canyon

Alden was born in New Jersey in 1916. He left home at about the age of 18 to attend the University of New Mexico. During his school years he took off some time and with a friend went to Mexico and saw quite a bit of it. He graduated and he and some college friends made a canoe trip down the Mackenzie River to the Arctic Circle. Not long after that he married a gal (my mother) and came to Portal with his new bride to take care of his new father-in-law's place.

Although he started out life as an Easterner, he spent most of his adult life in the West: Arizona, New Mexico, and Colorado for the most part. He wore out a lot of shoe soles and quite a few horse shoes trekking through the woods, mountains, and plains.

In the flyleaf of his book, A Portal to Paradise, *he referred to himself as a "failed farmer, bankrupt cattleman, one-time park ranger, and would be archaeologist." He was all of these things and a good deal more: He spent time as an officer in the U.S. Army, and although he was a professional archaeologist, he was also a pretty good geologist. He knew* a lot about the flora and fauna around here, and the basin and range country, and the edge of the Great Plains.

Alden Hayes at Mesa Verde.
Courtesy of Eric Hayes

Alden was an avid bird watcher and knew just about everything that flies or soars in these parts.

I was fortunate that he and I both lived long enough to become old men together or nearly so. That's when I got to know him better than I had before, and to realize how much he knew. Even as an old man he wasn't in the habit of procrastinating, and he was a good scholar, which is probably what made him so wise.

—*Eric Hayes*

Glossary

Accentor — any of several bird species in the Old World family of Prunellidae

Anabatic — moving upward or rising

Bajada — Spanish for "slope"; an alluvial slope at the base of a mountain, formed by several alluvial fans; the word alluvial relates to deposits of soil and sediments left by flowing water

Brumate — semi-hibernate; relates to reptiles, not mammals

Cremaster — a sharp spine at the end of the pupa

Convective — relating to the transfer of heat

Dendridic — branching like a tree

Diapause — a physiological condition of dormancy, can be caused by adverse environmental circumstances

Dorsum — the upper side of an animal or other upright organism

Endemic — restricted or peculiar to a locale or region

Evapotranspiration — the evaporation of water as well as transpiration from plants

Extirpations — extinctions in a specific locality, not globally

Felids — members of the Cat family

Geomorphology — study of landforms and how they are shaped

Geophysical — relating to physical properties and processes of the Earth

Hydrogeologic — concerning the distribution and movement of groundwater in rocks and soil

Irruptive — relating to incursions of larger than normal numbers of a species, particularly birds; an unusual migrant

Odonates — damselflies and dragonflies

Oviposition — the process of depositing or laying eggs, usually via an ovipositor

Parasitism — relating to one life form living off another

Physicochemical — relating to joint action of both physical and chemical processes

Physiography — physical geography

Proboscis — for moths and butterflies, the tube forming part of the mouth of some insects, a long hollow tongue

Refugia — plural of "refugium:" a refuge or location of an isolated or remnant population of a formerly more widespread species

Riparian – relating to the area near a stream, creek, or river

Solvation — interaction of molecules of a solvent with molecules or ions of a solute; interchangeable with "dissolution"

Statary — a period of about three weeks when colonies of army ants remain at the same nesting site; as opposed to nomadic, when colonies change nesting locations almost every night

Symbiosis — where two dissimilar life forms live together for mutual benefit

Talus — a sloping mass of rock debris

Urticating — irritating

Ventral — towards the belly, opposite of dorsal

Volant — flying or wings spread for flying

Vomeronasal organ — also Jacobson's organ, a part of the olfactory system of mammals, reptiles, and amphibians that can detect pheromones

Chiricahuas: Waiting on the World To Change

Oil painting by Sandy Urban

Further Reading

Chapter 1   Geology

Drewes, Harald, E.A. Du Bray and J.S. Pallister, *Geologic Map of the Portal Quadrangle and Vicinity, Cochise County, Southeast Arizona.* United States Geological Survey IMAP 2450, 1995.

Chapter 2   Hydrology

Arizona Department of Water Resources. "Southeastern Arizona Planning." *Arizona Water Atlas* 3, 2009.

Earman, Sam, Brian J.O.L. McPherson, Fred M. Phillips, Steve Ralser, James M. Herrin, and James Broska. "Tectonic Influences on Ground Water Quality: Insight from Complementary Methods." *Ground Water*, 354-71, 2008.

Reynolds, Glenn. "A Native American Water Ethic." *Transactions* 90: 143-61, 2003.

Chapter 3   Weather and Climate

Moon, William Least. *Blue Highways: A Journey into America.* Boston: Back Bay Books, 1999.

Sellers, William D., and Richard Hill. *Arizona Climate, 1931-1972.* Tucson: University of Arizona Press, 1974.

Sellers, William D., Richard H. Hill, and Margaret Sanderson-Rae, eds. *Arizona Climate The First Hundred Years.* Institute of Atmospheric Physics, University of Arizona, 1985.

Chapter 4   Skies

Astronomy Magazine

Sky and Telescope: The Essential Guide to Astronomy

www.astronomy.com.

www.conferringwiththesky.org to see images taken from the Portal area.

www.skyandtelescope.com

Chapter 5   Fire History

Gidwitz, Tom, and Abby N. *Counting Rings: Tree-ring Dating.* Tucson: Western National Parks Assoc., 2008.

Thybony, Scott. *Wildfire.* Tucson: Western National Parks Association, 2002.

www.wildlandfire.az.gov

Chapter 6   Habitat Zones

Brusca, Richard C., and Wendy Moore. *A Natural History of the Santa Catalina Mountains, Arizona, with an Introduction to the Madrean Sky Islands.* Tucson: Arizona-Sonora Desert Museum Press, 2013.

Gehlbach, Frederick R. *Mountain Islands and Desert Seas: A Natural History of the U.S.-Mexican Borderlands.* College Station: Texas A & M University Press, 1981.

Lowe, Charles H. *Arizona's Natural Environment: Landscapes and Habitats.* Tucson: University of Arizona Press, 1964.

Marshall, Joe T. *Birds of Pine-oak Woodland in Southern Arizona and Adjacent Mexico.* Berkeley: Cooper Ornithological Society, 1957.

Shreve, Forrest. *The Vegetation Of A Desert Mountain Range As Conditioned By Climatic Factors.* Whitefish: Kessinger Publishing, 2010.

Chapter 7   Trees, Shrubs, and Grasslands

Bennett, Peter S., and Michael R. Kunzmann. *An Annotated List of Vascular Plants of the Chiricahua Mountains, including the Pedregosa Mountains, Swisshelm Mountains, Chiricahua National Monument, and Fort Bowie National Historic Site.* Tucson: United States Geological Survey, Biological Resources Division, Cooperative Park Studies Unit, School of Renewable Natural Resources, University of Arizona, 1996.

Carter, Jack L., and Beth Dennis. *Trees and Shrubs of New Mexico.* Boulder, CO: Mimbres Pub, 1997.

Ferguson, George M., Aaron D. Flesch, and Thomas R. Van Devender. "Biogeography and Diversity of Pines in the Madrean Archipelago." *USDA Forest Service Proceedings RMRS-P-67*, 2012.

Rose, Frank S. *Mountain Trees of Southern Arizona: A Field Guide.* Tucson: Arizona-Sonora Desert Museum, 2012.

Chapter 8   Wildflower Walks in the Canyon

Epple, Anne Orth, and Lewis E. Epple. *A Field Guide to the Plants of Arizona.* Mesa, AZ: LewAnn Pub., 1995.

Ivey, Robert DeWitt. *Flowering Plants of New Mexico.* 3rd ed. Albuquerque, N.M.: R.D. Ivey, 1995.

Niehaus, Theodore F., and Charles L. Ripper. *A Field Guide to Southwestern and Texas Wildflowers.* Rev. ed. Boston: Houghton Mifflin, 1998.

Quinn, Meg. *Wildflowers of the Mountain Southwest.* Tucson: Rio Nuevo Publishers, 2003.

Rose, Frank, and Richard C. Brusca. *Mountain Wildflowers of Southern Arizona: A Field Guide to the Santa Catalina Mountains and Nearby Ranges.* Tucson: Arizona-Sonora Desert Museum Press, 2011.

Chapter 9   Mammals

Kays, Roland, and Don E. Wilson. *Mammals of North America.* 2nd ed. Princeton: Princeton University Press, 2009.

Arizona Natural Heritage Program (HDMS): Wildlife and Conservation at www.azgfd.gov

Chapter 10   Bats

Ivy, Jeannette. *The Vacationer's Guide to Bat Watching.* Austin: Bat Conservation Int'l, 1998.

Tuttle, Merlin D. *America's Neighborhood Bats*. Rev. ed. Austin: University of Texas Press, 1997.

Tyburec, Janet D. "Bats." In *A Natural History of the Sonoran Desert*, edited by Steven J. Phillips and Patricia Wentworth Comus, 461-472. Berkeley: University of California Press, 2000.

Wilson, Don E., and Merlin D. Tuttle. *Bats in Question: The Smithsonian Answer Book*. Washington, DC: Smithsonian Institution Press, 1997.

Arizona Game and Fish Department: http://www.azgfd.gov/w_c/bat_conserv_az_bats.shtml

Bat Conservation and Management: http://www.batmanagement.com/Programs/programcentral.html

Bat Conservation International: http://www.batcon.org/index.php/all-about-bats/species-profiles.html

Chapter 11   Jaguars
Brown, David E and Carlos López González. *Borderland Jaguars*. Salt Lake City: The University of Utah Press, 2001.

Childs, Jack L and Anna Mary Childs. *Ambushed on the Jaguar Trail: Hidden Cameras on the Mexican Border*. Tucson: Rio Nuevo Press, 2008.

Hayes, Alden. *A Portal to Paradise*. Tucson: The University of Arizona Press, 1999.

Glenn, Warner. *Eyes of Fire: Encounter with a Borderlands Jaguar*. El Paso: Printing Corner Press, 1996.

Chapter 12   Introduction to the Canyon Birds
Tucson Audubon Society. *Tucson Audubon Society's Finding Birds in Southeast Arizona*. 8th ed. Tucson: Tucson Audubon Society, 2011.

Taylor, Richard Cachor. *A Birder's Guide to Southeastern Arizona*. 5th ed. Colorado Springs, CO: American Birding Association, 2005.

https://list.arizona.edu/sympa/info/aznmbirds

http://birding.aba.org/maillist/AZ The Arizona-New Mexico Birding Listserv.

http://ebird.org/content/ebird/

Corman, Troy E. and Cathryn Wise-Gervais, eds. *Arizona Breeding Bird Atlas*. Albuquerque: University of New Mexico Press, 2005.

Phillips, Allan, Joe Marshall, and Gale Monson. *The Birds of Arizona*. Tucson: University of Arizona Press, 1964.

Chapter 13   Raptors
Snyder, Noel F. R., and Helen Snyder. *Raptors of North America: Natural History and Conservation*. St. Paul, MN: Voyageur Press, 2006.

Cartron, Jean-Luc E, ed. *Raptors of New Mexico*. Albuquerque: University of New Mexico Press, 2010.

Chapter 14   Extirpations and Introductions
Brown, David E. *Arizona Game Birds*. Tucson: University of Arizona Press, 1989.

Eaton, Stephen W. "Wild Turkey." In *Birds of North America, No 22*, edited by A. Poole, P. Stettenheim, and F. Gill. Washington, DC: American Ornithologists' Union, 1992.

Phillips, Allan R., Joe T. Marshall, and Gale Monson. *The Birds of Arizona*. Tucson: University of Arizona Press, 1964.

Snyder, Noel F.R., E.C. Enkerlin-Hoeflich, and M.A. Cruz-Nieto. "Thick-billed Parrot (*Rhynchopsitta pachyrhyncha*)." In *The Birds of North America, No. 406*, edited by A. Poole and F. Gill. Ithica, NY: Cornell Lab of Ornithology, 1999.

Snyder, Noel F.R., Susan E. Koenig, James Koschmann, Helen A. Snyder, and Terry B. Johnson. "Thick-billed Parrot Releases in Arizona." In *The Condor*, 845-862. Vol. 96. Cooper Ornithological Society, 1994.

Chapter 15   Hummingbirds

Gates, Larry, and Terrie Gates. *Enjoying Hummingbirds: In the Wild & in Your Yard*. Mechanicsburg, PA: Stackpole Books, 2007.

Howell, Steve N. G. *Hummingbirds of North America: The Photographic Guide*. Princeton: Princeton University Press, 2003.

Williamson, Sheri. *A Field Guide to Hummingbirds of North America*. Boston: Houghton Mifflin, 2002.

http://en.wikipedia.org/wiki/Hummingbird

Chapter 16   Elegant Trogons

Corman, Troy E., and Cathryn Athryn Wise-Gervais. "Elegant Trogon." In *Arizona Breeding Bird Atlas*, edited by, 264-265. Albuquerque: University of New Mexico Press, 2005.

Taylor, Richard Cachor. *Trogons of the Arizona Borderlands*. Tucson: Treasure Chest Publications, 1994.

Taylor, Richard Cachor. *Birds of Southeastern Arizona*. Seattle: R W Morse Company, 2010.

Chapter 17   Snakes

Brennan, Thomas C. and Andrew T. Holycross. *A Field Guide to Amphibians and Reptiles of Arizona*. Phoenix: Arizona Game and Fish Dept., 2006.

Degenhardt, William G., Charles W. Painter, and Andrew H Price. *Amphibians and Reptiles of New Mexico*. Albuquerque: University of New Mexico Press, 1996.

Chapter 18   Lizards

Brennan, Thomas C., and Andrew T. Holycross. *A Field Guide to Amphibians and Reptiles in Arizona*. Phoenix: Arizona Game and Fish Dept., 2006.

Jones, Lawrence L. C., and Robert E Lovich, eds. *Lizards of the American Southwest: A Photographic Field Guide*. Tucson: Rio Nuevo Publishers, 2009.

Stebbins, Robert C. *A Field Guide to Western Reptiles and Amphibians*. Edited by Roger Tory Peterson. 3rd ed. New York, N.Y.: Houghton Mifflin, 2003.

Chapter 19   Horned Lizards

Sherbrooke, Wade C. "Horned Lizard Responses to Diverse Threats from Diverse Predators: Mental Constructs and Cognitive Worlds." In *Reptiles in Research: Investigations of Ecology, Physiology, and Behavior from Desert to Sea*, edited by William I Lutterschmid, 177-196. Hauppauge NY: Nova Science Pub, 2013.

Sherbrooke, Wade C., and C. J. May. "Body-flip and Immobility Behavior in Regal Horned Lizards: A Gape-limiting Defense Selectively Displayed toward One of Two Snake Predators." *Herpetological Review* 39, no. 2: 156-62, 2008.

Sherbrooke, Wade C., K. Schwenk. "Horned Lizards (Phrynosoma) Incapacitate Dangerous Ant Prey with Mucus." *Journal of Experimental Zoology* 309A: 447-59, 2008.

Sherbrooke, Wade C., Andrew J. Scardino, Rocky Nys, and Lin Schwarzkopf. "Functional Morphology Of Scale Hinges Used To Transport Water: Convergent Drinking Adaptations In Desert Lizards (Moloch Horridus And Phrynosoma Cornutum)." In *Zoomorphology* 126: 89-102, 2007.

Sherbrooke, Wade C. *Introduction to Horned Lizards of North America.* Berkeley: University of California Press, 2003.

Chapter 20   Frogs

Behler, John L., and F. Wayne King. *The Audubon Society Field Guide to North American Reptiles and Amphibians.* New York: Knopf, 1979.

Brennan, Thomas C., and Andrew T. Holycross. *A Field Guide to Amphibians and Reptiles in Arizona.* Phoenix: Arizona Game and Fish Dept., 2006.

Rorabaugh, Jim. "Chiricahua Leopard Frog (*Lithobates chiricahuensis*) - Amphibians of Arizona." www.Reptilesofarizona.org.

Stebbins, Robert C. *A Field Guide to Western Reptiles and Amphibians: Field Marks of All Species in Western North America, including Baja California.* 2nd ed. Boston: Houghton Mifflin, 1985.

U.S. Fish and Wildlife Service. "Chiricahua Leopard Frog (*Rana chiricahuensis*) Draft Recovery Plan." Southwest Region - Arizona ES Field Office. January 1, 2006. www.fws. gov/southwest/es/arizona/CLF.htm.

Chapter 21   Ants

Moffett, Mark W. *Adventures among Ants: A Global Safari with a Cast of Trillions.* Berkeley: University of California Press, 2010.

Topoff, Howard. "Slave-Making Queens." *Scientific American*: 84-90, 1999.

Topoff, Howard. "Slave-making Ants." *American Scientist* 78: 520-28, 1990.

Chapter 22   Butterflies

Bailowitz, Richard A. *Butterflies of Southeastern Arizona.* Tucson: Sonoran Arthropod Studies, 1991.

Brock, James P., and Kenn Kaufman. *Kaufman Field Guide to Butterflies of North America.* New York, N.Y.: Houghton Mifflin, 2003.

Glassberg, Jeffrey. *Butterflies through Binoculars: The West: A Field Guide to the Butterflies of Western North America.* Oxford: Oxford University Press, 2001.

Chapter 23   Moths

http://nitro.biosci.arizona.edu/zeeb/butterflies/mothlist.html#Families An excellent website for both Southeast Arizona Moths and Butterflies, created by University of Arizona Entomology professor Bruce Walsh.

http://www.butterfliesandmoths.org Detailed website with information on all of the Butterflies and Moths of North America.

Chapter 24   Dragonflies

Dunkle, S. *Dragonflies through Binoculars: A Field Guide to Dragonflies of North America*. Oxford University Press, New York, 2000.

Paulson, D. *Dragonflies and Damselflies of the West*. Princeton University Press, Princeton, N.J., 2009.

Chapter 25   Other Invertebrates

Milne, Lorus Johnson, and Margery Joan Greene Milne. *National Audubon Society, Field Guide to North American Insects and Spiders*. New York: A.A. Knopf, 2000.

Resh, Vincent H. *Encyclopedia of Insects*. 2nd ed. Waltham: Academic Press, 2009.

Phillips, Steven, and Patricia Wentworth Comus, eds. *A Natural History of the Sonoran Desert*. Tucson: Arizona-Sonora Desert Museum Press, 1999.

White, Richard E. *A Field Guide to the Beetles of North America*. Boston: Houghton Mifflin Harcourt, 1998.

www.BugsofAmerica.com

Chapter 26   A Highway for Wildlife

Foreman, Dave. *Rewilding North America: A Vision for Conservation in the 21st Century*. Washington: Island Press, 2004.

Foreman, D. *Sky Islands Wildlands Network Conservation Plan*. Tucson: Wildlands Network, 2000. www.wildlandsnetwork.org

Hilty, Jodi A., William Z Lidicker, and Adina Merenlender. *Corridor Ecology: The Science and Practice of Linking Landscapes for Biodiversity Conservation*. Washington: Island Press, 2006.

Soulé, Michael E., and John Terborgh. *Continental Conservation: Scientific foundations of regional reserve networks*. Washington: Island Press, 1999.

Terborgh, John, and James A Estes. *Trophic Cascades: Predators, Prey, and the Changing Dynamics of Nature*. Washington: Island Press, 2010.

Western Wildway Network website: www.westernwildway.org

Chapter 27   Early Peoples

Hayes, Alden. *A Portal to Paradise*. Tucson: University of Arizona Press, 1999.

Reid, Jefferson and Stephanie Whittlesey. *The Archeology of Ancient Arizona*. Tucson: The University of Arizona Press, 1997.

Schaafsma, Polly. *Rock Art in New Mexico*. Santa Fe: Museum of New Mexico Press, 1992.

Chapter 28   Archaeology

Fish, Paul R, Suzanne K. Fish, and John H. Madsen. *Prehistory and early history of the Malpai Borderlands: Archaeological synthesis and recommendations*. Gen. Tech. Rep. RMRS-GTR-176. Fort Collins: U.S. Department of Agriculture, Forest Service, Rocky Mountain Research Station, 2006.

Hayes, Alden. *A Portal to Paradise*. Tucson: University of Arizona Press, 1999.

Coronado National Monument - http://www.nps.gov/coro/index.htm

Murray Springs Clovis Site San Pedro RNCA, US Department of the Interior Bureau of Land Management - http://www.blm.gov/az/st/en/prog/cultural/murray.html

Huckell, Bruce B. "A Fragmentary Clovis Point from Southwestern New Mexico." Kiva 37, no. 2 (1972): 114-116. - http://www.jstor.org/stable/30247612. http://commons.wikimedia.org/wiki/File:Anasazi-en.svg

http://azmemory.azlibrary.gov/cdm/singleitem/collection/cclrockart/id/39/rec/24

Chapter 29   Apaches and the U.S. Cavalry

General History

Sweeney, Edwin R. *From Cochise to Geronimo: The Chiricahua Apaches, 1874-1886*. Norman: University of Oklahoma Press, 2010.

Thrapp, Dan L. *The Conquest of Apacheria*. Norman: University of Oklahoma Press, 1967.

From the Military's Perspective

Bourke, John Gregory. *An Apache Campaign in the Sierra Madre; an Account of the Expedition in Pursuit of the Hostile Chiricahua Apaches in the Spring of 1883*. New York: Scribner, 1958.

From the Apache's Perspective

Betzinez, Jason. *I Fought with Geronimo*. Harrisburg: Stackpole, 1959.

Geronimo. *Geronimo, My Life*. Edited by S. M. Barrett. Mineola, N.Y.: Dover Publications, 2012.

Watt, Robert N. *Apache Tactics, 1830 - 86*. Oxford: Osprey, 2012.

Chapter 30   Two Early Settlers

Hayes, Alden. *A Portal to Paradise*. Tucson: University of Arizona Press, 1999.

Lekson, Stephen H. *Nana's Raid: Apache Warfare in Southern New Mexico, 1881*. El Paso: Texas Western Press, University of Texas at El Paso, 1987.

Morrow, R. W. *The Chiricahua Journals: Stories of Arizona Lawmen, Cowboys, & Miners*. Rev. and Expanded 2nd ed. Tucson: Chiricahua Press, 2010.

Utley, Robert M. *A Clash of Cultures: Fort Bowie and the Chiricahua Apaches*. Washington D.C.: National Park Service, 1977.

Chapter 31   Pioneer Graves

Hayes, Alden. *A Portal to Paradise*. Tucson: University of Arizona Press, 1999.

Hayes, Alden. *Resting in Paradise: Tales—tall and true— of the Paradise Cemetery and environs*. Portal, AZ: Paradise Cemetery Association, 1999.

Murphy, Kimrod. *The Devil Played Hell in Paradise: A Record of Some of the Settlers in the Chiricahua Mountain Region, Arizona, 1880-1980*. Portal, AZ: Banner Printing, 2010.

Chapter 32   Mining

Hayes, Alden. *A Portal to Paradise*. Tucson: University of Arizona Press, 1999.

Keith, Stanton B. *Index of Mining Properties in Cochise Cty, Ariz*. Tucson: Univ. of Ariz., 1973.

Morrow, R. W. *The Chiricahua Journals: Stories of Arizona Lawmen, Cowboys, & Miners*. Rev. and Expanded 2nd ed. Tucson: Chiricahua Press, 2010.

Murphy, Kimrod. *The Devil Played Hell in Paradise: A Record of Some of the Settlers in the Chiricahua Mountain Region, Arizona, 1880-1980*. Portal, AZ: Banner Printing, 2010.

Stidham, Maryan. "Teacher at Hilltop." *The Cochise Quarterly* vol. 20, no. 2, 1990.

Chapter 33   *Paradise Reminiscences*

Barnes, Will C. *Arizona Place Names*. Tucson: University of Arizona Press, 1988.

Hayes, Alden. *A Portal to Paradise*. Tucson: University of Arizona Press, 1999.

Hayes, Alden. *Resting in Paradise: Tales—tall and true— of the Paradise Cemetery and environs*. Paradise Cemetery Association, 1999.

Morrow, Carson, illustrated by Hayes, Eric. *The Chiricahua Bullsheet*. Portal: self-published news bulletin with 38 issues between May 7, 1957—July 17, 1959.

Sherman, James E, and Barbara H Sherman. "Paradise." In *Ghost Towns of Arizona*, 114-115. Norman: University of Oklahoma Press, 1969.

www.thegeorgewalkerhouse.com

Chapter 34   *Sawmills*

Bahre, Conrad Joseph. *A Legacy of Change: Historic Human Impact on Vegetation of the Arizona Borderlands*. Tucson: University of Arizona Press, 166-172, 1991.

Patt, Jonathan, "Early Sawmills of the Chiricahuas", *The Cochise County Historical Journal*, Vol. 43, No. 2: 29–41, 2013.

Wilson, John P. *Islands in the Desert a History of the Uplands of Southeastern Arizona*. Albuquerque, N.M.: University of New Mexico Press, 203-214, 1995.

Chapter 35   *U.S. Forest Service History*

Bahre, Conrad J. "Human Disturbance and Vegetation in Arizona's Chiricahua Mountains in 1902," *Desert Plants*, Vol. 11: 39-45, 1995. Gives a good discussion of Kellogg and Potter's 1902 inspection of the Chiricahuas.

Hayes, Alden. *A Portal to Paradise*. Tucson: University of Arizona Press, 1999.

Wilson, John P. *Islands in the Desert: A History of the Uplands of Southeastern Arizona*. Albuquerque: University of New Mexico Press, 1995. Presents a history of the mountains that comprise the Coronado National Forest.

Chapter 36   *Ranching*

Bailey, Lynn R. *The Unwashed Crowd, Stockmen and Ranches of the San Simon and Sulphur Springs Valleys, Arizona Territory, 1878-1900*. Westernlore Press, 2014.

Jordan, Terry G. *North American Cattle-Ranching Frontiers: Origins, Diffusion, and Differentiation*. Albuquerque: University of New Mexico Press, 1993.

Chapter 37   *Farming*

Bailey, Lynn R., and Don Chaput. *Cochise County Stalwarts: A Who's Who of the Territorial Years*. 2 vols. Tucson: Westernlore Press, 2000.

McEwan, Craig. "The Last 15 Years of C. S. Fly: From a Chiricahua Mountain Perspective." *The Cochise County Historical Journal*, Vol. 43, No. 2: 42–79, (Fall/Winter 2013).

Morrow, Carson, illustrated by Hayes, Eric. *The Chiricahua Bullsheet*. Portal: self-published news bulletin with 38 issues between May 7, 1957—July 17, 1959.

Morrow, R. W. *The Chiricahua Journals*. Tucson: Ghost River Images, 2009.

Murphy, Kimrod. *The Devil Played Hell in Paradise: A Record of Some of the Settlers in the Chiricahua Mountain Region, Arizona, 1880-1980*. Portal, AZ: Banner Printing, 2010.

Seymour, Deni. "Horse Herd Size and the Role of Horses Among the Mescalero Apache: A Response to Osborn." *From the Pueblos to the Southern Plains: Papers in Honor of Regge N. Wiseman*. Albuquerque: Archaeological Society of New Mexico, 2013.

Chapter 38   Early Visitors
Kumble, Peter Andrew. *The Vernacular Landscape of the Southwestern Guest Ranch*. Tucson: University of Arizona Press, 1991.

Hayes, Alden. *A Portal to Paradise*. Tucson: University of Arizona Press, 1999.

Guest Ranches on Lines of Southern Pacific. Southern Pacific, 1934. http://www.btcsd.org/About_BTCSD/essence/SP_Diamond_D.pdf

Travel Bureau, Arizona Highway Department. *Famous Arizona Ranches Welcome You*. Arizona Highway Department, 1939. http://azmemory.azlibrary.gov/cdm/ref/collection/statepubs/id/24197

Chapter 39   Game Wardens
Arizona Game and Fish Department website at: www.azgfd.gov

Morrow, Carson, illustrated by Hayes, Eric. *The Chiricahua Bullsheet*. Portal: self-published news bulletin with 38 issues between May 7, 1957 and July 17, 1959.

Morrow, R. W. *The Chiricahua Journals*. Tucson: Ghost River Images, 2009.

Murphy, Kimrod. *Lost Trails of the Arizona Game Rangers*. Sierra Vista: Banner Printing Center, 2005.

Tombstone Epitaph. Library of Congress website, *Chronicling America*, has territorial Arizona newspapers through statehood to 1922.

Wittig, Ainslee S. "Kim Murphy Reaches the End of the Trail: 'Legendary' Area Game Warden Hangs Up His Badge." *Seasons,* Vol. 13, No. 1 (Winter 1999): 11—13.

Chapter 40   Civilian Conservation Corps (CCC)
Audretsch, Robert W., and Sharon E. Hunt. *The Civilian Conservation Corps in Arizona*. Arcadia Publishing, 2014.

Otis, Alison T, William D Honey, Thomas C Hogg, and Kimberly K Lakin. *The Forest Service and the Civilian Conservation Corps: 1933-1942*. U.S. Dept. of Agriculture, Forest Service, 1986. The authors highlighted the Coronado National Forest (including the Chiricahuas) as one of three Forests given chapter-length discussion.   http://www.nps.gov/history/history/online_books/ccc/ccc/index.htm

Chapter 41   Portal Reminiscences
Hayes, Alden. *A Portal to Paradise*. Tucson: University of Arizona Press, 1999.

Murphy, Kimrod. *The Devil Played Hell in Paradise: A Record of Some of the Settlers in the Chiricahua Mountain Region, Arizona, 1880-1980*. Portal, AZ: Banner Printing, 2010.

Chapter 42   The Southwestern Research Station
Ascarza, William. *Chiricahua Mountains: History and Nature*. Charleston, S.C.: The History Press. 2014.

Heald, Weldon F. *The Chiricahuas Sky Island*. Tucson: Marguerite Bantin Publishing, 1993.

Lamberton, Ken. *Chiricahua Mountains: Bridging the Borders of Wilderness*. Tucson: The
University of Arizona Press, 2003.

Chapter 43   *Trails*

Chiricahua Mountains Hiking Trails: http://www.chiricahuatrails.com

Bootheel Maps: http://www.bootheelmaps.com

Chapter 44   *Everyday Life in the Canyon*

Basso, Keith H., *Wisdom Sits in Places: Landscape and Language Among the Western Apache*.
Albuquerque: University of New Mexico Press, 1996.

Granger, Byrd Howell. *Arizona Place Names*. Tucson: University of Arizona Press, 1982.

Authors

Abbott, Peg — I first came to Cave Creek Canyon in 1976 on a four-day field trip with my NAU college ornithology class. My professor, Russ Balda, was flipping pancakes at South Fork (in those days one could camp there) when an Elegant Trogon came in and posed for us all. That, the sheer beauty of the cliffs, the excitement of such rich natural history on every level, and the first Red-faced Warbler at the corner going into Barfoot Park cemented my bond here. After a busy career owning and guiding for a travel company, I was able to bring the business with me and settle in full time in 2002.

Alcock, John — I have been coming to Cave Creek Canyon often since 1973 to study one or another local insect or just to enjoy being in a reasonably remote area with wonderful trails and excellent bird watching. It is not irrelevant that the canyon is much cooler in summer than Tempe, Arizona, where my home is located close to my old workplace, Arizona State University. The dragonflies of Cave Creek kept me entertained for a number of glorious summers. Much more could be learned about these elegant, easily observable creatures. All that is needed is patience, an insect net and some paint markers.

Ashley, Bob —Bob Ashley has been interested in reptiles since he was a young Boy Scout in Grand Rapids, Michigan. In 2005 he and his wife Sheri began building the Chiricahua Desert Museum in Rodeo, New Mexico. It is now considered one of the premiere herpetological exhibits in the U.S. The collection features one of the largest groups of rare rattlesnakes anywhere in the world. Bob has a passion for all reptiles but most especially the beautiful creatures that reside in Cave Creek Canyon.

Bammann, Al — Al Bammann first visited the Chiricahua Mountains in 1975. He became a landowner here in 1989 and has been a full-time resident since 2006. Al retired from the BLM office in Vale, Oregon, where he was a wildlife biologist primarily working on riparian restoration projects.

Beno, Rick — Rick Beno operates his observatory, Conferring With the Sky, in Portal. Rick's early "career" in astronomy began when he was 9 years old with a 2" telescope. Periodic jumps in size and sophistication have culminated with his current 24" telescope. Rick graduated from UCSD with a degree in astrodynamics. He worked most of his career as an engineer designing navigation and simulation software. After retiring in 2003, he moved to Portal for access to the dark skies common in the area. Rick specializes in deep sky astrophotography, although he loves anything related to observing the sky. You can visit his passion for astronomy at "ConferringWiththeSky.org".

Brown, Wynne — Wynne Brown first came to Portal in 1972 as a volunteer at the Southwestern Research Station—an experience that changed her life. It was the first time she'd been to a place where a fascination with "creepy-crawlies" was considered normal. From that summer of drawing spider genitalia, she moved on to illustrating scientific papers, then to writing for magazines, then working for a newspaper as a copy editor. She loves bringing words and graphics together in a way that lets an author's concept shine. Working with the community on this book has been an honor!

Burchfield, Shane — Shane "Bugz" Burchfield is driven by a passion for wilderness, wildlife, and a desire for an outdoor office. As sole proprietor of the Portal-based business Bugs of America he removes unwanted invertebrates locally. He also locates, procures, and supplies zoos, nature centers, universities, researchers, and various educators worldwide with a diverse selection of live arthropods and related items. Education and conservation remain at the core of his personal and business priorities. He encourages everyone to walk wild and respect all living things. To learn more, go to BugsofAmerica.com or email us at BugsofAmerica@vtc.net.

Cavaliere, Bill — Historian Bill Cavaliere, vice-president of the Cochise County Historical Society, specializes in the Chiricahua Apaches. He frequently lectures at colleges, historical societies, and museums, and also guides history tours. He has written articles for numerous magazines and newspapers. His research has taken him all over the Southwest, as well as deep into Mexico. Bill retired in 2012 after 28 years in law enforcement, all on the border. He is the former sheriff of Hidalgo County, N. M. Prior to this he worked for the U.S. Forest Service in Cave Creek Canyon. He lives on a ranch near Portal.

Clark, Sheila — I grew up around the Portal area 2 miles from the Cienega on a farm where we grew crops like milo maize, sugar beets, and cotton. We also had horses, a milk cow, chickens, peacocks, goats, and sheep. My dad grew up in Glendale and moved here in 1957 to get away from the city environment. I never left the area; I always loved the mountains here.

Gates, Terrie and Larry— Terrie and Larry Gates came to the Chiricahuas as birdwatchers and stayed because they found the mountains emotionally and spiritually enriching. In a former life Larry was a psychology professor, and Terrie was an educator and mental health professional. They spend half the year in Portal and half near the South Carolina coast. The Gates's articles and bird photos have appeared in many publications, including their book, *Enjoying Hummingbirds: In the Wild and in Your Yard.*

Gillespie, Bill — Bill Gillespie has lived in southeastern Arizona for the past 30 years, though not in the Cave Creek area. He has long been fascinated by many different aspects of the Chiricahua Mountains: geology, plants, animals, and the history of human use, both before and after the arrival of Europeans. His occupation as archaeologist for the Coronado National Forest has allowed him an opportunity to explore many aspects of that long human history.

Grill, Frances Weaver — More than 15 years ago, my brother, my husband, and I were looking to buy a ranch together in the southwest. The search led us to the Noland ranch where we have been ranching since 1999. Having been a family nurse practitioner for nearly 30 years, practicing in rural Indiana, Kenya, and Costa Rica, and teaching community health nursing to college students, I was hoping to be able to open a practice locally. Finally, three years ago, after practicing in Willcox for 10 years, I was able to fulfill my dream by opening the Portal Clinic, owned by Walker Family Medicine of Willcox.

Grill, Peter James — When the government built a highway through our farm in Indiana, we decided to find a more sane place to live. Our requirements were simple: room for our animals, relatively remote, and an engaged community. Having a Masters Degree from Cornell in Rural Development, I was also looking to continue with the educational process while ranching. In addition to being on the school board, I have taught college courses at the ranch and ESL in Willcox. Living in the Portal area has met our expectations with the added benefit of waking up daily thankful for the beauty that surrounds us.

Hadley, Diana — Diana Hadley, historian, bilingual elementary school teacher, cheese-maker, and rancher, worked for many years as director of the Office of Ethnohistory at the Arizona State Museum. She raised her three children on a ranch on the Arizona-Sonora border, with no electricity or telephone and a 40-mile dirt road to the nearest town. She and her late husband, Peter Warshall, were among the founders of the Northern Jaguar Project. She first came to the Chiricahuas as a small child, snagged a few apples from the Maloney Orchard, and never dreamed that she would one day be lucky enough to have a home among the former apple trees.

Hayes, Eric — I was born in 1942 in the Phelps Dodge Hospital in Douglas. I was raised in the mouth of Cave Creek Canyon on what was then called the Sierra Linda Ranch. My granddad had bought the place about four years previously and was farming apples and grazing two milk cows on it. I went to school for the 1st through 8th grade in the Portal School (a one-room school) along with a varying number of other young scholars. One year the Hilltop Mine was operating, which brought the enrollment up to 26 kids. The next year the mine closed, and there were four of us: my brother and I, and two sisters. We left the neighborhood when I was about 15, but after living in other parts of the country for a little more than 30 years, I came back to the mouth of Cave Creek Canyon again, and I am still here.

Hernbrode, Gerry — I warn my visitors, "Be careful. The Canyon is addictive. Once you've been here, you will always be drawn back." Portal is a perfect setting for a writer such as I. The Canyon's beauty, calm but abundant, forms a perfect backdrop for the caring and interesting folks one meets daily at the Post Office. As a bonus, Jeanne Williams, resident and author of more than 70 published books, has been my mentor. The Writers' Group that meets weekly offers support, advice and friendship. Good neighbors! Great natural beauty! Good fortune!

Julian, JoAnn — After retiring from careers in education, JoAnn Julian and her husband, Doug, moved to Portal to pursue their passion for birding. They soon became active members of the community. JoAnn brought her experience as a teacher and junior high school principal to the San Simon School Board where she served for four years, two as the president. She is also active in the women's service organization, Sew What?, Portal Rescue, and the Chiricahua Gallery.

Lewis, Winston — Winston's family roots go back to 1862 in the Chiricahua Mountains, and he and his wife Jackie are carrying on the tradition of being Paradise "Mountaineers." Winston supports the mountain residence working in Las Cruces, driving home on weekends to trap hummingbirds, coach birdwatchers, and share the town's history of mines, men, bars, bordellos, hippies, and lawmen with birders and other casual visitors.

Maddox, Bob — Growing up in the Midwest, I often tagged along with my Dad on the golf course and fishing outings. Time outdoors stimulated my interest in weather and thunderstorms. At college I majored in meteorology and went to work for the U.S. Weather Bureau and spent most of eight Air Force years in Omaha, forecasting severe weather. After the military, I was a storm and flood researcher and was director of NOAA's National Severe Storms Laboratory. I met my wife (Katie Hirschboeck, a professor at the University of Arizona) because of her interest in floods. I have retired in Tucson but have a second career as a bookseller, dealing in collectible books.

McEwan, Craig — Craig lived on a midwestern Missouri cattle farm, a region once violently rocked by the Civil War. With failing health, he and his wife Juvy moved here in 2004. They established a house and garden and attempted to raise cattle, pigs, goats, turkeys, chickens, and guineas. Chickens fit McEwan's temperament, if only Coyotes would eat something different. Like their home, Craig's health has slowly been built—thanks to exercise (hiking with friends and running) and gratitude—to where he feels more comfortable. Neither structure will ever reach completion; the house needs replacement windows, and Craig's frame could use a new hip.

Miller, Barbara — Learning the plants and plant communities wherever I am is one of my greatest passions. Before retiring from my elementary school teaching in the Tempe area, I spent much of my free time in the surrounding Sonoran Desert. Now I am growing my gardens here and watching nature grow its gardens in the canyons and mountains around me. Finding a new plant to identify is a good game to play, and the 20-plus years here surrounded with the natural world has been a gift in my life.

Minchak, Sharon — My love of geology is fueled by a deep satisfaction that comes from understanding the world around me, in a very literal sense. Rocks tell a 5-billion-year story and offer human beings the chance to hold a part of that timeless story in our hands. I was introduced to the Portal area by my aunt and uncle, Jean and Don Wadsworth, who spent decades birdwatching in the area prior to building a home here in 2001. My husband and children and I have many wonderful memories of time spent in this beautiful place.

Moe, Mel — A retired wildlife biologist, I moved to the Rodeo–Portal area in 2008. I was attracted to the area by Cave Creek Canyon and its diversity of plants, wildlife, and geology. I have been interested in mammals since doing research on predator-prey relationships in graduate school. Native American studies have been a hobby of mine since taking a great archeology course in college. I spend much of my time visiting local archeological sites and reading the literature on native peoples of North America.

Patt, Jonathan — After moving to the Portal area ten years ago, I have in recent years become an avid hiker and explorer of the Chiricahua Mountains and a regular member of the Portal/Rodeo Hiking Group. Working as a freelance web developer, I currently spend much of my free time researching and writing a new hiking guide for the area, going on multi-day backpacking trips, and volunteering with the Forest Service to do trail maintenance.

Peters, Reed — Reed Peters first came to Arizona in the 1980s and realized this was a fascinating state. Visiting the Chiricahuas in a monsoon thunderstorm in 1996, he determined to come back and camp someday. Instead he bought Cave Creek Ranch in 1998 and still has not camped here. His family encouraged an interest in nature, which Cave Creek Canyon feeds every day, but he wishes he had taken a biology course along with all the history and classics. The canyon is an outdoor classroom that never closes; too bad this student forgets half of what he learns every day!

Quinn, Ron — Dr. Ron Quinn has been coming to the Chiricahua Mountains since 1967, first as a graduate student, and then as class leader, forest fire researcher, and local resident. He felt drawn to the immense beauty and biodiversity of the Chiricahuas the first time he saw them, a love affair that has lasted for a lifetime. He and Barbara Ellis-Quinn met and married at the Southwestern Research Station, and built a straw bale house in Portal where they reside for half of each year. Ron has done fire ecology research in southern and northern California, northwestern and southeastern Arizona, and southern Europe.

Ridgway, Harry — Dr. Harry Ridgway lives and works with his wife Polly in Rodeo, New Mexico—Portal's sister community where unsavory souls are reportedly seen from time to time. Harry is a modern-day cyber-alchemist involved in suspicious government-sanctioned programs, often involving water security. Polly is a past-life regression therapist, and they are both devoted conspiracy theorists and UFO aficionados. As small remote communities with dark night skies, Rodeo and Portal both offer some insulation from government spying and disinformation campaigns; but it is not perfect, and that is why we must pay special attention to our local water resources.

Sherbrooke, Wade — Thirty-eight years ago I came to Portal in search of horned lizards and their stories. The search was not easy. I'm still looking for secrets. Sometimes I get a peek into the unknown, so I look for more. Being in the right place at the right time helps. Sometimes I don't even ask a question; a revelation just appears. They taught me to pay attention and not let my mind jump too quickly. It doesn't do well grasping everything out there, way beyond its capacity. But there is a lot of joy along the path. What more can I ask?

Simon, Carol — Carol Simon first visited Cave Creek Canyon in 1964, on a spring vacation field trip led by her southern California high school biology teacher. That summer she was a volunteer at the Southwestern Research Station and her life was set. During that time she decided to be a biologist, and her future college choice was was influenced by SWRS scientists. In addition, she met life-long friends, her future Ph.D. advisor, and her future husband, Howard Topoff. Carol returned to Cave Creek Canyon often, for camping, hiking, research, and finally to live, becoming a permanent full-time resident of the canyon in 2002.

Snyder, Helen — Helen Snyder spent her childhood in trees trying to get close to birds. In 1967 she and her husband were on their camping honeymoon and fell in love with the Chiricahuas and its abundant, diverse raptor population. Southwestern Research Station Director Vince Roth offered them a tour of the lab and that settled it—they returned two years later with a National Geographic grant to study Cooper's Hawks. Since then she and Noel have studied California Condors, Snail Kites, Puerto Rican and Thick-billed Parrots, Apache Goshawks, and Peregrine Falcons. Helen and Noel have lived in Portal, Arizona since 1986.

Snyder, Noel — Noel Snyder, now retired and living in Portal, spent most of his professional career leading field conservation programs for endangered birds for various governmental and private organizations. The species involved have included the Puerto Rican Parrot, the Everglade (Snail) Kite, the California Condor, and the Thick-billed Parrot. With his wife Helen and other collaborators he has published many papers and books on these and other species. As a Portal resident, he led the successful fight in the 1990s to prevent Cave Creek Canyon from becoming an open-pit gold mine, and he was a co-founder of the Chiricahua Regional Council.

Stoltz, Zola — A long-distance romance brought Zola Stoltz to Portal, a romance with a good-looking Air Force recruit with black hair and green eyes. She and

Pat Stoltz (aka Maloney) spent as much time as possible building/fixing the Maloney Homestead, despite being stationed in Libya, Spain, Ohio, Oregon, Colorado, and Arizona. They built a garage to live in until a proper house could be built, but Pat died without being able to live his dream—that of spending his last days in his "home." Zola turned that garage into a house and added a smaller version for the garage. At least Pat's soul can rest in Portal.

Taylor, Rick — Rick Taylor moved to the Chiricahuas after finishing his masters in creative writing at the U of A in 1974, working as a Park Service lookout and on a trail crew for the Forest Service. While researching and writing *Hiking Trails and Wilderness Routes of the Chiricahua Mountains*, he'd fallen for birds, especially the Elegant Trogon. He hiked up to 500 miles each summer for eight years conducting research throughout the Sky Islands of southeastern Arizona, summarizing that research in *Trogons of the Arizona Borderlands*. Rick now leads birding tours throughout the world, but his heart and home are still in the Chiricahuas.

Thompson, Bruce — BAlvarius is the *nom-de-plume* of a local biologist managing an estate in the San Simon valley. Moving to the area in order to build a business, he uses photography to explore the landscape and test ideas of how people see. Trying to make a living in the sparsely settled Bootheel of New Mexico leads one to consider how others who lived during the past in the area provided for themselves and their families. This consideration leads naturally to an exploration of the past in an effort to make a living in the present.

Topoff, Howard — Howard Topoff grew up in Brooklyn, New York. He began his research career on ants in the Chiricahua Mountains in 1964, the year the first Beatles' album was released in the United States. As a graduate student at the American Museum of Natural History in New York City, he began field research on ants at the Southwestern Research Station, which is owned and operated by the Museum. For 33 years, he was also a professor of psychology at the City University of New York. He retired to Portal in 2002, where he continues research on the behavior of social insects.

Tyburec, Janet — Janet Debelak Tyburec is not a resident but has been visiting Cave Creek annually each May since 1992, catching and recording bats. Despite this long association, many people have probably never met her. Like a bat, she's most active at night. Her favorite species is the Pallid Bat, a burly "giant," notorious for feeding on centipedes and scorpions. She once caught one that was missing an eye, had teeth worn down to stubby nubs, big old arthritic-looking knees, and more scars than a Hollywood action hero. She figures it was either the oldest living Pallid Bat, or the unluckiest one.

Vacariu, Kim — Kim Vacariu is the Western Director for the Wildlands Network, an international conservation group working to establish a system of connected wildlife habitat across North America. He is currently working to protect the habitat corridor that runs from the Blue Range Wolf Recovery Area in New

Mexico's Gila Mountain complex south through the Chiricahua and Peloncillo Mountains to the Sierra Madre Occidental in northern Mexico. Kim is also the founder and organizer of the annual Chiricahua-Peloncillo Heritage Days events, celebrating the region's natural and cultural heritage. He lives with his wife, Lorraine, in the Sulphur Canyon area south of Portal.

Van Buskirk, Mike — When I was 8 years old I read a children's book called *All About Butterflies and Moths*. It fascinated me completely and created a life-long interest in Lepidoptera. In 1971 I became a student volunteer at the Southwestern Research Station. During that summer Vince Roth encouraged my study of Sphinx Moths (Sphingidae). It was the best summer of my life! I have been returning to the Chiricahuas and the other Sky Islands almost every year since to continue research on the biology of Sphinx moths. I am grateful to write this chapter on Cave Creek Canyon moths.

Warshall, Peter — Peter Warshall, aka Dr. Watershed, was a biologist, anthropologist, writer, science editor for the *Whole Earth Catalog*, editor of *Whole Earth Magazine*, designer of the savannah in Biosphere Two, and author of the Dreaming New Mexico project. A self-described maniacal naturalist, others thought of him as a "biogladiator" in recognition of his many years of fearless environmental advocacy. As co-discoverer of the Mt. Graham Red Squirrel, he fought for many years to protect the squirrel, preserve Apache sacred sites, and prevent the construction of more telescopes on the Pinaleño range. Armed with a new Ph.D. from Harvard, he first came to the Chiricahuas in the 1970s as a cook on one of Rich Stalkup's bird trips, and determined to live here one day.

Webster, Richard — Richard Webster guides birdwatching tours for Field Guides Incorporated in faraway places, and then happily returns to the home he shares with Rose Ann Rowlett in Portal. Once home, he immediately wants to go birding again, and again, and again, because in the Chiricahua region there is something interesting to see, photograph, or record every morning, the processing of which occupies much of the time that remains after re-filling the hummingbird feeders.

Jeanne Williams — "I have learned and been happy." *The Once and Future King* by T. H. White.

Wilson, Dawn — I came to this amazingly beautiful area in 2003 when I became director of the Southwestern Research Station. As director, my goals have been to increase research and educational opportunities for students and scientists that are drawn to this area because of its incredibly high biodiversity. As a scientist, my research currently focuses on the reintroduction of a threatened species, the Chiricahua Leopard Frog. This collaborative effort focuses on the restoration and management of perennial wetlands that benefit not only the leopard frog, but other species whose life cycles depend on permanent riparian habitats.

Zweifel, Dick — Fran and I first visited the Chiricahuas on our honeymoon in 1956 and returned at every opportunity, often to continue my research at the Southwestern Research Station. I was a Curator of Amphibians and Reptiles in the American Museum of Natural History in New York City from 1954-1989; Fran was a biological illustrator there when we met. We retired to Paradise in 1989, and the great biological diversity in the Chiricahuas enslaved us: I with research on amphibians and reptiles and on butterflies, Fran as my essential field assistant and illustrator as well as a host of myriad civic opportunities.

Chiricahua Place Names Quiz—Answers

1. A);
2. A) Although the definite answer cannot be confirmed, "cave" seems to be the most plausible explanation.
3. E) The tallest peak sometimes referred to as Portal High Point is adjacent to the southwest of Portal Peak (which is about 30 feet shorter).
4. B);
5. C);
6. A) Four species live on or near the mountain.
7. B);
8. C) However, there should be an honorable mention for "B)"
9. A);
10. A) or C)

Give yourself a bonus point if you knew both canyons named for serious lawbreakers. "Black Jack" Tom Ketchum was a notorious train robber, who died by hanging in 1900. Tombstone resident, "Buckskin" Frank Leslie—who managed a ranch in the canyon that bears his name—was convicted in the alcohol-induced shootings of his girlfriend, who died, and a ranch hand. After serving some time in the penitentiary, he was released early with a governor's pardon. He sometimes worked in law-enforcement and scouting for the army. As for D)—sorry, none of the Beatles ever broke any laws in Cochise County.

Awards granted to Place Name Scholars: 1st Place—11 correct answers out of 10 questions entitles you to be an honorary "Chiricahuan." If you got more than 12 answers correct, you may be delusional. 2nd Place—10 out of 10 means you have a legitimate claim to argue that you are an honorary "Chiricahuan." 3rd Place—9 out of 10: you deserve an extra marshmallow 'round the campfire. 4th Place—8 out of 10 means you should make your own Sky Island Quiz. To everyone else—a bit of wisdom: Keep studying, because toasted marshmallows taste really good.

Supporting Patrons

Anonymous
Robert Abrams
Astrid and Earl Berkson
Nancy and Jim Carpenter
Sally and John Carr
Sandra and Tad Dale
Orchid Davis
Nancy and Thomas Denney
Teri Denson
Rene and Tony Donaldson
Elbrock Water Systems LLC
Barbara Walker and Phil Feigin
Roger Funk
Janice Hurd and Marvin Goldfogel
Claudia Kirscher
Jan and David Labiner
Mary and Jon Lacey
Jim Lee
Diane and Michael Lilley
Jill Faulkner and Graham Manley
Christine and Brendan McCooey
Barb and Pete Miller
Mt. Diablo Audubon Society
Douglas Noffsinger
Pat Owens
Linda Pretty and John Pouy
Rodeo Tavern
Rodeo Store & Café
Rene and Ben Roush
Catherine Sandell
San Francisco/Portland Royal Academy
Delia Scholes and Ed Newbold
Carol Simon and Howard Topoff
Bruce Taubert
The Magic Brush
Lorraine Titus and Kim Vacariu
Suzanne Winckler and David Smith
Carol Woods
Sherry and Bob Zoellick

Major Sponsors

Anonymous

Anonymous

Anonymous

Barbara and William Bickel

David Brooks

Bill Chilson

Kate and Bud Fackelman

Andrea Gessner Friedman and Richard Friedman

Mary and Donald Kesterson

Louisiana State Arthropod Museum

John McQuillan Charitable Fund

Sandy and Scott Menough

New Mexico Friends of Cave Creek Canyon

New Mexico Land Conservancy

Karen and Randy Norrick of Portal Rodeo Realty

Pat and Lee Perkinson

Portal Peak Lodge, Store & Café

Paula Baldwin and Thomas Roseman

Sky Island Alliance

Steven and William Stiffler

Southwestern Research Station

Tucson Audubon Society

Jan and Tom Vargo